The Wordsworth
Book of 19th Century Verse

The Wordsworth
Book of 19th Century Verse

*Edited, with an Introduction,
by Tim Cook*

Wordsworth Poetry Library

INTRODUCTION

The aim of this anthology is to give the lover of poetry as comprehensive and varied a picture as possible of the nineteenth century in verse. Because it confines itself to verse written between 1801 and 1900, it excludes the earlier poems of Blake and the remarkable achievement of Coleridge and Wordsworth in *Lyrical Ballads* (1798). These will be represented in a companion anthology, already in preparation, covering the eighteenth century. This will give readers the opportunity to see how extraordinary those early Romantic poems were in the context of what was being written at the time.

The word 'verse' is used instead of 'poetry' in the title because many of the pieces included, for instance lighter work by Hood or Gilbert, may fall short of the expectations raised by the loftier word. Nevertheless, most items in the selection have long had their admirers, and though none may appeal to all tastes, nineteenth century concerns, prejudices and preferences being what they were, readers should find plenty here to involve, move or amuse them.

Over fifty poets, British, Irish and American, have been included. Since the intention has been to give space to as many individual voices as possible, the number of pages given to the greatest names of the century, Wordsworth, Shelley, Keats, Byron, Tennyson and Browning has had to be limited, and some poems that you might expect to be here are omitted. However these are very easily accessible in collections of their work already available from Wordsworth Editions. In this anthology some of their mid-length poems are given complete; others are represented by appropriate extracts. Small but characteristic sections of very long poems such as Wordsworth's *Prelude* and Byron's *Don Juan* will be found in relevant sections of the anthology.

The Arrangement of the Poems

An anthologist faces several choices in arranging the poems he or she has collected. Works can be grouped by poet, printing each poet in chronological order with the verse selected; one can print all the poems chosen in order according to the dates of composition or publication, if known, intermingling poems by different poets; or one can arrange them by category or theme, so that poems on related topics by different poets can be compared. The option chosen here is the last, with the poems printed as nearly as possible in chronological order within each section.

This choice of options of course raises the difficulty that many poems fall into more than one category. Tennyson's *In Memoriam*, for instance, is probably the greatest expression in Victorian literature of the struggle between faith and doubt which tormented the minds of many educated people once Sir Charles Lyell, the geologist, and others had called into question the Bible's account of the creation of life on earth and the time-scale over which this took place. These doubts were reinforced by critical analyses of the biblical texts and an increasing tendency to question the moral values embodied in them and in the teachings of the Churches.

In this collection Tennyson's masterpiece is placed in Section 3, Faith, Doubt, Despair & Hope, but it could equally well have appeared in Section 8, Thoughts & Memories of Death. Some of the poet's 'short swallow-flights of song' are more appropriate to one section, the rest to the other, or perhaps to Section 5, Responses to the Natural World. However it is clearly best to keep the selected lyrics from the poem together in one section. No doubt some readers will have objections to other placings, but most will, one hopes, see the reason for them.

The Political and Social Situation

The collection begins with poems reflecting the enthusiasm for change and reform that still inspired many young writers at the beginning of a century with vivid memories of the French Revolution. The Battle of Waterloo and the final overthrow of Napoleon led eventually to the confirmation of Britain's status as a world power, yet it was a country still dominated by an upper class and hereditary aristocracy very unwilling to share its power with the growing middle classes, let alone the workers on whose poorly paid labour the accelerating industrial revolution depended. Castlereagh and the Lord Chancellor Eldon, both figuring in Shelley's *Mask of Anarchy,* represented the system at its most repressive under a king, by then sick and helpless, whose refusal to accept reasonable change had been blamed for the loss of the American colonies over a quarter of a century earlier.

From revolutionary, prophetic, satirical and enthusiastic poetry generated by events before Victoria's reign, and a few later flashes of the revolutionary spirit, including one attacking similar complacencies across the Atlantic, we move to a series of poems exploring social issues or commenting on social attitudes throughout the century. Charles Lamb's doggerel ballad highlights the chasm between the well-to-do classes and the poor; Clare points to the hardship suffered by country labourers as a result of the Enclosure Acts; Hood, in his crusading mode, seeks to arouse society's compassion for working-class women forced to choose between appallingly low-paid work and a life on the streets; Elizabeth Barrett Browning similarly uses all the resources of rhetoric and sentiment to make her male brethren aware of exploited children toiling away in abominable conditions.

After the mid-century, when some of these abuses had been put right, but England had moved further into bourgeois smugness, we have Clough's succinctly cynical comment on the hypocrisies of an officially Christian society (compare his brief portrait of it with Samuel Butler's powerful later prose satire *Erewhon*), Hardy's double-edged and blackly humorous view of the career opportunities offered to a 'raw country girl' in the metropolis, and Amy Levy's striking protest at over two millennia of intellectual undervaluing and oppression of her sex.

The Position of Women

Indeed, the nineteenth century was a time in which women poets as well as novelists were really beginning to challenge male domination of the literary scene effectively, even though it was only gradually that they began to be granted access to higher education. Besides including a fairly representative selection of work by women poets with whose names readers may be familiar, such as Elizabeth Barrett Browning, Christina Rossetti and the Brontës, this anthology contains, in its various sections, poems by women writers not widely remembered today, ranging from the unsophisticated favourite of the Victorian middle classes Eliza Cook to the Cambridge educated Levy, whose suicide in 1889 cut short the development of an unusual talent.

However, in an anthology of nineteenth-century verse in the English language, there is one woman poet whose work, though hardly varied in form, surely surpasses all those writing on this side of the Atlantic in originality of mind and vision, and that is Emily Dickinson. So original was she that she was advised not to try to have her poems published, with the result that many have appeared slowly in print over the course of this century, and some of the very best remain unavailable for this anthology.

Science and Religion

Dickinson is, naturally, one of the poets represented in the third section of the anthology, where the nineteenth-century crisis in Christian belief is the central theme, though the section includes a variety of states of mind, ranging from Dickinson's own powerful description of near-mental breakdown, paralleling similar cries of spiritual anguish by Christina Rossetti and Gerard Manley Hopkins, to Browning's expressions of determined optimism and Newman's submission to the Divine will.

After the emotional and spiritual switchback ride of Section 3, the next section offers the reader some moments of relaxation in the shape of verse designed primarily to amuse and entertain. Ann Taylor's 'Meddlesome Matty' anticipates Hilaire Belloc, Barham's 'Jackdaw of Rheims' has long been a popular favourite, and Thackeray's potted Goethe and Peacock's parody of a Celtic war chant are equally well-known. However, Lamb's 'Farewell to Tobacco' will strike particular chords of sympathy in a century of increasing hostility to the weed, and the items by Hood (again commenting with characteristically black humour on a macabre social phenomenon of the time) and Praed anticipate Gilbert's ingenuity with words in the later part of the century, as does Thackeray's stage Irish account of that central event of the century, the Great Exhibition of 1851, planned by the Prince Consort and housed in Paxton's Crystal Palace, then located in Hyde Park.

Man and the Natural World

Section 5 brings in traditional sources of poetic inspiration such as the weather, the seasons and the different forms of life from animals and birds to plants and insects. England in particular was of course far less urbanised than it is today, and birds such as the skylark and thrush, now becoming relatively rare through intensive farming and destruction of habitat, were far more familiar to the general public than they are today. Poets such as Wordsworth, Tennyson and Clare in England and Dickinson in America lived particularly close to nature, and it is present in much of their imagery. (Some of Wordsworth's most striking evocations of the natural world are not in fact printed here, but will be found in the passages from *The Prelude* included in the later section on Childhood.) Although Dickinson lived in long settled Massachusetts, other American poets such as William Cullen Bryant knew the prairies before the great mass movement westward and revelled in their as yet unspoilt Edenic quality, while aware of and sympathetic to the already partly dispossessed Indian tribes whose domains they had been.

For Shelley such subjects as the West Wind and the Skylark, though admired in themselves, become symbols of revolution and spiritual rebirth, while for Keats natural phenomena and creatures inspire meditations on the cycles of nature, the impermanence of beauty and the allure of death; for Hopkins, on the other hand, they are the supreme evidence of the existence of a beneficent Creator, and man's encroachment on them is to be resisted and deplored. Wordsworth and Hopkins, together with Hardy, are the poets who perhaps most anticipate the environmental concerns of the present century. Indeed Rachel Carson, in her seminal book *Silent Spring,* pointed out that modern farming practices were in danger of wiping out much of the subject matter of poetry in English.

From the natural world we move, in Section 6, to the cities, and London in particular, which was, during the century, to become very different from the city Wordsworth admired from Westminster Bridge. Eliza Cook paints a picture more recognisable to readers of Dickens, while George Eliot's vision of the people from her London drawing room somewhat anticipates T. S. Eliot's gloomy post-1918 crowds in *The Waste Land*. It is not until we reach Amy Levy that we meet someone who actually prefers London life, though Oscar Wilde's aesthetic sensibility is excited by the city's Whistler-like colour schemes.

From Childhood to the Grave

In the seventh section, Views of Childhood, another subject perpetually fascinating to the writers of the century is explored. The section begins with Wordsworth's great Ode, in which under the influence of writers as diverse as Rousseau and Henry Vaughan he sees infancy as a state of Edenic blessedness. However, much of the section gives a less portentous and more realistic, if far less moving and inspired, picture of childhood, ranging from the paternal exasperation amusingly described by Tom Hood to George Eliot's, Eliza Cook's and William Barnes's nostalgically autobiographical pieces.

From one end of life we move to the other, with a selection of poems reacting in different ways to deaths of people of very different ages and status, and with varying degrees of dignity, the most artless being Eliza Cook's vastly popular 'Old Arm-chair', which some readers will feel keeps rather inappropriate company with Shelley's great and passionate ode on the death of Keats and Walt Whitman's powerful and moving lament on the death of that titan of the age, Abraham Lincoln. Most of the other poems included here deal with more personal emotions, with Emily Dickinson, one of the very finest lyricists on this subject, represented by two pieces.

Love

In Varieties of Love & its Aftermath, the section that follows, relations between men and women are explored in many different forms, from the lyrical sentimentality of Tom Moore and the mutual affection of the Brownings to the mad possessiveness of 'Porphyria's Lover', the disillusionment of a failed marriage in Meredith's cynically titled Modern Love and the unsatisfied longings of Dickinson and Levy. Most of the poems here speak for themselves, and will be responded to by anyone who has experience of the vagaries of what W. B. Yeats said is, along with religion, one of the only two forces which really stir human beings to the depths. He was himself to become one of the greatest poets of the century to come, and some of his early work is included here.

War and Empire

The section on love is followed by its opposite, war, a subject often written about in the nineteenth century, though rarely with anything approaching the de-heroicising realism of the 1914–18 war poets. The century had begun with the defeat by British naval power of Napoleon's fleet, and the Peninsular War and had been followed ten years later by the final victory at Waterloo. Byron gives a brief account of this from the standpoint of an onlooker, but it is Thomas Hood's grim humour which comes closest, though in dubious taste, to deglamorising the event and indicating its human cost. Tennyson's line both in describing a legendary naval exploit of the past and in celebrating the heroic idiocy of the Light Brigade at Balaclava is more one of traditional glorification, while Clough provides a fairly dispassionate civilian view of the fight for the short-lived Roman Republic involving Garibaldi.

Only Walt Whitman, with his actual battlefield experience, makes the realities of war vivid in all their harrowing detail, though, unlike his Great War successors, he has no moral doubts. However, for Britons, the most important wars of the century were those brought about by the steady expansion of the Empire, wars celebrated in the work of Kipling and Newbolt, who between them helped to sustain that ideology of imperialism which Disraeli had envisioned when having Victoria proclaimed Empress of India in 1876 by celebrating the ideal of the self-sacrificing English gentleman born to civilise the world and in all circumstances to 'play up, play up and play the game'.

After such noise and violence, a lighter hearted section seemed appropriate (though it begins with yet more fighting!). This, the eleventh one, is devoted to another kind of writing in which the Victorians achieved distinction: nonsense and parody, with Edward Lear and Lewis Carroll as the supreme exponents. The section concludes with A. E. Housman's brief parody of a Greek tragedy which acts as an appropriate bridge to the next section.

Past and Imagined Worlds

Here nineteenth-century Classicism is less frivolously represented, by poems inspired in one way or another by the contemporary fascination with the ancient civilisations of Greece and Rome. Whereas the Augustans had, as the name implies, taken Rome as their primary model, the Romantics were more interested in the intellectual and literary achievements and aesthetic standards of the Greeks. Shelley's revolutionary Prometheus (see Section 2) was inspired by them, and Keats, who lacked the Classical education enjoyed by his better-off contemporaries was profoundly moved by their myths and their art, as his poetry shows.

On the other hand, for a rather more conventional patriot like Tennyson, who to some extent seems to see himself as the Victorian Virgil, the Romans as well as the Greeks provided inspiration, though in 'Parnassus', a poem that makes a very different use of mythology, he sees all the centuries of Classically inspired culture fading into insignificance in the face of new scientific advances. Meanwhile other poets such as Landor and Dowson cast themselves and their mistresses in the roles of Classical poets and their lovers and, towards the end of the century, Swinburne shocked bourgeois sensibilities by imaginatively rejecting Christianity in favour of the pagan values that preceded it.

Many nineteenth-century poets were equally fascinated by the medieval world which had been brought back into literary consciousness by the discoveries of Bishop Percy and others in the previous century. Sir Walter Scott had continued the tradition of interest in the age of chivalry and poets such as Tennyson saw the Arthurian legends as fulfilling the same role in Victorian culture as the legend of Aeneas' flight from Troy and early victories in Italy had fulfilled in the Roman Empire.

Others were interested in the narrative, dramatic and psychological possibilities of the traditional medieval ballad form or in the symbolic possibilities of the ghosts, fairies and other supernatural beings of early folklore. A further area of interest was that of dreams and visions, pioneered by Coleridge in *Kubla Khan*, though the ones printed here have little in common with that poem's exotic orientalism. In the thirteenth section of the anthology examples of all these kinds of writing will be found, from Keats's hauntingly foreboding ballad, via Browning's version of a knightly quest set in an increasingly sinister landscape, to Christina Rossetti's erotic goblins and Meredith's vision of the wandering and frustrated Lucifer.

Verse Characterisations

Another kind of poem much favoured by nineteenth-century poets described a person met or known by the poet, or revealed a character in depth through allowing him or her to speak for themselves. Browning was of course the supreme master of the latter form in his dramatic monologues, though for length reasons only two are given here. Other writers were, however, able to produce striking portraits in different modes: for example Gerard Manley Hopkins' almost sculptural evocation of the strength and good looks of his ploughman, and Tennyson's remarkable recreation of the feelings of a bereaved mother in his latish poem 'Rizpah'. One or two poems included in this section are actually concerned with portraits as works of art.

The penultimate section is mainly devoted to portraits of another kind: the self-revelations of the characters created by that good-humoured satirist of the latter part of the century W. S. Gilbert, without whom no collection of the century's verse would be complete. It begins with a litttle known but entertaining early Bab Ballad and goes on to some characteristic mockery of the law, Parliament and the aesthetic movement in songs familiar in their operatic settings by Sullivan.

Conclusion

Finally, we leave the century with four poems written in its last five years, all of them singularly free of the sense of hope and enthusiasm which inspired the idealistic poets writing at its start, all of them anticipating, in one way or another the problems and the changed world which Britain was to confront within the next two decades. Indeed, on balance, the mid to late nineteenth century, as seen through the eyes of its major versifiers, was far from being the self-confident era often looked back to nostalgically in these economically uncertain and politically disillusioned times.

Note on texts

Where available to the editor, nineteenth-century texts have been used, with occasional emendations where there appears to have been a misprint or a lack of clarity in punctuation. Where later versions of poems are still in copyright, earlier published versions are given. Where possible the known or probable date of composition, or failing that publication, is given at the end of a poem.

Tim Cook
Kingston University

DATES RELEVANT TO THE ANTHOLOGY

1776 American Declaration of Independence

1789 French Revolution begins

1800 Battle of Hohenlinden at end of French Revolutionary Wars

1804 Napoleon crowned Emperor

1805 Battle of Trafalgar

1812 Napoleon's retreat from Russia

1808–14 Peninsular War including siege of Corunna

1815 Battle of Waterloo

1819 Peterloo Massacre

1820 Death of George III (after reigning since 1760)

1827 Resignation of Lord Liverpool, Tory Premier since 1812

1830 Death of George IV

Sir Charles Lyell publishes his *Principles of Geology*

Indian Removal Act: Relocation of Indian Tribes in US

1832 Votes in Britain extended to most middle-class males

1837 Accession of Queen Victoria

1844 First of Factory Acts, pioneered by Lord Shaftesbury, to limit working hours

1848 Formation of Pre-Raphaelite Brotherhood

Garibaldi involved in short-lived Roman Republic

1849 Foundation of Bedford College for women in London

1851 Great Exhibition in Crystal Palace

1852 Louis Napoleon crowned Emperor Napoleon III of France

1854–6 Crimean War (Battle of Balaclava 1854)

1857–8 Indian Uprising ('Mutiny')

1859 Charles Darwin publishes *On the Origin of Species*

1861 Victoria widowed by death of her Consort, Prince Albert

1861–5 American Civil War

1865 Assassination of President Abraham Lincoln

1867 on Votes in Britain gradually extended to working-class males

1869 Foundation of Girton College, Cambridge

1870 Franco–Prussian War: Fall of Napoleon III

1876 Victoria becomes Empress of India

1877 Whistler's work exhibited at new Grosvenor Gallery

1880–1 First Boer War

1882 Married Women's Property Act, lessening financial dependence

1887 Victoria's Golden Jubilee

1897 Victoria's Diamond Jubilee

1898 Spanish–American War

1899–1902 Second Boer War

1900 Death of Oscar Wilde

1901 Death of Queen Victoria

CONTENTS

3 FAITH, DOUBT, MELANCHOLY, DESPAIR & HOPE

4 THE LIGHTER SIDE

6 THE URBAN SCENE

7 VIEWS OF CHILDHOOD

8 THOUGHTS & MEMORIES OF DEATH

9 VARIETIES OF LOVE
& ITS AFTERMATH

10 WARS, ANCIENT
& MODERN

11 THE WORLD OF
NONSENSE & PARODY

12 ECHOES OF GREECE & ROME

13 MEDIEVALISM, LEGEND, DREAM,
NIGHTMARE & THE SUPERNATURAL

1
PROPHETS, ROMANTICS
& REVOLUTIONARIES

London 1802

Milton! thou shouldst be living at this hour:
England hath need of thee; she is a fen
Of stagnant waters: altar sword and pen,
Fireside, the heroic wealth of sword and bower,
Have forfeited their ancient English dower
Of ancient happiness. We are selfish men;
O raise us up, return to us again;
And give us manners, virtue, freedom, power.
Thy soul was like a Star, and dwelt apart;
Thou hadst a voice whose sound was like the sea:
Pure as the naked heavens, majestic, free,
So didst thou travel on life's common way,
In cheerful godliness; and yet thy heart
The lowliest duties on herself did lay.

WILLIAM WORDSWORTH

Jerusalem

And did those feet in ancient time
Walk upon England's mountains green
And was the holy Lamb of God
In England's pleasant pastures seen
And did the Countenance Divine
Shine forth upon our clouded hills
And was Jerusalem builded here
Among these dark Satanic mills?

Bring me my Bow of burning Gold
Bring me my Arrows of Desire
Bring me my Spear: O clouds unfold
Bring me my Chariot of Fire
I shall not cease from mental fight
Nor shall my sword sleep in my hand
Till we have built Jerusalem
In England's green and pleasant Land

WILLIAM BLAKE (c. 1804)

Auguries of Innocence

To see a world in a grain of sand
And a heaven in a wild flower,
Hold infinity in the palm of your hand
And eternity in an hour.
A robin redbreast in a cage
Puts all Heaven in a rage,
A dovehouse full of doves and pigeons
Shudders Hell through all its regions.
A dog starved at his master's gate
Predicts the ruin of the state.
A horse misused upon the road
Calls to Heaven for human blood
Each outcry of the hunted hare
A fibre from the brain doth tear,
A skylark wounded in the wing
A cherubim does cease to sing.
The gamecock clipped and armed for fight
Does the rising sun affright,
Every wolf's and lions howl
Raises from Hell a human soul.
The wild deer wandering here and there
Keep the human soul from care.
The lamb misused breeds public strife
And yet forgives the butcher's knife.
The bat that flits at close of eve
Has left the brain that won't believe,
The owl that calls upon the night
Speaks the unbeliever's fright,
He who hurts the little wren
Shall never be beloved by men.
He who the ox to wrath has moved
Shall never be by woman loved.
The wanton boy that kills the fly
Shall feel the spider's enmity.
He who torments the chafer's sprite
Weaves a bower in endless night,
The caterpillar on the leaf

Repeats to thee thy mother's grief,
Kill not the moth not butterfly,
For the Last Judgement draweth nigh,
He who shall train the horse to war
Shall never pass the polar bar,
The beggar's dog and widow's cat –
Feed them and thou wilt grow fat,
The gnat that sings his summer's song
Poison gets from slander's tongue,
The poison of the snake and newt
Is the sweat of envy's foot;
The poison of the honey bee
Is the artist's jealousy.
The prince's robes and beggar's rags
Are toadstools on the miser's bags.
A truth that's told with bad intent
Beats all the lies you can invent.
It is right that it should be so;
Man was made for joy and woe,
And when this we rightly know
Through the world we safely go.
Joy and woe are woven fine
A clothing for the soul divine.
Under every grief and pine
Runs a joy with silken twine.
The babe is more than swaddling bands:
Throughout all these human lands
Tools were made and born were hands:
Every farmer understands.
Every tear from every eye
Becomes a babe in eternity;
This is caught by females bright
And returned to its own delight.
The bleat, the bark, bellow and roar
Are waves that beat on Heaven's shore.
The babe that weeps the rod beneath
Writes *Revenge!* in realms of death.
The beggar's rags flutt'ring in air
Does to rags the heavens tear.
The soldier armed with sword and gun

Palsied strikes the summer's sun.
The poor man's farthing is worth more
Than all the gold on Afric's shore.
One mite wrung from the labourer's hands
Shall buy and sell the miser's lands;
Or if protected from on high
Does that whole nation sell and buy.
He who mocks the infant's faith
Shall be mocked in age and death.
He who shall teach the child to doubt
The rotting grave shall ne'er get out.
He who respects the infants's faith
Triumphs over hell and death.
The child's toys and the old man's reasons
Are the fruits of the two seasons.
The questioner who sits so sly
Shall never know how to reply.
He who replies to words of doubt
Doth put the light of knowledge out.
The strongest poison ever known
Came from Caesar's laurel crown.
Nought can deform the human race
Like to the armour's iron brace.
When golden gems adorn the plough
To peaceful arts shall envy bow.
A riddle, or the cricket's cry,
Is to doubt a fit reply.
The emmet's inch and eagle's mile
Make lame philosophy to smile.
He who doubts from what he sees
Will ne'er believe, do what you please.
If the sun and moon should doubt
They'd immediately go out.
To be in a passion to you good may do,
But no good if a passion is in you.
The whore and gambler by the state
Licensed build that nation's fate.
The harlot's cry from street to street
Shall weave old England's winding sheet;
The winner's shout and loser's curse

Dance before dead England's hearse.
Every night and every morn
Some to misery are born
Every morn and every night
Some are born to sweet delight.
Some are born to sweet delight,
Some are born to endless night.
We are led to believe a lie
When we see not through the eye
Which was born in a night to perish in a night,
When the soul slept in beams of light.
God appears and God is light
To those poor souls who dwell in night
But does a human form display
To those who dwell in beams of day.

WILLIAM BLAKE (c.1804)

Wordsworth remembers
the French Revolution

Bliss was it in that dawn to be alive
But to be young was very Heaven! O times
In which the meagre, stale, forbidding ways
Of custom, law and statute, took at once
The attraction of a country in romance!
When Reason seemed the most to assert her rights
When most intent on making of herself
A prime enchantress – to assist the work
Which then was going forward in her name!
Not favoured spots alone, but the whole Earth
The beauty wore of promise – that which sets
(As at some moment might not be unfelt
Among the bowers of Paradise itself)
The budding rose above the rose full blown.
What temper at the prospect did not wake
To happiness unthought of? The inert
Were roused, and lively natures rapt away.
They who had fed their childhood upon dreams,
The playfellows of fancy, who had made

All powers of swiftness, subtlety and strength
Their ministers, – who in lordly wise had stirred
Among the grandest objects of the sense,
And dealt with whatsoever they found there
As if they had within some lurking right
To wield it; – they, too, who of gentle mood
Had watched all gentle motions, and to these
Had fitted their own thoughts, schemers more mild
And in the region of their peaceful selves;–
Now was it that *both* found, the meek and lofty
Did both find, helpers to their hearts desire,
And stuff at hand, plastic as they could wish,–
Were called upon to exercise their skill,
Not in Utopia,– subterranean fields, –
Or some secreted island, Heaven knows where!
But in the very world, which is the world
Of all of us,– the place where, in the end,
We find our happiness, or not at all!

from THE PRELUDE, Book 11, Lines 108–24 (1805)

Sonnet: England in 1819

An old, mad, blind, despised and dying king –
Princes, the dregs of their dull race, who flow
Through public scorn, mud from a muddy spring –
Rulers who neither see, nor feel, nor know,
But leech-like to their fainting country cling,
Till they drop, blind in blood, without a blow, –
A people starved and stabbed in the untilled field, –
An army, which liberticide and prey
Make as an untilled field to all who wield,–
Golden and sanguine laws, which tempt and slay;
Religion Christless, Godless– a book sealed;
A Senate, – Time's worst statute unrepealed, –
Are graves, from which a glorious Phantom may
Burst to illumine our tempestuous day.

PERCY BYSSHE SHELLEY

from *A Vision of Judgement*

1

Saint Peter sat by the celestial gate,
    His keys were rusty and the lock was dull,
So little trouble had been given of late;
    Not that the place by any means was full,
But since the Gallic era, eighty-eight
    The devils had ta'en a longer stronger pull,
And a 'pull altogether' as they say
At sea, which drew most souls another way.

2

The angels all were singing out of tune
    And hoarse with having little else to do,
Excepting to wind up the sun and moon,
    Or curb a runaway young star or two,
Or wild colt of a comet, which too soon
    Broke out of bounds o'er the ethereal blue,
Splitting some planet with its playful tail,
As boats are sometimes by a wanton whale.

3

The guardian seraphs had retired on high,
    Finding their charges past all care below
Terrestrial business fill'd nought in the sky
    Save the recording angel's black bureau;
Who found, indeed, the facts to multiply
    With such rapidity of vice and woe,
That he had stripped off both his wings in quills
And yet was in arrear of human ills.

4

His business so augmented of late years,
    That he was forced, against his will, no doubt,
(Just like those cherubs, earthly ministers)
    For some resource to turn himself about,
And claim the help of his celestial peers,
    To aid him ere he should be quite worn out

By the increased demand for his remarks;
Six angels and twelve saints were named his clerks.

5

This was a handsome board, at least for heaven;
    And yet they had even then enough to do,
So many conqueror's cars were daily driven,
    So many kingdoms fitted up anew;
Each day, too, slew its thousands, six or seven,
    Till at the crowning carnage, Waterloo,
They threw their pens down in divine disgust –
The page was so besmeared with blood and dust.

6

This by the way; 'tis not mine to record
    What angels shrink from; even the very devil
On this occasion his own work abhorred
    So surfeited with the infernal revel;
Though he himself had sharpened every sword,
    It almost quench'd his innate sense of evil.
(Here Satan's sole good work deserves insertion –
Tis that he has both generals in reversion.)

7

Let's skip a few short years of hollow peace,
    Which peopled earth no better, hell as wont,
And heaven none– they form the tyrant's lease,
    With nothing but new names inscribed upon't;
'Twill one day finish; meantime they increase
    'With seven heads and ten horns', and all in front
Like Saint John's foretold beast; but ours are born
Less formidable in the head than horn.

8

In the first year of freedom's second dawn
    Died George the Third; although no tyrant, one
Who shielded tyrants, till each sense withdrawn
    Left him nor mental nor external sun;
A better farmer ne'er brushed dew from lawn,
    A worse king never left a realm undone!
He died – but left his subjects still behind,
One half as mad – and t'other no less blind.

9

He died! His death made no great stir on earth:
   His burial made some pomp; there was profusion
Of velvet, gilding, brass, and no great dearth
   Of aught but tears – save those shed by collusion.
For these things may be bought at their true worth;
   Of elegy there was the due infusion,
Bought also; and the torches, cloaks and banners,
Heralds and relics of old Gothic manners,

10

Formed a sepulchral melodrame. Of all
   The fools who flocked to swell or see the show,
Who cared about the corpse? The funeral
   Made the attraction, and the black the woe,
There throbbed not there a thought which pierced the pall;
   And when the gorgeous coffin was laid low,
It seem'd the mockery of hell to fold
The rottenness of eighty years in gold.

    *   *   *   *   *

16

Saint Peter sat by the celestial gate,
   And nodded o'er his keys; when, lo! there came
A wondrous noise he had not heard of late –
   A rushing noise of wind, and stream, and flame;
In short a noise of things extremely great,
   Which would have made aught save a saint exclaim;
But he, with first a start and then a wink,
Said, 'There's another star gone out, I think!'

17

But ere he could return to his repose,
   A cherub flapped his right wing o'er his eyes –
At which St Peter yawn'd, and rubb'd his nose;
   'Saint Porter,' said the angel, 'prithee rise!'
Waving a goodly wing, which glowed, as glows
   An earthly peacock's tail, with heavenly dyes:
To which the saint replied, 'Well, what's the matter?
'Is Lucifer come back, with all this clatter?'

18

'No,' quoth the cherub; 'George the Third is dead.'
  'And who is George the Third?' replied the apostle:
'What George? What Third?' 'The king of England,' said
  The angel. 'Well, he won't find kings to jostle
Him on his way; but does he wear his head?
  Because the last we saw here had a tustle,
And ne'er would have got into Heaven's good graces
Had he not thrown his head in all our faces.

19

'He was, if I remember, king of France;
  That head of his, which could not keep a crown
On earth, yet ventured in my face to advance
  A claim to those of martyrs – like my own;
If I had had my sword, as I had once
  When I cut ears off, I had cut him down;
But having but my keys and not my brand,
I only knocked his head from out his hand.

20

'And then he set up such a headless howl,
  That all the saints came out and took him in;
And there he sits by St Paul, cheek by jowl;
  That fellow Paul, the parvenu! The skin
Of St Bartholomew, which makes his cowl
  In heaven and upon earth redeemed his sin,
So as to make a martyr, never sped
Better than did this weak and wooden head.

21

'But had it come up here upon his shoulders,
  There would have been a different tale to tell;
The fellow feeling in the saint's beholders
  Seems to have acted on them like a spell,
And so this very foolish head heaven solders
  Back on its trunk: it may be very well,
And seems the custom here to overthrow
Whatever has been wisely done below.'

22

The angel answered, 'Peter, do not pout:
    The king who comes has head and all entire,
And never knew much what it was about –
    He did as doth the puppet – by its wire,
And will be judged like all the rest no doubt;
    My business and your own is not to inquire
Into such matters, but to mind our cue –
Which is to act as we are told to do.'

23

While thus they spake, the angelic caravan,
    Arriving like a rush of mighty wind,
Cleaving the fields of space, as doth the swan
    Some silver stream (say Ganges, Nile or Inde,
Or Thames, or Tweed) and midst them an old man
    With an old soul, and both extremely blind,
Halted before the gate, and in his shroud
Seated their fellow traveller on a cloud.

24

But bringing up the rear of this bright host
    A spirit of a different aspect waved
His wings, like thunder-clouds above some coast
    Whose barren beach with frequent wrecks is paved;
His brow was like the beach when tempest-toss'd;
    Fierce and unfathomable thoughts engraved
Eternal wrath on his immortal face,
And where he gazed a gloom pervaded space.

25

As he drew near, he gazed upon the gate
    Ne'er to be entered more by him or Sin,
With such a glance of supernatural hate,
    As made Saint Peter wish himself within;
He patter'd with his keys at a great rate,
    And sweated through his apostolic skin:
Of course his perspiration was but ichor,
Or some such other spiritual liquor.

26

The very cherubs huddled all together,
    Like birds when soars the falcon; and they felt
A tingling to the top of every feather,
    And formed a circle like Orion's belt
Around their poor old charge; who scarce knew whither
    His guards had led him, though they gently dealt
With royal *manes*, (for by many stories,
And true, we learn the angels are all Tories).

27

As things were in this posture, the gate flew
    Asunder, and the flashing of its hinges
Flung over space an universal hue
    Of many-coloured flame, until its tinges
Reached even our speck of earth, and made a new
    Aurora Borealis spread its fringes
O'er the North Pole; the same seen when ice-bound
By Captain Parry's ship in 'Melville's Sound'.

28

And from the door thrown open issued beaming
    A beautiful and mighty Thing of Light,
Radiant with glory, like a banner streaming
    Victorious from some world-o'erthrowing fight:
My poor comparisons must needs be teeming
    With earthly likenesses, for here the night
Of clay obscures our best conceptions saving
Joanna Southcote, or Bob Southey, raving.

29

'Twas the archangel Michael; all men know
    The make of angels and archangels, since
There's scarce a scribbler has not one to show,
    From the fiends' leader to the angels' prince:
There also are some altar pieces, though
    I really can't say that they much evince
One's inner notions of immortal spirits;
But let the connoisseurs explain *their* merits.

*   *   *   *   *

35

The spirits were in neutral space, before
   The gate of heaven; like eastern thresholds is
The place where Death's grand cause is argued o'er,
   And souls despatched to that world or to this;
And therefore Michael and the other wore
   A civil aspect, though they did not kiss,
Yet still between his darkness and his Brightness
There passed a mutual glance of great politeness.

36

The Archangel bow'd, not like a modern beau,
   But with a graceful Oriental bend,
Pressing one radiant arm just where below
   The heart in good men is suppos'd to tend;
He turn'd as to an equal, not too low,
   But kindly; Satan met his ancient friend
With more hauteur, as might an old Castilian
Poor noble meet a mushroom rich civilian.

37

He merely bent his diabolic brow,
   An instant; and then raising it, he stood
In act to assert his right or wrong, and show
   Cause why King George by no means could or should
Make out a case to be exempt from woe
   Eternal more than other kings, endued
With better sense and hearts, whom history mentions,
Who long have 'paved Hell with their good intentions'.

38

Michael began, 'What would'st thou with this man,
   Now dead, and brought before the Lord? What ill
Hath he wrought since his mortal race began,
   That thou canst claim him? Speak! and do thy will
If it be just: if in this earthly span
   He hath been greatly failing to fulfil
His duties as a king and mortal, say,
And he is thine; if not, let him have way.'

39

'Michael!' replied the Prince of Air, 'even here,
 Before the Gate of him thou servest must
I claim my subject: and will make appear
 That as he was my worshipper in dust,
So shall he be in spirit, although dear
 To thee and thine, because nor wine nor lust
Were of his weaknesses; yet on his throne
He reigned o'er millions to serve me alone.

40

'Look to our earth, or rather *mine*; it was
 Once, more thy master's; but I triumph not
In this poor planet's conquest; nor alas!
 Need he thou servest envy me my lot:
With all the myriads of bright worlds which pass
 In worship round him, he may have forgot
Yon weak creation of such paltry things:
I think few worth damnation save their kings, –

41

'And these but as a kind of quit-rent, to
 Assert my right as lord: and even had
I such an inclination, 'twere (as you
 Well know) superfluous, they are grown so bad
That hell has nothing better left to do
 Than leave them to themselves: so much more mad
And evil, by their own internal curse,
Heaven cannot make them better, nor I worse.

42

'Look to the earth, I said, and say again
 When this old, blind, mad, helpless, weak,
  poor worm
Began in youth's first bloom and flush to reign,
 The world and he both wore a different form,
And much of earth and all the watery plain
 Of ocean called him king: through many a storm
His isles had floated on the abyss of time;
For the rough virtues chose them for their clime.

43

'He came to his sceptre young; he leaves it old:
   Look to the state in which he found his realm,
And left it; and his annals too behold,
   How to a minion first he gave the helm;
How grew upon his heart a thirst for gold,
   The beggar's vice, which can but overwhelm
The meanest hearts; and for the rest but glance
Thine eye along America and France.

44

' 'Tis true, he was a tool from first to last
   (I have the workmen safe); but as a tool
So let him be consumed. From out the past
   Of ages, since mankind have known the rule
Of monarchs – from the bloody rolls amass't
   Of sin and slaughter – from the Caesars' school,
Take the worst pupil; and produce a reign
More drench'd with gore, more cumber'd with the slain.

45

'He ever warr'd with freedom and the free;
   Nations as men, home subjects, foreign foes,
So that they uttered the word "Liberty!"
   Found George the Third their first opponent. Whose
History was ever stained as his will be
   With national and individual woes?
I grant his household abstinence; I grant
His neutral virtues, which most monarchs want;

46

'I know he was a constant consort; own
   He was a decent sire, and middling lord,
All this is much, and most upon a throne;
   As temperance, if at Apicius' board,
Is more than at an anchorite's supper shown.
   I grant him all the kindest can accord;
And this was well for him, but not for those
Millions who found him what oppression chose.

47

'The New World shook him off; the Old yet groans
   Beneath what he and his prepared if not
Completed; he leaves heirs on many thrones
   To all his vices, without what begot
Compassion for him – his tame virtues: drones
   Who sleep, or despots, who have now forgot
A lesson which shall be retaught them, wake
Upon the thrones of earth; but let them quake!'

*   *   *   *   *

GEORGE GORDON, LORD BYRON (1821)

Compare this reaction to the death of George III (an answer to a poem with the same title by the poet laureate Southey) with the more humorously contemptuous one to the death of his son George IV by Winthrop Mackworth Praed in Section 4 below.

from *The Mask of Anarchy*

*Written on the occasion of the
massacre at Manchester*

1

As I lay asleep in Italy
There came a voice from over the Sea,
And with great power it forth led me
To walk in the visions of Poesy.

2

I met Murder on the way –
He had a mask like Castlereagh –
Very smooth he looked, yet grim;
Seven bloodhounds followed him:

3

All were fat; and well they might
Be in admirable plight,
For one by one and two by two,
He tossed them human hearts to chew
Which from his wide cloak he drew.

4

Next came Fraud, and he had on,
Like Eldon, an ermined gown,
His big tears, for he wept well
Turned to millstones as they fell.

5

And the little children who
Round his feet played to and fro,
Thinking every tear a gem,
Had their brains knocked out by them.

6

Clothed with the Bible, as with light,
And the shadows of the night,
Like Sidmouth, next Hypocrisy
On a crocodile rode by.

7

And many more Destructions played
In this ghastly masquerade,
All disguised, even to the eyes,
Like Bishops, lawyers, peers or spies.

8

Last came Anarchy; he rode
On a white horse, splashed with blood;
He was pale, even to the lips
Like Death in the Apocalypse.

9

And he wore a kingly crown;
And in his hand a sceptre shone;
On his brow this mark I saw –
'I AM GOD AND KING AND LAW!'

10

With a pace stately and fast,
Over English lands he passed,
Trampling to a mire of blood
The admiring multitude.

11

And a mighty troop around,
With their trampling shook the ground,
Waving each a bloody sword,
For the service of their Lord.

12

And with glorious triumph they
Rode through England proud and gay,
Drunk as with intoxication
On the wine of desolation.

13

O'er fields and towns, from sea to sea,
Passed the Pageant, swift and free,
Tearing up and trampling down
Till they came to London town.

14

And each dweller, panic stricken
Felt his heart with terror sicken
Hearing the tempestuous cry
Of the triumph of Anarchy.

15

For with pomp to meet him came,
Clothed in arms like blood and flame,
The hired murderers who did sing
'Thou art God and Law and King.

16

'We have waited, weak and lone
For thy coming Mighty One!
Our purses are empty, our swords are cold,
Give us glory, and blood, and gold.'

17

Lawyers and priests, a motley crowd,
To the earth their pale brows bowed;
Like a bad prayer not over loud,
Whispering – 'Thou art Law and God.' –

18

Then all cried with one accord,
'Thou art King and God and Lord;
Anarchy to thee we bow,
Be thy name made holy now!'

19

And Anarchy, the Skeleton,
Bowed and grinned to everyone,
As well as if his education
Had cost ten millions to the nation.

20

For he knew the Palaces
Of our kings were rightly his;
His the sceptre, crown and globe
And the gold inwoven robe.

21

So he sent his slaves before
To seize upon the Bank and Tower,
And was proceeding with intent
To meet his pensioned Parliament

22

When one fled past, a maniac maid
And her name was Hope, she said:
But she looked more like Despair,
And she cried out in the air:

23

'My father Time is old and grey
With waiting for a better day:
See how idiot like he stands,
Fumbling with his palsied hands!

24

'He has had child after child,
And the dust of death is piled
Over everyone but me –
Misery, oh, Misery!'

25

Then she lay down in the street,
Right before the horses' feet,
Expecting with a patient eye,
Murder, Fraud and Anarchy.

26

When, between her and her foes,
A mist, a light, an image rose,
Small at first, and weak and frail
Like the vapour of a vale:

27

Till, as clouds grow on the blast,
Like tower-crowned giants striding fast,
And glare with lightnings, as they fly,
And speak with thunder to the sky,

28

It grew – a Shape arrayed in mail
Brighter than the viper's scale,
And upborne on wings whose grain
Was as the light of sunny rain.

29

On its helm seen far away,
A planet, like the Morning's, lay;
And those plumes its light rained through
Like a shower of crimson dew.

30

With step as soft as dew it passed
O'er the heads of men – so fast
That they knew the presence there,
And looked, – but all was empty air.

31

As flowers beneath May's footstep waken,
As stars from Night's loose hair are shaken,
As waves arise when loud winds call,
Thoughts sprung where'er that step did fall.

32

And the prostrate multitude
Looked – and ankle-deep in blood,
Hope, that maiden most serene,
Was walking with a quiet mien:

33

And Anarchy the ghastly birth
Lay, dead earth, upon the earth;
The Horse of Death, tameless as wind,
Fled, and with his hoofs did grind
To dust the murderers thronged behind.

*   *   *   *   *

P. B. SHELLEY (1819)

This poem, which concludes with a supernatural voice urging the English people to unite and resist the tyranny of the few, was inspired by the Peterloo Massacre of 1819 in which eleven protesters at a mass meeting demanding Parliamentary reforms were killed by the Manchester Yeomanry.

from *Prometheus Unbound*

The speech of the Spirit of the Hour

As I have said, I floated to the earth:
It was, as it is still, the pain of bliss
To move, to breathe, to be; I wandering went
Among the haunts and dwellings of mankind,
And first was disappointed not to see
Such mighty change as I had felt within
Expressed in outward things; but soon I looked,
And behold, thrones were kingless, and men walked
One with the other even as spirits do,
None fawned, none trampled; hate, disdain or fear,
Self-love or self-contempt, on human brows
No more inscribed as o'er the gate of hell,
'All hope abandon ye who enter here;'
None frowned, none trembled, none with eager fear
Gazed on another's eye of cold command
Until the subject of a tyrant's will
Became, worse fate, the abject of his own,
Which spurred him, like an outspent horse, to death.
None wrought his lips in truth-entangling lines
Which smiled the lie his tongue disdained to speak;
None with firm sneer, trod out in his own heart
The sparks of love and hope, till there remained
Those bitter ashes, a soul self-consumed,
And the wretch crept a vampire among men,
Infecting all with his own hideous ill;
None talked that common, false, cold, hollow talk
Which makes the heart deny the *yes* it breathes,
Yet question that unmeant hypocrisy
With such a self-mistrust as has no name.
And women, too, frank, beautiful and kind
As the free heaven which rains fresh light and dew
On the wide earth, past; gentle radiant forms,
From custom's evil taint exempt and pure;
Speaking the wisdom once they could not think,

Looking emotions they once feared to feel,
And changed to all which once they dared not be,
Yet being now, made earth like heaven; nor pride,
Nor jealousy, nor envy, nor ill shame,
The bitterest of those drops of treasured gall,
Spoilt the sweet taste of the nepenthe, love.

Thrones, altars, judgement seats, and prisons; wherein,
And beside which, by wretched men were borne
Sceptres, tiaras, swords and chains, and tomes
Of reasoned wrong, glozed on by ignorance,
Were like those monstrous and barbaric shapes,
The ghosts of a no-more-remembered fame,
Which, from their unworn obelisks, look forth
In triumph o'er the palaces and tombs
Of those who were their conquerors: mouldering round,
These imaged to the pride of kings and priests
A dark yet mighty faith, a power as wide
As is the world it wasted, and are now
But an astonishment; even so the tools
And emblems of its last captivity,
Amid the dwellings of the peopled earth,
Stand not o'erthrown, but unregarded now.
And those foul shapes, abhorred by god and man,–
Which, under many a name and many a form
Strange, savage, ghastly, dark and execrable
Were Jupiter, the tyrant of the world;
And which the nations, panic-stricken, served
With blood, and hearts broken by long hope, and love
Dragged to his altars soiled and garlandless,
And slain amid men's unreclaiming tears,
Flattering the thing they feared, which fear was hate,–
Frowned, mouldering fast o'er their abandoned shrines;
The painted veil, by those who were, called life,
Which mimicked, as with colours idly spread,
All men believed or hoped, is torn aside;
The loathsome mask has fallen, the man remains
Sceptreless, free, uncircumscribed, but man
Equal, unclassed, tribeless and nationless,
Exempt from awe, worship, degree, the king

Over himself; just, gentle, wise: but man
Passionless? – no, yet free from guilt or pain,
Which were, for his will made or suffered them,
Nor yet exempt, though ruling them like slaves,
From chance and death, and mutability,
The clogs of that which else might oversoar
The loftiest star of unascended heaven,

PERCY BYSSHE SHELLEY (1819)

The Lost Leader

1

Just for a handful of silver he left us
   Just for a riband to stick in his coat
Found the one gift of which fortune bereft us
   Lost all the others she lets us devote;
They, with the gold to give, doled him out silver,
   So much was theirs who so little allowed:
How all our copper had gone for his service!
   Rags, were they purple, his heart had been proud!
We that had loved him so, followed him, honoured
      him,
   Lived in his mild and magnificent eye,
Learned his great language, caught his clear accents,
   Made him our pattern to live and to die!
Shakespeare was of us, Milton was for us,
   Burns, Shelley were with us, – they watch from
      their graves!
He alone breaks from the van and the freemen,
   He alone sinks to the rear and the slaves!

2

We shall march prospering, – not thro' his presence;
    Songs may inspirit us, – not from his lyre;
Deeds will be done, – while he boasts his quiescence,
    Still bidding crouch, when the rest bade aspire;
Blot out his name, then, record one lost soul more,
    One task more declined, one more footpath untrod,
One more devils'-triumph and sorrow for angels,
    One more wrong to man, one more insult to God!
Life's night begins: let him never come back to us!
    There would be doubt, hesitation and pain,
Forced praise on our part – the glimmer of twilight,
    Never glad confident morning again!
Best fight on well, for we taught him, strike gallantly,
    Menace our heart ere we master his own;
Then let him receive the new knowledge and wait us,
    Pardoned in heaven, the first by the throne!

ROBERT BROWNING (1843)

Written on Wordsworth's acceptance of the laureateship.

For Righteousness' Sake

*Inscribed to friends under arrest for
treason against the Slave Power*

The age is dull and mean. Men creep,
    Not walk; with blood too pale and tame
    To pay the debt they owe to shame;
Buy cheap, sell dear; eat, drink, and sleep
    Down-pillowed, deaf to moaning want;
Pay tithes for soul-insurance; keep
    Six days to Mammon, one to Cant.

In such a time give thanks to God,
   That somewhat of the holy rage
   With which the prophets in their age
On all its decent seemings trod,
   Has set your feet upon the lie,
That man and ox and soul and clod
   Are market stock to sell and buy.

The hot words from your lips, my own,
   To caution trained might not repeat;
   But if some tares amongst the wheat
Of generous thought and deed were sown,
   No common wrong provoked your zeal;
The silken gauntlet that is thrown
   In such a quarrel rings like steel.

The brave old strife the fathers saw
   For Freedom calls for men again
   Like those who battled not in vain
For England's charter, Alfred's law;
   And right of speech and trial just
Wage in your name their ancient war
   With venal courts and perjured trust.

God's ways seem dark, but, soon or late,
   They touch the shining hills of day;
   The evil cannot brook delay,
The good can well afford to wait.
   Give ermined knaves their hour of crime;
Ye have the future grand and great,
   The safe appeal of Truth to Time!

JOHN GREENLEAF WHITTIER

A Song in Time of Order

Push hard across the sand,
　For the salt wind gathers breath;
Shoulder and wrist and hand,
　Push hard as the push of death.

The wind is an iron that rings,
　The foamheads loosen and flee;
It swells and welters and swings,
　The pulse of the tides of the sea.

And up on the yellow cliff
　The long corn flickers and shakes;
Push, for the wind holds stiff,
　And the gunwale dips and rakes.

Good hap to the fierce fresh weather,
　The quiver and beat of the sea!
While three men hold together,
　The kingdoms are less by three.

Out to the sea with her there,
　Out with her over the sand;
Let the kings keep the earth for their share!
　We have done with the sharers of land.

They have tied the world in a tether,
　They have bought over God with a fee;
While three men hold together,
　The kingdoms are less by three.

We have done with the kisses that sting,
　The thief's mouth red from the feast,
The blood on the hands of the king
　And the lie at the lips of the priest.

Will they tie the winds in a tether,
    Put a bit in the jaws of the sea?
While three men hold together,
    The kingdoms are less by three.

Let our flag run out straight in the wind!
    The old red shall be floated again
When the ranks that are thin shall be thinned,
    When the names that were twenty are ten;

When the devil's riddle is mastered
    And the galley bench creaks with a Pope,
We shall see Bonaparte the bastard
    Kick heels with his throat in a rope.

While the shepherd sets wolves on his sheep
    And the emperor halters his kine,
While Shame is a watchman asleep
    And Faith is a keeper of swine,

Let the wind shake our flag like a feather,
    Like the plumes of the foam of the sea!
While three men hold together,
    The kingdoms are less by three.

All the world has its burdens to bear,
    From Cayenne to the Austrian whips;
Forth, with the rain in our hair
    And the salt sweet foam on our lips;

In the teeth of the glad hard weather,
    In the blown wet face of the sea;
While three men hold together,
    The kingdoms are less by three.

ALGERNON CHARLES SWINBURNE (1852)

Bonaparte here is Louis Napoleon who came to power in France by
a *coup d'état* in 1851 and was crowned as Napoleon III in 1852.

A Death Song

What cometh here from west to east awending?
And who are these, the marchers stern and slow?
We bear the message that the rich are sending
Aback to those who bade them wake and know.
Not one, not one, but thousands must they slay,
But one and all if they would dusk the day.

We asked them for a life of toilsome earning,
They bade us bide their leisure for our bread;
We craved to speak to tell our woeful learning:
We come back speechless, bearing back our dead.
Not one, not one, nor thousands must they slay,
But one and all, if they would dusk the day.

They will not learn; they have no heart to hearken.
They turn their faces from the eyes of fate;
Their gay-lit halls shut out the skies that darken,
But lo! this dead man knocking at the gate.
Not one, not one, nor thousands must they slay,
But one and all if they would dusk the day.

Here lies the sign that we shall break our prison;
Amidst the storm he won a prisoner's rest;
But in the cloudy dawn the sun arisen
Brings us our day of work to win the best.
Not one, not one, nor thousands must they slay,
But one and all, if they would dusk the day.

                                    WILLIAM MORRIS (1887)

Written for the funeral of a man who died from injuries received
while demonstrating for freedom of speech in Trafalgar Square.

2
POEMS OF
SOCIAL COMMENT
& OBSERVATION

A Ballad

In a costly palace Youth goes clad in gold
In a wretched workhouse Age's limbs are cold:
There they sit, the old men by a shivering fire,
Still close and closer cowering, warmth is their desire.

In a costly palace, when the brave gallants dine,
They have store of venison with old canary wine,
With singing and music, to heighten the cheer;
Coarse bits, with grudging are the pauper's best fare.

In a costly palace Youth is still caressed
By a train of attendants, which laugh at my young
    Lord's jest;
In a wretched workhouse the contrary prevails:
Does Age begin to prattle? – no man hearkens to his tales.

In a costly palace, if the child with a pin
Do but chance to prick a finger, straight the doctor is
    called in;
In a wretched workhouse, men are left to perish
For want of proper cordials, which their old age might
    cherish.

In a costly palace Youth enjoys his lust;
In a wretched workhouse, Age, in corners thrust,
Thinks upon the former days, when he was well to do,
Had children to stand by him, both friends and
    kinsmen too.

In a costly palace, Youth his temples hides
With a new-devised peruke that reaches to his sides;
In a wretched workhouse Age's crown is bare,
With a few thin locks just to fence out the cold air.

In peace, as in war, 'tis our young gallant's pride
To walk, each one, in the streets with a rapier by his side,
That none to do them injury may have pretence;
Wretched Age, in poverty, must brook offence.

CHARLES LAMB

Enclosure

Far spread the moory ground a level scene,
Bespread with rush and one eternal green
That never felt the rage of wandering plough,
Though centuries' wreathed spring's blossoms on its brow,
Autumn met plains that stretched them far away
In unchecked shadows of green, brown and grey.
Unbounded freedom ruled the wandering scene,
Nor fence of ownership crept in between
To hide the prospect of the gazing eye:
Its only bondage was the circling sky.
One mighty flat, undwarfed by bush and tree,
Spread its faint shadow of immensity
And lost itself, which seemed to eke its bounds
In the blue mist the horizon's edge surrounds.

Now this sweet vision of my boyish hours
Free as spring clouds and wild as summer flowers
Is faded all – a hope that blossomed free
And hath been once no more shall ever be.
Inclosure came and trampled on the grave
Of labour's rights, and left the poor a slave.
And memory's pride, ere want to wealth did bow,
Is both the shadow and the substance now.
The sheep and cows were free to range as then
Where change might prompt, nor felt the bonds of men.
Cows went and came with evening, morn and night
To the wild pasture, as their common right
And sheep, unfolded with the rising sun,
Heard the swains shout, and felt their freedom won,
Tracked the red fallow field and heath and plain
Then met the brook and drank and roamed again:
While the glad shepherd traced their tracks along,
Free as the lark, and happy as her song.
But now all's fled, and flats of many a dye
That seemed to lengthen with the following eye,
Moors loosing from the sight far smooth and blea,
Where swoopt the plover in its pleasure free,

Are vanished now, with heaths once wild and gay
As poets' visions of life's early day.
Like mighty giants of their limbs bereft,
    The sky bound moors in mangled garbs are left
Fence now meets fence in owners' little bounds
Of field and meadow, large as garden-grounds,
In little parcels little minds to please,
With men and flocks imprisoned, ill at ease.
For with the poor scared freedom bade farewell,
And fortune hunters totter where they fell,
They dreamed of riches in the rebel scheme
And find too truly that they did but dream.

JOHN CLARE (c. 1823)

This is the version in the 1935 edition of Clare's poetry. A longer,
somewhat different version entitled 'The Moors' is available in the
new standard edition.

The Song of the Shirt

With fingers weary and worn,
    With eyelids heavy and red,
A Woman sat in unwomanly rags,
    Plying her needle and thread –
        Stitch! stitch! stitch!
In poverty, hunger and dirt,
And still with a voice of dolorous pitch
    She sang the Song of the Shirt!

'Work! work! work!
While the cock is crowing aloof!
    And work – work – work,
Till the stars shine through the roof!
    It's O! to be a slave
    Along with the barbarous Turk,
Where woman has never a soul to save,
    If this is Christian work!

'Work! work! work!
Till the brain begins to swim;
    Work – work – work
Till the eyes are heavy and dim!
Seam and gusset and band,
    Band and gusset and seam,
Till over the buttons I fall asleep,
    And sew them on in a dream!

'O! Men with Sisters dear!
    O! Men with Mothers and Wives!
It is not linen you're wearing out,
    But human creatures' lives!
        Stitch – stitch – stitch,
    In poverty, hunger and dirt,
Sewing at once, with a double thread,
    A Shroud as well as a Shirt.

'But why do I talk of Death?
    That Phantom of grisly bone,
I hardly fear his terrible shape,
    It seems so like my own –
    It seems so like my own,
    Because of the fasts I keep,
Oh! God! that bread should be so dear,
    And flesh and blood so cheap!

'Work – work – work!
    My labour never flags;
And what are its wages? A bed of straw,
    A crust of bread – and rags,
That shattered roof, – and this naked floor –
    A table – a broken chair –
And a wall so blank, my shadow I thank
    For sometimes falling there!

'Work – work – work!
From weary chime to chime,
    Work – work – work,
As prisoners work for crime!
    Band, and gusset, and seam,
    Seam, and gusset, and band,
Till the heart is sick, and the brain benumb'd,
    As well as the weary hand.

'Work – work –work
In the dull December light,
    And work, work, work,
When the weather is warm and bright –
While underneath the eaves
    The brooding swallows cling
As if to show me their sunny backs
    And twit me with the spring.

'Oh! but to breathe the breath
Of the cowslip and primrose sweet –
    With the sky above my head,
And the grass beneath my feet,

For only one short hour
   To feel as I used to feel,
Before I knew the woes of want
   And the walk that costs a meal!

'Oh! but for one short hour!
   A respite, however brief!
No blessed leisure for Love or Hope,
   But only time for Grief!
A little weeping would ease my heart,
   But in their briny bed
My tears must stop, for every drop
   Hinders needle and thread!

'Seam, and gusset, and band,
Band, and gusset, and seam,
   Work, work, work,
Like the Engine that works by Steam!
A mere Machine of iron and wood
   That toils for Mammon's sake –
Without a brain to ponder and craze
   Or a heart to feel – and break!'

With fingers weary and worn,
   With eyelids heavy and red,
A Woman sat, in unwomanly rags,
   Plying her needle and thread –
      Stitch! stitch! stitch!
   In poverty, hunger and dirt.,
And still with a voice of dolorous pitch,
Would that its tone could reach the Rich! –
   She sang the Song of the Shirt!

THOMAS HOOD (1843)

The Cry of the Children

1

Do you hear the children weeping, O my brothers,
    Ere the sorrow comes with years?
They are leaning their young heads against their mothers,
    And that cannot stop their tears,
The young lambs are bleating in the meadows,
    The young birds are chirping in the nest,
The young fawns are playing with the shadows,
    The young flowers are blowing toward the west –
But the young, young children, O my brothers,
    They are weeping bitterly!
They are weeping in the playtime of the others,
    In the country of the free.

2

Do you question the young children in the sorrow,
    Why the tears are falling so?
The old man may weep for his tomorrow
    Which is lost in Long Ago;
The old tree is leafless in the forest,
    The old year is ending in the frost,
The old wound, if stricken, is the sorest,
    The old hope is hardest to be lost.
But the young young children, O my brothers,
    Do you ask them why they stand
Weeping sore before the bosoms of their mothers,
    In our happy Fatherland?

3

They look up with their pale and sunken faces,
    And their looks are sad to see,
For the man's hoary anguish draws and presses
    Down the cheeks of infancy.
'Your old earth,' they say, 'is very dreary;
    Our young feet,' they say, 'are very weak!
Few paces have we taken, yet are weary –

Our grave-rest is very far to seek.
Ask the aged why they weep, and not the children;
    For the outside earth is cold;
And we young ones stand in our bewildering,
    And the graves are for the old.'

4

'True,' say the children, 'it may happen
    That we die before our time;
Little Alice died last year – her grave is shapen
    Like a snowball, in the rime.
We looked into the pit prepared to take her:
    Was no room for any work in the close clay!
From the sleep wherein she lieth, none will wake her,
    Crying, "Get up, little Alice! it is day."
If you listen by that grave in sun and shower,
    With your ear down, little Alice never cries;
Could we see her face, be sure we would not know her,
    For the smile has time for growing in her eyes:
And merry go her moments, lulled and stilled in
    The shroud by the kirk-chime!
It is good when it happens,' say the children,
    'That we die before our time.'

5

Alas, alas, the children! They are seeking
    Death in life, as best to have;
They are binding up their hearts away from breaking,
    With a cerement from the grave.
Go out, children, from the mine and from the city,
    Sing out, children, as the little thrushes do;
Pluck you handfuls of the meadow cowslips pretty,
    Laugh aloud, to feel your fingers let them through!
But they answer, 'Are your cowslips of the meadows
    Like our weeds anear the mine?
Leave us quiet in the dark of the coal shadows,
    From your pleasures fair and fine!

6

'For, oh,' say the children, 'we are weary,
        And we cannot run or leap;
If we cared for any meadows, it were merely
        To drop down in them and sleep.
Our knees tremble sorely in the stooping,
        We fall upon our faces, trying to go;
And underneath our heavy eyelids drooping,
        The reddest flower would look as pale as snow;
For all day we drag our burden, tiring
        Through the coal dark underground –
Or, all day, we drive the wheels of iron
        In the factories, round and round.

7

'For, all day the wheels are droning, turning, –
        Their wind comes in our faces, –
Till our hearts turn, – our head with pulses burning,
        And the walls turn in their places;
Turns the sky in the high window blank and reeling,
        Turns the long light that drops adown the wall,
Turn the black flies that crawl along the ceiling,
        All are turning, all the day, and we with all.
And all day, the iron wheels are droning,
        And sometimes we could pray,
"O, ye wheels" (breaking out in a mad moaning),
        "Stop! be silent for today!" '

8

Ay! be silent! Let them hear each other breathing
        For a moment, mouth to mouth!
Let them touch each other's hands, in a fresh wreathing
        Of their tender human youth!
Let them feel that this cold metallic motion
        Is not all the life God fashions or reveals;
Let them prove their living souls against the notion
        That they live in you, or under you, O wheels! –
Still, all day, the iron wheels go onward,
        Grinding life down from its mark;

And the children's souls, which God is calling sunward,
    Spin on blindly in the dark.

9

Now tell the poor young children, O my brothers,
    To look up to Him and pray;
So the blessed One, who blesseth all the others,
    Will bless them another day.
They answer, 'Who is God, that he should hear us,
    While the rushing of the iron wheels is stirred?
When we sob aloud, the human creatures near us
    Pass by, hearing not, or answer not a word.
And we hear not (for the wheels in their resounding)
    Strangers speaking at the door.
Is it likely God, with angels singing round Him
    Hears our weeping any more?

10

'Two words indeed, of praying we remember,
    And at midnight's hour of harm,
"Our Father," looking upward in the chamber,
    We say softly, for a charm.
We know no other words, except "Our Father,"
    And we think that, in some pause of angels' song,
God may pluck them with the silence sweet to gather,
    And hold both within his right hand, which is
        strong.
"Our Father!" If he heard us, he would surely
    (For they call him good and mild)
Answer, smiling down the steep world very purely,
    "Come and rest with me, my child."

11

'But no!' say the children, weeping faster,
    'He is speechless as a stone;
And they tell us, of his image is the master
    Who commands us to work on.
Go to!' say the children, – 'up in Heaven,
    Dark, wheel-like, turning clouds are all we find.

Do not mock us; grief has made us unbelieving –
      We look up for God, but tears have made us blind.'
Do you hear the children weeping and disproving,
      O my brothers, what ye preach?
For God's possible is taught by his world's loving,
      And the children doubt of each.

12

And well may the children weep before you!
      They are weary ere they run;
They have never seen the sunshine nor the glory
      Which is brighter than the sun.
They know the grief of man, without its wisdom;
      They sink in man's despair, without its calm;
Are slaves, without the liberty in Christdom,
      Are martyrs by the pang, without the palm, –
Are worn, as if with age, yet unretrievingly
      The harvest of its memories cannot reap, –
Are orphans of the earthly love and heavenly.
      Let them weep! Let them weep!

13

They look up, with their pale and sunken faces,
      And their look is dread to see,
For they mind you of their angels in high places,
      With eyes turned on Deity! –
'How long,' they say, 'how long, O cruel nation,
      Will you stand, to move the world, on a child's
        heart, –
Stifled down with a mailed heel its palpitation,
      And tread onward to your throne amid the mart?
Our blood splashes upward, O gold-heaper,
      And your purple shows your path!
But the child's sob in the silence curses deeper
      Than the strong man in his wrath.'

                  ELIZABETH BARRETT BROWNING (1843)

The Bridge of Sighs

One more unfortunate
Weary of breath
Rashly importunate
Gone to her death!

Take her up tenderly,
Lift her with care;
Fashioned so slenderly
Young and so fair!

Look at her garments
Clinging like cerements;
While the wave constantly
Drips from her clothing;
Take her up instantly
Loving, not loathing.

Touch her not scornfully;
Think of her mournfully,
Gently and humanly;
Not of the stains of her –
All that remains of her
Now is pure womanly.
Make no deep scrutiny
Into her mutiny:
Rash and undutiful;
Past all dishonour,
Death has left on her
Only the beautiful.

Still, for all slips of hers,
One of Eve's family –
Wipe those poor lips of hers
Oozing so clammily.

Loop up her tresses
Escaped from the comb,
Her fair auburn tresses,
While wonderment guesses:
Where was her home?

Who was her father?
Who was her mother?
Had she a sister?
Had she a brother?
Or was there a dearer one
Still, and a nearer one
Yet than all other?

Alas! for the rarity
Of Christian charity
Under the sun!
O! It was pitiful!
Near a whole city full,
Home she had none.

Sisterly, brotherly,
Fatherly, motherly
Feelings had changed:
Love, by hard evidence,
Thrown from its eminence,
Even God's providence
Seeming estranged.
Where the lamps quiver
So far in the river,
With many a light
From window and casement,
From garret and basement,
She stood, with amazement,
Houseless, by night.

The bleak wind of March
Made her tremble and shiver;
But not the dark arch,
Or the black flowing river:

Mad from life's history,
Glad to death's mystery
Swift to be hurl'd –
Anywhere, anywhere
Out of the world!

In she plunged boldly,
No matter how coldly
The rough river ran
Over the brink of it, –
Picture it, think of it,
Dissolute Man!
Lave in it, drink of it,
Then, if you can!

Take her up tenderly,
Lift her with care;
Fashioned so slenderly
Young and so fair!
Ere her limbs frigidly
Stiffen too rigidly,
Decently, kindly,
Smooth and compose them;
And her eyes, close them,
Staring so blindly!

Dreadfully staring
Through muddy impurity,
As when with the daring
Last look of despairing
Fixed on futurity.

Perishing gloomily,
Spurred by contumely
Cold inhumanity
Burning insanity
Into her rest.
– Cross her hands humbly,
As if praying dumbly,
Over her breast.

Owning her weakness,
Her evil behaviour,
And leaving, with meekness,
Her sins to her Saviour.

THOMAS HOOD (Published 1844)

The Latest Decalogue

Thou shalt have one God only; who
Would be at the expense of two?
No graven images may be
Worshipped, except the currency;
Swear not at all; for, for thy curse
Thine enemy is none the worse;
At church on Sunday to attend
Will serve to keep the world thy friend;
Honour thy parents; that is, all
From whom advancement may befall;
Thou shalt not kill; but need'st not strive
Officiously to keep alive;
Do not adultery commit;
Advantage rarely comes of it;
Thou shalt not steal; an empty feat,
When it's so lucrative to cheat;
Bear not false witness, let the lie
Have time on its own wings to fly;
Thou shalt not covet, but tradition
Approves all forms of competition.

ARTHUR HUGH CLOUGH (1862)

The Ruined Maid

'O, Melia, my dear, this does everything crown!
Who could have supposed I should see you in Town?
And whence such fair garments, such prosperi-ty?' –
'O didn't you know I'd been ruined?' said she.

– 'You left us in tatters, without shoes or socks,
Tired of digging potatoes, and spudding up docks;
And now you've gay bracelets and bright feathers three!'
'Yes, that's how we dress when we're ruined,' said she.

– 'At home in the barton you said "thee" and "thou,"
And "thik oon", and "theas oon", and "t'other"; but now
Your talking quite fits 'ee for high compa-ny!'
'Some polish is gained with one's ruin,' said she.

– 'Your hands were like paws then, your face blue and
    bleak
But now I'm bewitched by your delicate cheek,
And your little gloves fit as on any la-dy!' –
'We never do work when we're ruined,' said she

– 'You used to call home life a hag-ridden dream,
And you'd sigh and you'd sock; but at present you seem
To know not of megrims and melancho-ly!' –
'True. One's pretty lively when ruined,' said she.

– 'I wish I had feathers, a fine sweeping gown,
And a delicate face, and could strut about Town!' –
'My dear – a raw country girl, such as you be,
Cannot quite expect that. You ain't ruined,' said she.

THOMAS HARDY (1866)

from *Xantippe*

This poem, although set in Ancient Greece, with Socrates' legendarily shrewish wife Xanthippe as narrator, clearly reflects Amy Levy's view of the condescending attitude of intellectual men to women in her own age. I have therefore placed it here rather than in Section 12, Echoes of Greece and Rome. The 'subtle herb' mentioned at the end of the passage is the hemlock which Socrates was made to drink when condemned to death for his teachings.

> I do remember how, one summer's eve,
> He, seated in an arbour's leafy shade,
> Had bade me bring fresh wineskins . . .
>   As I stood
> Ling'ring upon the threshhold, half concealed
> By tender foliage, and my spirit light
> With draughts of sunny weather, did I mark
> An instant the gay group before mine eyes.
> Deepest in shade, and facing where I stood,
> Sat Plato, with his calm face and low brows
> Which met above the narrow Grecian eyes,
> The pale thin lips just parted to the smile,
> Which dimpled that smooth olive of his cheek.
> His head a little bent, sat Sokrates,
> With one swart finger raised admonishing,
> And on the air were borne his changing tones.
> Low lounging at his feet, one fair arm thrown
> Around his knee (the other, high in air
> Brandished a brazen amphor, which yet rained
> Bright drops of ruby on the golden locks
> And temples with their fillets of the vine)
> Lay Alkibiades the beautiful.
> And thus, with solemn tone, spake Sokrates:
> 'This fair Aspasia, which our Pericles
> Hath brought from realms afar, and set on high
> In our Athenian city, hath a mind,
> I doubt not, of a strength beyond her race,
> And makes employ of it, beyond the way
> Of women nobly gifted: woman's frail, —

Her body rarely stands the test of soul;
She grows intoxicate with knowledge; throws
The laws of custom, order, 'neath her feet,
Feasting at life's great banquet with wide throat.'
Then sudden, stepping from my leafy screen,
Holding the swelling wine-skin o'er my head,
With breast that heaved and eyes and cheeks aflame,
Lit by a fury and a thought I spake:
'By all great powers about us! can it be
That we poor women are empirical?
That gods who fashioned us did strive to make
Beings too fine, too subtly delicate,
With sense that thrilled response to ev'ry touch
Of nature's, and their task is not complete?
That they have sent their half-completed work
To bleed and quiver here upon the earth?
To bleed and quiver, and to weep and weep,
To beat its soul against the marble walls
Of men's cold hearts, and then at last to sin!'
  I ceased, the first hot passion stayed and stemmed
And frighted by the silence: I could see,
Framed by the arbour foliage, which the sun,
In setting, softly gilded with rich gold,
Those upturned faces, and those placid limbs;
Saw Plato's narrow eyes and niggard mouth,
Which half did smile, and half did criticise,
One hand held up, the shapely fingers framed
To gesture of entreaty – 'Hush, I pray,
Do not disturb her, let us hear the rest;
Follow her mood, for here's another phase
Of your black-browed Xantippe . . .'
                    Then I saw
Young Alkibiades, with laughing lips
And half shut eyes, contemptuous shrugging up
Soft snowy shoulders, till he brought the gold
Of flowing ringlets round about his breasts.
But Socrates, all slow and solemnly,
Raised, calm, his face to mine, and sudden spake:
'I thank thee for the wisdom which thy lips
Have thus let fall amongst us: prythee tell

From what high source, from what philosophies
Didst cull the sapient notion of thy words?'
Then stood I, straight and silent for a breath,
Dumb, crushed with all that weight of cold contempt;
But swiftly in my bosom there uprose
A sudden flame, a merciful fury sent
To save me; with both angry hands I flung
The skin upon the marble, where it lay
Spouting red rills and fountains on the white;
Then all unheeding faces, voices, eyes,
I fled across the threshold, hair unbound –
White garment stained to redness – beating heart
Flooded with all the rising tide of hopes
Which once had gushed out golden, now sent back,
Swift to their sources, never more to rise . . .
I think I could have borne the weary life,
The narrow life within the weary walls,
If he had loved me; but he kept his love
For this Athenian city and her sons;
And haply for some stranger-woman, bold
With freedom, thought and glib philosophy . . .
Ah me! the long, long weeping through the nights,
The weary watching for the pale-eyed dawn,
Which only brought fresh grieving; then I grew
Fiercer, and cursed from outy my inmost heart
The Fates which marked me an Athenian maid.
Then faded that vain fury; hope died out;
A huge despair was stealing on my soul,
A sort of fierce acceptance of my fate, –
He wished a household vessel – well 'twas good,
For he should have it! He should have no more
The yearning treasure of a woman's love,
But just the baser treasure which he sought.
I called my maidens, ordered out the loom,
And spun unceasing from the morn till eve;
Watching all keenly over warp and woof,
Weighing the white wool with a jealous hand.
I spun until, methinks, I spun away
The soul from out my body, the high thoughts
From out my spirit; till at last I grew

As ye have known me, – eye exact to mark
The texture of the spinning; ear all keen
For aimless talking when the moon is up,
And ye should be a-sleeping; tongue to cut
With quick incision, 'thwart the merry words
Of idle maidens . . .
                  Only yesterday
My hands did cease from spinning; I have wrought
My dreary duties, patient till the last.
The gods reward me! Nay, I will not tell
The after years of sorrow: wretched strife
With grimmest foes – sad Want and Poverty; –
Nor yet the time of horror, when they bore
My husband from the threshold; nay, nor when
The subtle weed had wrought its deadly work.
Alas! alas! I was not there to soothe
The last great moment; never any thought
Of her that loved him – save at least the charge,
All earthly, that her body should not starve . . .
You weep, you weep; I would not that ye wept;
Such tears are idle; with the young, such grief
Soon grows to gratulation, as, 'her love
Was withered by misfortune; mine shall grow
All nurtured by the loving,' or, 'her life
Was wrecked and shattered – mine shall smoothly sail.'
Enough, enough. In vain! in vain! in vain!
The gods forgive me! Sorely have I sinned
In all my life. A fairer fate befall
You all that stand there . . .
                Ha! the dawn has come;
I see a rosy glimmer – nay! it grows dark;
Why stand ye so in silence? throw it wide,
The casement, quick; why tarry? – give me air –
O fling it wide, I say, and give me light!

                           AMY LEVY (Published 1881)

Pericles, whose mistress Aspasia was renowned for her intellect, was the greatest statesman in the Athenian democracy. Xantippe protests that other women should not be regarded as merely 'empirical' (i.e. able to learn only from practical experience alone and not capable of abstract reasoning).

The Widow at Windsor

'Ave you 'eard of the Widow at Windsor
  With a hairy gold crown on 'er 'ead?
She 'as ships on the foam – she 'as millions at 'ome
  An' she pays us poor beggars in red.
(Ow, poor beggars in red!)
There's 'er nick on the cavalry 'orses,
  There's 'er mark on the medical stores –
An' er troopers you'll find with a fair wind be'ind
  That takes us to various wars.
    (Poor beggars, barbarious wars!)
    Then 'ere's to the Widow at Windsor,
      An 'ere's to the stores and the guns,
      The men and the 'orses that make up the forces
      O' Missis Victorier's sons.
    (Poor beggars! Victorier's sons!)

Walk wide o' the Widow at Windsor,
  For 'alf o' Creation she owns;
We 'ave bought 'er the same with the sword an' the
    flame,
  'An we've salted it down with our bones.
(Poor beggars! – it's blue with our bones!)
Hands off o' the sons o' the Widow
  Hands off o' the goods in 'er shop,
For the Kings must come down and the Emperors
    frown
  When the Widow at Windsor says 'Stop!'
    (Poor beggars! we're sent to say 'Stop!')
      Then 'ere's to the Lodge o' the Widow,
        From the Pole to the Tropics it runs –
      To the Lodge that we tile with the rank and the
        file,
        An' open in form wi' the guns.
      (Poor beggars! – it's always they guns!)

We 'ave 'eard o' the Widow at Windsor,
   It's safest to leave 'er alone:
For 'er sentries we stand by the sea an' the land
   Wherever the bugles are blown.
(Poor beggars, an' don't we get blown!)
    Take 'old o' the Wings o' the Mornin'
     An' flop round the earth till you're dead;
      But you won't get away from the tune that they play
      To the bloomin' old rag over'ead.
        (Poor beggars! – it's 'ot over'ead!)
         Then 'eres to the sons o' the Widow,
          Wherever, 'owever they roam.
         'Eres all they desire, 'an if they require
         A speedy return to their 'ome.
        (Poor beggars, they'll never see 'ome!)

RUDYARD KIPLING

Kipling would not normally be seen as a poet of social protest, but from his time in India he did come to sympathise with the lot of the ordinary soldiers serving in remote corners of empire. Queen Victoria was said to have been sufficiently unamused by this poem to deny Kipling the Laureateship.

3
FAITH, DOUBT, MELANCHOLY, DESPAIR & HOPE

See also, especially, the opening stanzas of Tennyson's *In Memoriam* in Section 8 and poems 34, 54–6 and 113 of that sequence.

Dejection: An Ode

Late, late yestreen I saw the new Moon,
With the old Moon in her arms;
And I fear, I fear, my master dear!
We shall have a deadly storm.

BALLAD OF SIR PATRICK SPENCE

1

Well, if the bard was weather-wise, who made
  The grand old ballads of Sir Patrick Spence,
This night so tranquil now, will not go hence
Unroused by winds, that ply a busier trade
Than those which mold yon cloud in lazy flakes,
Or the dull sobbing draft, that moans and rakes
Upon the strings of this Aeolian lute,
    Which better far were mute.
  For lo! the New-moon winter-bright!
  And over-spread with phantom light,
  (With swimming phantom light o'erspread,
  But rimmed and circled by a silver thread)
I see the old Moon in her lap foretelling
  The coming on of rain and squally blast.
And oh! that even now the gust were swelling,
  And the slant night-shower driving loud and fast!
Those sounds that oft have raised me, whilst they awed,
    And sent my soul abroad,
Might now perhaps their wonted impulse give,
Might startle this dull soul and make it move and live!

2

A grief without a pang, dull cold and drear,
  A stifled, drowsy., unimpassioned grief,
  Which finds no natural outlet, no relief,
    In word or sigh or tear –
Oh Lady!, in this wan and heartless mood,
To other thoughts by yonder throstle wooed,
  All this long eve, so balmy and serene,

Have I been gazing on the western sky,
    And its peculiar tint of yellow-green:
And still I gaze – and with how blank an eye!
And those thin clouds above, in flakes and bars,
That give away their motion to the stars;
Those stars, that glide behind them, or between,
Now sparkling, now bedimmed, but always seen:
Yon crescent Moon, as fixed as if it grew
In its own cloudless, starless lake of blue;
I see them all so excellently fair,
I see, not feel, how beautiful they are!

3

        My genial spirits fail;
        And what can these avail
To lift the smothering weight from off my breast?
        It were a vain endeavour
        Though I should gaze forever
On that green light that lingers in the West:
I may not hope from outward forms to win
The passion and the life whose fountains are within.

4

O Lady! we receive but what we give,
And in our life alone does Nature live:
Ours is her wedding garment, ours her shroud!
    And would we aught behold, of higher worth,
Than that inanimate cold world allowed
To the poor loveless ever-anxious crowd,
    Ah! from the soul itself must issue forth
A light, a glory, a fair luminous cloud
        Enveloping the Earth –
And from the Soul itself must there be sent
    A sweet and potent voice, of its own birth,
Of all sweet sounds the life and element!

5

O pure of heart! thou need'st not ask of me
What this strong music in the soul may be!
What, and wherein it doth exist,
This light, this glory, this fair luminous mist,
This beautiful and beauty-making power.
   Joy, virtuous Lady! Joy that ne'er was given
Save to the pure, and in their purest hour,
Life and Life's effluence, cloud at once and shower,
Joy., Lady, is the spirit and the power,
Which wedding Nature to us gives in dower
     A new Earth and new Heaven,
Undreamt of by the sensual and the proud –
Joy is the sweet voice, Joy the luminous cloud –
       We in ourselves rejoice!
And thence flows all that charms or ear or sight,
   All melodies the echoes of that voice,
All colours a suffusion from that light.

6

There was a time when, though my path was rough,
   This joy within me dallied with distress,
And all misfortunes were but as the stuff
   Whence Fancy made me dreams of happiness:
For hope grew round me, like the twining vine,
And fruits and foliage, not my own, seemed mine.
But now afflictions bow me down to earth:
Nor care I that they rob me of my mirth;
     But oh! each visitation
Suspends what nature gave me at my birth,
   My shaping spirit of Imagination.
For not to think of what I needs must feel,
   But to be still and patient all I can;
And haply by abstruse research to steal
   From my own nature all the natural man –
   This was my sole resource, my only plan:
Till that which suits a part infects the whole,
And now is almost grown the habit of my soul.

7

Hence, viper thoughts that coil around my mind,
  Reality's dark dream!
I turn from you, and listen to the wind,
  Which long has raved unnoticed. What a scream
Of agony by torture lengthened out
That lute sent forth! Thou Wind, that rav'st without,
  Bare crag or mountain tairn, or blasted tree,
Or pine grove whither woodman never clomb,
Or lonely house, long held the witches' home,
  Methinks were fitter instruments for thee,
Mad lutanist! who in this month of showers,
Of dark brown gardens, and of peeping flowers,
Mak'st devils' yule, with worse than wintry song,
The blossoms, buds, and timorous leaves among.
  Thou actor, perfect in all tragic sounds!
Thou mighty poet, e'en to frenzy bold!
   What tell'st thou now about?
   'Tis of the rushing of a host in rout,
  With groans of trampled men, with smarting wounds –
At once they groan with pain, and shudder with the cold!
But hush! there is a pause of deepest silence!
  And all that noise, as of a rushing crowd,
With groans and tremulous shudderings – all is over –
It tells another tale, with sounds less deep and loud!
   A tale of less affright,
   And tempered with delight,
As Otway's self head framed the tender lay –
   'Tis of a little child
   Upon a lonesome wild,
Not far from home, but she hath lost her way:
And now moans low in bitter grief and fear,
And now screams loud, and hopes to make her mother hear.

8

'Tis midnight, but small thoughts have I of sleep
Full seldom may my friend such vigils keep!
Visit her, gentle Sleep, with wings of healing,
  And may this storm be but a mountain birth,

May all the stars hang bright above her dwelling,
    Silent, as though they watched the sleeping Earth!
        With light heart may she rise,
        Gay fancy, cheerful eyes,
    Joy lift her spirit, joy attune her voice;
To her may all things live, from pole to pole,
Their life the eddying of her living soul!
Dear Lady, friend devoutest of my choice,
Thus may'st thou ever, evermore rejoice.

SAMUEL TAYLOR COLERIDGE (1802)

The Lady was Sara Hutchinson, with whom Coleridge, who had been unhappily married to Sara Fricker for seven years, was in love.

Elegiac Stanzas

*Suggested by a picture of Peele Castle, in a Storm,
painted by Sir George Beaumont*

I was thy neighbour once, thou rugged Pile,
Four summer weeks I dwelt in sight of thee;
I saw thee every day; and all the while
Thy form was sleeping on a glassy sea.

So pure the sky, so quiet was the air!
So like, so very like, was day to day!
Whene'er I looked, thy Image was still there;
It trembled, but it never passed away.

How perfect was the calm! It seemed no sleep;
No mood, which season takes away or brings;
I could have fancied that the mighty Deep
Was even the gentlest of all gentle Things.

Ah! THEN if mine had been the Painter's hand,
To express what then I saw; and add the gleam,
The light that never was, on sea or land,
The consecration, and the Poet's dream,

I would have planted thee, thou hoary Pile,
Amid a world how different from this
Beside a sea which could not cease to smile,
On tranquil land, beneath a sky of bliss.

Thou shouldst have seemed a treasure-house divine
Of peaceful years, a chronicle of heaven; –
Of all the sunbeams that did ever shine
The very sweetest had to thee been given.

A Picture it had been of lasting ease,
Elysian quiet, without toil or strife;
No motion but the moving tide, a breeze,
Or merely silent Nature's breathing life.

Such, in the fond illusion of my heart,
Such Picture would I at that time have made;
And seen the soul of truth in every part,
A steadfast peace that might not be betrayed.

So once it would have been, – 'tis so no more;
I have submitted to a new control;
A power is gone which nothing can restore;
A deep distress hath humanised my Soul.

Not for a moment could I now behold
A smiling sea and be what I have been:
The feeling of my loss will ne'er be old;
This, which I know, I speak with mind serene.

Then, Beaumont, Friend! who would have been the Friend.
If he had lived, of Him whom I deplore,
This work of thine I blame not, but commend;
This sea in anger, and that dismal shore.

O 'tis a passionate Work! – yet wise and well,
Well chosen is the spirit that is here;
That hulk which labours in the deadly swell,
This rueful sky, this pageantry of fear!

And this huge Castle, standing here sublime,
I love to see the look with which it braves,
Cased in the lightning armour of old Time,
The lightning, the fierce wind, and trampling waves.

Farewell, farewell the heart that lives alone,
Housed in a dream, at distance from the Kind!
Such happiness, wherever it be known,
Is to be pitied, for 'tis surely blind.

But welcome fortitude and patient cheer,
And frequent sights of what is to be borne!
Such sights, or worse, as are before me here, –
Not without hope we suffer and we mourn.

WILLIAM WORDSWORTH (1806)

Written after the death of his brother at sea.

I Wish I was by that Dim Lake

I wish I was by that dim Lake
Where sinful souls their farewell take
Of this vain world, and half-way lie
In death's cold shadow, ere they die.
There, there, far from thee,
Deceitful world, my home should be;
Whence, come what might of gloom and pain,
False hope should ne'er deceive again.

The lifeless sky, the mournful sound
Of unseen waters falling round;
The dry leaves quiv'ring o'er my head,
Like man, unquiet ev'n when dead!

These, ay, these shall wean
My soul from life's deluding scene,
And turn each thought, o'ercharged with gloom,
Like willows, downward tow'rds the tomb.

As they, who to their couch at night
Would win repose, first quench the light,
So must the hopes, that keep this breast
Awake, be quench'd, ere it can rest.
Cold, cold, this heart must grow,
Unmoved by either joy or woe,
Like freezing founts, where all that's thrown
Within their current turns to stone.

THOMAS MOORE

The Pillar of the Cloud

Lead kindly light amid the encircling gloom
   Lead Thou me on!
The night is dark and I am far from home –
   Lead Thou me on!
Keep Thou my feet: I do not ask to see
The distant scene, – one step enough for me.

I was not ever thus, nor pray'd that Thou
   Shouldst lead me on.
I lov'd to choose and see my path; but now
   Lead Thou me on!
I lov'd the garish day, and spite of fears,
Pride ruled my will: remember not past years.

So long Thy power hath blest me, sure it still
   Will lead me on,
O'er moor and fen, o'er crag and torrent, till
   The night is gone;
And with the morn those angel faces smile
Which I have lov'd long since and lost awhile.

JOHN HENRY (later Cardinal) NEWMAN (1833)

O Take this World away from Me

O take this world away from me;
Its strife I cannot bear to see,
Its very praises hurt me more
Than e'er its coldness did before,
Its hollow ways torment me now
And start a cold sweat on my brow,
Its noise I cannot bear to hear,
Its joy is trouble to my ear,
Its ways I cannot bear to see
Its crowds are solitudes to me.
Oh how I long to be agen
That poor and independent man,
With labour's lot from morn till night
And books to read at candle light,
That followed labour in the field
From light to dark when toil could yield
Real happiness with little gain,
Rich thoughtless health unknown to pain;
Though, leaning on my spade to rest,
I've thought how richer folk were blest
And knew not quiet was the best.

JOHN CLARE (before 1836)

Mezzo Cammin

Boppard on the Rhine. August 25, 1842

Half of my life is gone, and I have let
 The years slip from me and have not fulfilled
 The aspiration of my youth, to build
Some tower of song, with lofty parapet.
Not indolence, nor pleasure, nor the fret
 Of restless passions that would not be stilled,
 But sorrow, and a care that almost killed,
Kept me from what I may accomplish yet;

Though, half-way up the hill I see the Past
   Lying beneath me with its sounds and sights, –
   A city in the twilight dim and vast,
With smoking roofs, soft bells and twinkling lights, –
   And hear above me, on the autumnal blast
   The cataract of Death, far thundering from the heights.

HENRY WADSWORTH LONGFELLOW (1842)

The Nameless One

Roll forth, my song, like the rushing river,
   That sweeps along to the mighty sea;
God will inspire me while I deliver
     My soul of thee!

Tell thou the world, when my bones lie whitening
   Amid the last homes of youth and eld,
That once there was one whose veins ran lightning
     No eye beheld.

Tell how his boyhood was one drear night-hour,
   How shone for him, through all his griefs and gloom,
No star of all heaven sends to light our
     Path to the tomb.

Roll on my song, and to after ages
   Tell how, disdaining all that earth can give
He would have taught men, from wisdom's pages,
     The way to live.

And tell how, trampled derided, hated,
   And worn by weakness, disease and wrong,
He fled for shelter to God, who mated
     His soul with song

– With song which alway, sublime or vapid,
   Flowed like a rill in the morning beam,
Perchance not deep, but intense and rapid:
     A mountain stream.

Tell how this Nameless, condemned for years long
  To herd with demons from hell beneath,
Saw things that made him, with groans and tears, long
    For even death.

Go on to tell how, with genius wasted,
  Betrayed in friendship, befooled in love,
With spirit shipwrecked, and young hopes blasted,
    He still, still strove;

Till, spent with toil, dreeing death for others
  (And some whose hands should have wrought for him
If children live not for sires and mothers),
    His mind grew dim;

And he fell far through that pit abysmal,
  The gulf and grave of Maginn and Burns,
And pawned his soul for the devil's dismal
    Stock of returns.

But yet redeemed it in days of darkness,
  And shapes and signs of the final wrath,
When death, in hideous and ghastly starkness,
    Stood on his path.

And tell how now, amid wreck and sorrow,
  And want, and sickness, and houseless nights,
He bides in calmness the silent morrow
    That no ray lights.

And lives he still, then? Yes! Old and hoary
  At thirty-nine, from despair and woe,
He lives, enduring what future story
    Will never know.

Him grant a grave to, ye pitying noble,
  Deep in your bosoms; there let him dwell!
He, too, had tears for all in trouble,
    Here and in hell.

JAMES CLARENCE MANGAN (died 1849)

I Am

I am – yet what I am none cares or knows,
   My friends forsake me like a memory lost;
I am the self consumer of my woes.
   They rise and vanish in oblivions host,
Like shadows in love – frenzied stifled throes
And yet I am, and live like vapours tost

Into the nothingness of scorn and noise,
   Into the living sea of waking dreams,
Where there is neither sense of life or joys,
   But the vast shipwreck of my life's esteems;
And e'en the dearest, that I love the best –
Are strange – nay, rather stranger than the rest.

I long for scenes where man has never trod.
   A place where woman never smile or wept;
There to abide with my creator, God,
   And sleep as I in childhood sweetly slept:
Untroubled and untroubling where I lie,
    The grass below – above the vaulted sky.

                         JOHN CLARE (by 1846)

No Coward Soul is Mine

No coward soul is mine,
No trembler in the world's storm-troubled sphere
I see heaven's glories shine
And Faith shines equal, arming me from Fear

O God within my breast
Almighty, ever-present Deity,
Life that in me hast rest,
As I, Undying Life, have power in Thee.

Vain are the thousand creeds
That move men's hearts, unutterably vain,
Worthless as withered weeds,
Or idlest froth amid the boundless main

To waken doubt in one
Holding so fast by thy infinity,
So surely anchored on
The steadfast rock of Immortality.

With wide, embracing love
Thy spirit animates eternal years,
Pervades and broods above,
Changes, sustains, dissolves, creates and rears.

Though Earth and moon were gone
And suns and universes ceased to be,
And Thou wert left alone
Every Existence would exist in Thee.

There is not room for death,
Nor atom that his might could render void,
Since Thou art Being and Breath,
And what Thou art may never be destroyed.

                              EMILY BRONTË (1846)

Say Not the Struggle Naught Availeth

Say not the struggle naught availeth
    The labour and the wounds are vain,
The enemy faints not nor faileth,
    And as things have been they remain.

If hopes were dupes, fears may be liars;
    It may be, in yon smoke concealed,
Your comrades chase e'en now the fliers,
    And, but for you, possess the field.

For, while the tired waves, vainly breaking,
   Seem here no painful inch to gain,
Far back, through creeks and inlets making,
   Comes silent, flooding in, the main.

And not by eastern windows only,
   When daylight comes, comes in the light,
In front, the day climbs, slow, how slowly,
   But westward look, the land is bright!

ARTHUR HUGH CLOUGH (1849)

song from *The Princess*

Tears, idle tears, I know not what they mean,
Tears from the depths of some divine despair
Rise in the heart and gather to the eyes
In looking on the happy Autumn fields
And thinking of the days that are no more.

Fresh as the first beam glittering on a sail,
That brings our friends up from the underworld
Sad as the last which reddens over one
That sinks with all we love below the verge;
So sad, so fresh, the days that are no more.

Ah, sad and strange as in dark summer dawns
The earliest pipe of half awaken'd birds
To dying ears, when unto dying eyes
The casement slowly grows a glimmering square;
So sad, so strange, the days that are no more.

Dear as remembered kisses after death,
And sweet as those by hopeless fancy feign'd
On lips that are for others; deep as love,
Deep as first love, and wild with all regret;
O Death in Life, the days that are no more.

ALFRED, LORD TENNYSON (1847)

Dover Beach

The sea is calm tonight.
The tide is full, the moon lies fair
Upon the straits; – on the French coast the light
Gleams and is gone; the cliffs of England stand,
Glimmering and vast, out in the tranquil bay.
Come to the window, sweet is the night air!
Only, from the long line of spray
Where the sea meets the moon-blanched land,
Listen! you hear the grating roar
Of pebbles which the waves draw back and fling,
At their return, up the high strand,
Begin and cease, and then again begin,
With tremulous cadence slow, and bring
The eternal note of sadness in.

Sophocles long ago
Heard it on the Aegean, and it brought
Into his mind the turbid ebb and flow
Of human misery; we
Find also in the sound a thought,
Hearing it by this distant northern sea.

The Sea of Faith
Was once, too, at the full, and round earth's shore
Lay like the folds of a bright girdle furled.
But now I only hear
Its melancholy, long, withdrawing roar,
Retreating, to the breath
Of the night-wind, down the vast edges drear
And naked shingles of the world.

Ah love, let us be true to one another! for the world,
    which seems
To lie before us like a land of dreams,
So various, so beautiful, so new,
Hath really neither joy, nor love, nor light,
Nor certitude, nor peace, nor help for pain;

And we are here as on a darkling plain
Swept with confused alarms of struggle and flight,
Where ignorant armies clash by night.

MATTHEW ARNOLD (c. 1851)

Introspective

I wish it were over, the terrible pain,
Pang after pang, again and again;
First the shattering ruining blow,
Then the probing steady and slow.

Did I wince? I did not faint:
My soul broke but was not bent:
Up I stand like a blasted tree
By the shore of the shivering sea.

On my boughs neither leaf nor fruit,
No sap in my utmost root,
Brooding in an anguish dumb
On the short past and the long to-come.

Dumb I was when the ruin fell,
Dumb I remain and will never tell;
Oh my soul, I talk with thee,
But not another the sight must see.

I did not start when the torture stung,
I did not faint when the torture wrung;
Let it come tenfold if come it must,
But I will not groan when I bite the dust.

CHRISTINA ROSSETTI (1857)

I Felt a Funeral

I felt a funeral in my brain,
And mourners to and fro,
Kept treading, treading, till it seemed
That sense was breaking through.

And when they all were seated,
A service, like a drum
Kept beating, beating, till I thought
My mind was going numb.

And then I heard them lift a box,
And creak across my soul
With those same boots of lead, again,
Then space began to toll,

As all the heavens were a bell,
And being but an ear,
And I, and Silence, some strange race
Wrecked, solitary, here.

EMILY DICKINSON (1861)

I Know that He Exists

I know that He exists.
Somewhere, in silence.
He has hid his rare life
From our gross eyes.

'Tis an instant's play.
'Tis a fond ambush
Just to make bliss
Earn her own surprise!

But should the play
Prove piercing earnest, –
Should the glee glaze
In Death's stiff stare,

Would not the fun
Look too expensive?
Would not the jest
Have crawled too far?

EMILY DICKINSON (1862)

My Life Closed Twice

My life closed twice before its close:
It yet remains to see
If Immortality unveil
A third event to me,

So huge, so hopeless to conceive
As these that twice befell.
Parting is all we know of heaven
And all we need of hell.

EMILY DICKINSON

Up-Hill

Does the road wind up-hill all the way?
    Yes, to the very end.
Will the day's journey take the whole long day?
    From morn to night, my friend,

But is there for the night a resting-place?
    A roof for when the slow dark hours begin.
May not the darkness hide it from my face?
    You cannot miss that inn.

Shall I meet other wayfarers at night?
    Those who have gone before.
Then must I knock, or call when just in sight?
    They will not keep you standing at that door.

Shall I find comfort, travel sore and weak?
    Of labour you will find the sum.
Will there be beds for me and all who seek?
    Yea, beds for all who come.

CHRISTINA ROSSETTI (1861)

I Chafe at Darkness

I chafe at darkness in the night
    But when 'tis light
Hope shuts her eyes; the clouds are pale;
The fields stretch cold into a distance hard:
    I wish again to draw the veil
    Thousand-starred.

Am I of them whose blooms are shed,
    Whose fruits are spent,
Who from dead eyes see Life half dead, –
Because desire is feeble discontent?
    Ah, no! desire and hope should die,
    Thus were I.

But in me something clipped of wing,
    Within its ring
Frets; for I have lost what made
The dawn-breeze magic, and the twilight beam
    A hand with tidings o'er the glade
    Waving seem.

GEORGE MEREDITH (1862)

Prospice

Fear death? – to feel the fog in my throat,
  The mist in my face,
When the snows begin, and the blasts denote
  I am nearing the place,
The power of the night, the press of the storm,
  The post of the foe:
Where he stands, the Arch Fear in a visible form,
  Yet the strong man must go;
For the journey is done and the summit attained
  And the barriers fall,
Though a battle's to fight ere the guerdon be gained,
  The reward of it all.
I was ever a fighter, so – one fight more,
  The best and the last!
I would hate that death bandaged my eyes and
    forebore
  And bade me creep past.
No let me taste the whole of it, fare like my peers,
  The heroes of old,
Bear the brunt in a minute, pay glad life's arrears
  Of pain, darkness and cold.
For sudden the worst turns the best to the brave,
  The black minute's at end,
And the elements rage, the fiend-voices that rave,
  Shall dwindle, shall blend,
Shall change, shall become first a peace out of pain,
  Then a light, then thy breast,
O thou soul of my soul! I shall clasp thee again,
  And with God be the rest!

ROBERT BROWNING (1864)

Hap

If but some vengeful god would call to me
From up the sky, and laugh, 'Thou suffering thing,
Know that thy sorrow is my ecstasy,
That thy love's loss is my hate's profiting!'

Then would I bear it, clench myself and die,
Steeled by the sense of ire unmerited;
Half eased, in that a Powerfuller than I
Had willed and meted me the tears I shed,

But not so. How arrives it joy lies slain,
And why unblooms the best hope ever sown?
– Crass Casualty obstructs the sun and rain,
And dicing Time for gladness casts a moan . . .
These purblind doomsters had as readily strown
Blisses about my pilgrimage as pain.

THOMAS HARDY (1866)

The Middle Watch of the Night

1

I woke in the night and the darkness was heavy and deep;
    I had known it was dark in my sleep,
        And I rose and looked out,
And the fathomless dark was all sparkling, set thick round about
With the ancient inhabiters silent and wheeling too far
For man's heart, like a voyaging frigate, to sail where remote
        In the sheen of their glory they float,
Or man's soul, like a bird, to fly near, of their beams to partake,
            And dazed in their wake,
        Drink day that is born of a star.
I murmured, 'Remoteness and greatness, how deep you are set
        How afar in the rim of the whole;
You know nothing of me, or of man, nor of earth, O, nor yet
Of our light-bearer – drawing the marvellous moons as they roll,

    Of our regent the sun.
I look on you trembling, and think, in the dark with my soul,
How small is our place 'mid the kingdoms and nations of God;
   These are greater than we, every one.'
And there falls a great fear, and a dread cometh over, that cries
'O my hope! Is there any mistake?
Did He speak? Did I hear? Did I listen aright if He spake?
Did I answer Him duly? For surely I now am awake,
   If never I woke until now.'
And a light, baffling wind, that leads nowhither, plays on my brow.
As a sleep, I must think on my day, of my path as untrod,
Or trodden in dreams, in a dreamland whose coasts are a doubt;
Whose countries recede from my thoughts, as they grope round
  about,
   And vanish, and tell me not how.
Be kind to our darkness, O Fashioner, dwelling in light,
   And feeding the lamps of the sky;
Look down upon this one, and let it be sweet in Thy sight,
   I pray Thee, tonight.
O watch whom Thou madest to dwell on its soil, Thou Most High!
For this is a world full of sorrow (there may be but one);
Keep watch o'er its dust, else Thy children for aye are undone,
For this is a world where we die.

     2

With that, a still voice in my spirit that moved and that yearned
   (There fell a great calm while it spake),
I had heard it erewhile, but the noises of life are so loud,
That sometimes it dies in the cry of the street and the crowd:
To the simple it cometh, – the child, or asleep, or awake,
And they know not from whence; of its nature the wise never
  learned
By his wisdom; its secret the worker ne'er earned
By his toil; and the rich among men never bought with his gold;
   Nor the times of its visiting monarchs controlled,
   Nor the jester put down with his jeers
(For it moves where it will), nor its season the aged discerned
   By thought, in the ripeness of years.

O elder than reason and stronger than will!
A voice when the dark world is still:
Whence cometh it? Father Immortal, Thou knowest! and we –
We are sure of that witness, that sense which is sent us of Thee;
For it moves, and it yearns in its fellowship mighty and dread,
And let down to our hearts it is touched by the tears that we shed;
It is more than all meanings, and over all strife;
On its tongue are the laws of our life,
And it counts up the times of the dead.

3

I will fear you, O stars, nevermore.
I have felt it! Go on, while the world is asleep,
Golden islands fast moored in God's infinite deep,
Hark, hark, to the words of sweet fashion, the harpings of yore!
How they sang to him, seer and saint in the faraway lands:
'The heavens are the work of thy hands;
They shall perish but Thou shalt endure;
Yes, they shall all wax old –
But Thy throne is established, O God, and Thy years are made sure;
They shall perish, but Thou shalt endure –
They shall pass like a tale that is told.'

Doth he answer, the Ancient of Days?
Will he speak in the tongue and the fashion of men?
(Hist! hist! while the heaven-hung multitudes shine in His praise,
His language of old.) Nay, He spoke with them first; it was then
They lifted their eyes to His throne:
'They shall call on Me, "Thou art our Father, our God, Thou alone!"
For I made them, I led them in deserts and desolate ways;
I have found them a Ransom Divine;
I have loved them with love everlasting, the children of men;
I swear by Myself, they are Mine.'

JEAN INGELOW (Published 1874)

Invictus

Out of the night that covers me,
    Black as the Pit from pole to pole
I thank whatever gods may be
    For my unconquerable soul.

In the fell clutch of circumstance
    I have not winced nor cried aloud.
Under the bludgeonings of chance
    My head is bloody but unbowed.

Beyond this place of wrath and tears
    Looms but the Horror of the shade,
And yet the menace of the years
    Finds and shall find me unafraid.

It matters not how strait the gate,
    How charged with punishments the scroll
I am the master of my fate:
    I am the captain of my soul.

W. E. HENLEY (1875)

No worst, there is none

No worst, there is none. Pitched past pitch of grief,
More pangs will, schooled at forepangs, wilder wring.
Comforter, where is your comforting?
Mary, mother of us, where is your relief?
My cries heave, herds long; huddle in a main, a chief
Woe, world sorrow; on an age old anvil wince and sing –
Then lull, then leave off. Fury had shrieked 'No ling-
ering! Let me be fell; force I must be brief.'

O the mind, mind has mountains; cliffs of fall
Frightful, no-man-fathomed. Hold them cheap
May who ne'er hung there. Nor does long our small
Durance deal with that steep or deep. Here! creep,
Wretch, under a comfort serves in a whirlwind: all
Life death does end and each day dies with sleep.

GERARD MANLEY HOPKINS (1885)

I wake and feel the fell of dark

I wake and feel the fell of dark, not day.
What hours, O what black hours we have spent
This night! what sights you, heart, saw; ways you went!
And more must in yet longer light's delay.
With witness I speak this. But where I say
Hours I mean years, mean life. And my lament
Is cries countless, cries like dead letters sent
To dearest him that lives, alas! away.

I am gall, I am heartburn. God's most deep decree
Bitter would have me taste: my taste was me;
Bones built in me, flesh filled, blood brimmed the curse.
Self-yeast of spirit a dull dough sours. I see
The lost are like this, and their scourge to be
As I am mine, their sweating selves; but worse.

GERARD MANLEY HOPKINS (1885)

Vastness

Many a hearth upon our dark globe sighs after many a vanished
    face,
Many a planet by many a sun may roll, with the dust of a
    vanished race.

Raving politics, never at rest – as this earth's poor history runs, –
What is it all but a toiling of ants, in the gleam of a million
    million of suns?

Lies upon this side, lies upon that side, truthless violence
    mourned by the Wise,
Thousands of voices drowning his own in a popular torrent of
    lies upon lies;

Stately purposes, valour in battle, glorious annals of army and
    fleet,
Death for the right cause, death for the wrong cause, trumpets
    of victory groans of defeat;

Innocence seethed in her mother's milk and Charity setting the
    martyr aflame;
Thraldom who walks with the banner of freedom, and recks not
    to ruin a realm in her name.

Faith at her zenith, or all but lost in the gloom of doubts that
    darken the schools;
Craft with a bunch of all-heal in her hand, follow'd up by her
    vassal legion of fools;

Trade flying over a thousand seas, with her spice and her
    vintage, her silk and her corn;
Desolate offing, sailorless harbours, famishing populace,
    wharves forlorn.

Star of the morning, Hope in the sunrise; gloom of the evening,
    Life at a close;
Pleasure who flaunts on her wide down-way, with her flying
    robe and her poisoned rose;

Pain that has crawled from the corpse of Pleasure, a worm
    which writhes all day, and at night
Stirs up again in the heart of the sleeper, and stings him back to
    the curse of the light;

Wealth with his wines and his wedded harlots; honest Poverty,
    bare to the bone;
Opulent Avarice, lean as Poverty; Flattery gilding the rift in a
    throne;

Fame blowing out from her golden trumpet a jubilant challenge
    to Time and to Fate;
Slander, her shadow, sowing the nettle on all the laurel'd graves
    of the great;

Love for the maiden, crown'd with marriage, no regrets for
    aught that has been;
Household happiness, gracious children, debtless competence,
    golden mean;

National hatreds of whole generations, and pigmy spites of the
    village spire,
Vows that will last to the last death-rackle, and vows that are
    snapt in a moment of fire;

He that has lived for the lust of the minute, and died in the
    doing it, flesh without mind;
He that has nailed all flesh to the Cross, till Self died out in the
    love of his kind;

Spring and Summer and Autumn and Winter, and all these old
    revolutions of earth;
All new-old revolutions of Empire – change of the tide – what is
    all of it worth?

What the philosophies, all the sciences, poesy, varying voices of
    prayer?
All that is noblest, all that is basest, all that is filthy with all that
    is fair?

What is it all, if we all of us end but in being our own corpse-
    coffins at last,
Swallowed in Vastness, lost in Silence, drowned in the deeps of
    a meaningless Past?

What but a murmur of gnats in the gloom, or a moment's anger
    of bees in their hive? –

               *   *   *   *   *

Peace, let it be, for I loved him for ever; the dead are not dead,
    but alive.

                              ALFRED, LORD TENNYSON (Published 1889)

Crossing the Bar

Sunset and evening star,
    And one clear call for me!
And may there be no moaning at the bar,
    When I put out to sea,

But such a tide as moving seems asleep,
    Too full for sound and foam,
When that which drew from out the boundless
        deep
    Turns again home.

Twilight and evening bell,
    And after that the dark!
And may there be no sadness of farewell,
    When I embark;

For tho' from out our bourne of Time and Place
    The flood may bear me far,
I hope to see my Pilot face to face,
    When I have crost the bar.

                              ALFRED, LORD TENNYSON (1889)

Epilogue

At the midnight in the silence of the sleeptime,
    When you set your fancies free,
Will they pass to where – by death, fools think,
    imprisoned –
Low he lies who once so loved you, whom you loved so,
                – Pity me?

Oh, to love so, be so loved, yet so mistaken!
    What had I on earth to do
With the slothful, with the mawkish, the unmanly?
Like the aimless, helpless, hopeless, did I drivel
                – Being, who?

One who never turned his back but marched breast
    forward,
    Never doubted clouds would break,
Never dreamed, though right were worsted wrong would
    triumph,
Held we fall to rise, are baffled to fight better,
                – Sleep to wake.

No, at noonday in the bustle of man's work-time,
    Greet the unseen with a cheer!
Bid him forward, breast and back as either should be,
'Strive and thrive!' cry 'Speed, – fight on, fare ever
                There as here!'

                      ROBERT BROWNING (1889)

In Tenebris

Wintertime nighs
But my bereavement pain
It cannot bring again:.
      Twice no-one dies.

Flower petals flee;
But, since it once hath been,
No more that severing scene
      Can harrow me.

Birds faint in dread:
I shall not lose old strength
In the lone frost's black length;
      Strength long since fled!

Leaves freeze to dun;
But friends can not turn cold
This season as of old
      For him with none.

Tempests may scath;
But love can not make smart
Again this year his heart
      Who no heart hath.

Black is night's cope
But death will not appal
One who past doubtings all
      Lives in unhope.

THOMAS HARDY (1895–6)

4
THE LIGHTER SIDE

Meddlesome Matty

Oh how one ugly trick has spoiled
   The sweetest and the best!
Matilda, though a pleasant child
   One ugly trick possessed,
Which like a cloud before the skies
   Hid all her better qualities.

Sometimes she'd lift the teapot lid,
   To peep at what was in it,
Or tilt the kettle, if you did,
   But turn your back a minute;
In vain you told her not to touch,
   Her trick of meddling grew so much.

Her Grandmama went out one day,
   And by mistake she laid
Her spectacles and snuff-box gay
   Too near the little maid,
'Ah well,' thought she, 'I'll try them on,
   As soon as Grandmama is gone.'

Forthwith she placed upon her nose
   The glasses large and wide;
And looking round, as I suppose,
   The snuff-box too she spied.
'Oh, what a pretty box is this!
   I'll open it,' said little Miss.

'I know that Grandmama would say
   "Don't meddle with it, dear";
But then, she's far enough away,
   And no one else is near;
Besides, what can there be amiss
   In opening such a box as this?'

So thumb and finger went to work
    To move the stubborn lid,
And presently a mighty jerk
    The mighty mischief did;
For all at once, ah, woeful case!
    The snuff came puffing in her face.

Poor eyes, poor nose, poor mouth and chin
    A dismal sight presented;
And as the snuff got further in,
    Sincerely she repented;
In vain she ran about for ease,
    She could do nothing else but sneeze,

She dashed the spectacles away,
    To wipe her tingling eyes,
And as in twenty bits they lay,
    Her grandmama she spies; –
'Heyday! and what's the matter now?'
    Cries Grandmama, with lifted brow.

Matilda, smarting with the pain,
    And tingling still, and sore,
Made many a promise to refrain
    From meddling evermore;
And 'tis a fact, as I have heard,
    She ever since has kept her word.

ANN TAYLOR (1810)

Anne and Jane Taylor were pioneering children's writers. This anticipates by over a century the similar *Cautionary Tales* of Hilaire Belloc.

A Farewell to Tobacco

May the Babylonish curse
Straight confound my stammering verse,
If I can a passage see
In this word perplexity,
Or a fit expression find,
Or a language in my mind
(Still the phrase is wide or scant)
To take leave of thee, GREAT PLANT!
Or in any terms relate
Half my love or half my hate:
For I hate, yet love thee so,
That whichever thing I show,
The plain truth will seem to be
A constrained hyperbole,
And the passion to proceed
More from a mistress than a weed.

Sooty retainer to the vine,
Bacchus black servant, negro fine;
Sorcerer, that makes us dote upon
Thy begrimed complexion,
And for thy pernicious sake,
More and greater oaths to break
Than reclaimed lovers take
'Gainst women: thou thy siege dost lay
Much too in the female way,
While thou suck'st the labouring breath
Faster than kisses or than death.

Thou in such a cloud dost bind us,
That our worst foes cannot find us,
And ill fortune, that would thwart us,
Shoots at rovers, shooting at us;
While each man, through thy heightening steam,
Does like a smoking Aetna seem,
And all about us does express
(Fancy and wit in richest dress)
A Sicilian fruitfulness.

Thou through such a mist doth show us
That our best friends do not know us,
And for those allowed features
Due to reasonable creatures,
Liken'st us to fell Chimeras,
Monsters that, who see us fear us;
Worse than Cerberus or Geryon,
Or who first loved a cloud, Ixion.

Bacchus we know, and we allow
His tipsy rite, but what art thou,
That but by reflex canst show
What his deity can do,
As the false Egyptian spell
Aped the true Hebrew miracle?
Some few vapours thou mays't raise,
The weak brain may serve to amaze,
But to the reins and nobler heart
Canst nor life nor heat impart.

Brother of Bacchus, later born,
The old world was sure forlorn
Wanting thee, that aidest more
The god's victories than before
All his panthers, and the brawls
Of his piping Bacchanals.
These, as stale, we disallow,
Or judge of thee meant: only thou
His true Indian conquest art;
And for ivy round his dart
The reformed god now weaves
A finer thyrsus of thy leaves.

Scent to match thy rich perfume
Chemic art did ne'er presume
Through her quaint alembic strain,
None so sovereign to the brain.
Nature that did in thee excel,
Framed again no second smell.
Roses, violets, but toys
For the smaller sort of boys,

Or for greener damsels meant;
Thou art the only manly scent.

Stinking'st of the stinking kind,
Filth of the mouth and fog of the mind,
Africa that brags her foison,
Breeds no such prodigious poison,
Henbane, nightshade, both together,
Hemlock, aconite . . .

           Nay rather,
Plant divine, of rarest virtue;
Blisters on the tongue would hurt you.
'Twas but in a sort I blamed thee;
None e'er prospered who defamed thee;
Irony all and feigned abuse,
Such as perplex'd lovers use,
At a need, when, in despair
To paint forth their fairest fair,
Or in part but to express
That exceeding comeliness
Which their fancies so doth strike,
They borrow language of dislike;
And instead of 'Dearest Miss',
'Jewel', 'Honey', 'Sweetheart', 'Bliss',
And those forms of old admiring,
Call her 'Cockatrice' and 'Siren',
'Basilisk' and all that's evil,
'Witch', 'Hyena', 'Mermaid', 'Devil',
'Ethiop Wench' and 'Blackamoor'.
'Monkey', 'Ape' and twenty more;
'Friendly Traitress', 'Loving Foe' –
Not that she is truly so,
But no other way they know
A contentment to express,
Borders so upon excess,
That they do not rightly wot
Whether it be pain or not.

Or, as men constrained to part
With what's nearest to their heart,

While their sorrow's at the height,
Lose discrimination quite,
And their hasty wrath let fall,
To appease their frantic gall,
On the darling thing whatever
Whence they feel it death to sever
Though it be, as they, perforce,
Guiltless of the sad divorce.

For I must (nor let it grieve thee,
Friendliest of plants, that I must) leave thee.
For thy sake, TOBACCO, I
Would do anything but die,
And but seek to extend my days
Long enough to sing thy praise.
But as she, who once hath been
A king's consort is a queen
Ever after, nor will bate
Any tittle of her state,
Though a widow, or divorced,
So I, from my converse forced,
The old name and style retain
A right Katherine of Spain;
And a seat, too, 'mongst the joys
Of the blest Tobacco Boys;
Where, though I, by sour physician,
Am debarred the full fruition
Of thy favours, I may catch
Some collateral sweets, and snatch
Sidelong odours, that give life
Like glances from a neighbour's wife;
And still live in the by-places
And the suburbs of thy graces;
And in thy borders take delight,
An unconquered Canaanite.

CHARLES LAMB (Published 1818)

The War Song of Dinas Vawr

The mountain sheep are sweeter
But the valley sheep are fatter.
We therefore deemed it meeter
To carry off the latter.
We made an expedition;
We met an host and quelled it;
We forced a strong position,
And killed the men who held it.

On Dyfed's richest valley
Where herds of kine were browsing,
We made a mighty sally
To furnish our carousing.
Fierce warriors rushed to meet us;
We met them and o'erthrew them;
They struggled hard to beat us;
But we conquered them and slew them.

As we drove our prize at leisure
The king marched forth to catch us;
His rage surpassed all measure,
But his people could not match us.
He fled to his hall pillars;
And ere our force we led off
Some sacked his house and cellars
While others cut his head off.

We there in strife bewildering
Spilt blood enough to swim in;
We orphaned many children
And widowed many women
The eagles and the ravens
We glutted with our foemen;
The heroes and the cravens,
The spearmen and the bowmen.

We brought away from battle,
And much their land bemoaned them,
Two thousand head of cattle
And the head of him that owned them:
Ednyfed king of Dyfed,
His head was borne before us;
His wine and beasts supplied our feasts
And his overthrow our chorus.

THOMAS LOVE PEACOCK (1829)

The Sorrows of Werther

Werther had a love for Charlotte
Such as words could never utter;
Would you know how first he met her?
She was cutting bread and butter.

Charlotte was a married lady,
And a moral man was Werther,
And for all the wealth of Indies,
Would do nothing for to hurt her.

So he sighed and pined and ogled,
And his passion boiled and bubbled,
Till he blew his silly brains out
And no more by it was troubled.

Charlotte, having seen his body
Borne before her on a shutter,
Like a well-conducted person,
Went on cutting bread and butter.

WILLIAM MAKEPEACE THACKERAY

This is Thackeray's summary of Goethe's novel, which was
very popular at the time.

Epitaph on the late King
of the Sandwich Islands

Translated from the original of Crazee Rattee,
his Majesty's Poet Laureate

Beneath this marble, mud or moss,
   Whiche'er his subjects shall determine,
Entombed in Eulogies and dross,
   The Island king is food for vermin;
Preserved by scribblers, and by salt,
   From Lethe and sepulchral vapours,
His body fills his father's vault,
   His character the daily papers.

Well was he framed for royal seat;
   Kind to the meanest of his creatures,
With tender heart, and tender feet,
   An open purse and open features;
The ladies say, who laid him out,
   And earned thereby the usual pensions,
They never wreathed a shroud about
   A corpse of more genteel dimensions.

He warred with half a score of foes,
   And shone, by proxy, in the quarrel;
Enjoyed hard fights, and soft repose,
   And deathless debt, and deathless laurel:
His enemies were scalped and flayed,
   Where'er his soldiers were victorious;
And widows wept, and paupers paid,
   To make their sovereign ruler glorious.

And days were set apart for thanks,
   And prayers said by pious readers,
And laud was lavished on the ranks,
   And land was lavished on their leaders;
Events are writ by History's pen,
   And causes are too much to care for;

Fame talks about the where and when,
    And Folly asks the why and wherefore.

In peace he was immensely gay,
    And indefatigably busy;
Preparing gew-gaws every day,
    And shows to make his subjects dizzy;
And hearing the reports of guns,
    And signing the reports of gaolers;
And making up recipes for buns,
    And patterns for the army tailors.

And building carriages and boats,
    And streets and chapels and pavilions;
And regulating all the coats,
    And all the principles of millions;
And drinking homilies and gin,
    And chewing pork and adulation;
And looking backwards upon sin,
    And looking forwards to salvation.

The people in his happy reign,
    Were blest beyond all other nations,
Unharmed by foreign axe or chain,
    Unhealed by civil innovations;
They served the usual logs and stones,
    With all the usual rights and terrors;
And swallowed all their father's bones,
    And swallowed all their fathers' errors.

When a fierce mob with clubs and knives,
    Declared that nothing should content them,
But that their representatives
    Should actually represent them,
He interposed the proper checks,
    By sending troops, with drums and banners,
Cut short their speeches and their necks,
    And broke their heads, to mend their manners.

And when Dissension flung her stain
    Upon the light of Hymen's altar,
And Destiny made Cupid's chain

As galling as the hangman's halter,
He passed a most domestic life,
    By many mistresses berfriended,
And did not put away his wife,
    For fear the priests might be offended.

And thus, at last he sunk to rest,
    Amid the blessings of his people;
And sighs were heaved from every breast,
    And bells were tolled from every steeple;
And loud was every public throng,
    His brilliant character adorning;
And poets raised a mourning song,
    And clothiers raised the price of mourning.

His funeral was very grand,
    Followed by many robes and maces,
And all the great ones of the land,
    Struggling, as heretofore, for places.
And every loyal Minister
    Was there with signs of purse-felt sorrow,
Save Pozzy, his Lord Chancellor,
    Who promised to attend tomorrow.

Peace to his dust! his fostering care
    By grateful hearts shall long be cherished;
And all his subjects shall declare
    He lost a grinder when he perished.
They, when they look upon the lead,
    In which a people's love hath shrined him,
Shall say, when all the worst is said,
    Perhaps he leaves a worse behind him!

WINTHROP MACKWORTH PRAED (1825)

The King of the Sandwich Islands did in fact die in London in 1824, but Praed's poem actually refers to George IV, formerly the Prince Regent. His notes tell us that the bones of parents are eaten as a mark of respect in the islands (but that in modern nations their prejudices are swallowed), and that islanders have teeth extracted as a sign of mourning. The King's marriage to Caroline of Brunswick was famously unhappy.

Mary's Ghost

A pathetic ballad

'Twas in the middle of the night
 To sleep poor William tried:
When Mary's ghost came stealing in,
 And stood at his bedside.

O William dear! O William dear!
 My rest eternal ceases;
Alas! my everlasting peace
 Is broken into pieces.

I thought the last of all my cares
 Would end with my last minute;
But though I went to my long home,
 I didn't stay long in it.

The body-snatchers they have come,
 And made a snatch at me;
It's very hard them kind of men
 Won't let a body be!

You thought that I was buried deep,
 Quite decent-like and chary,
But from her grave in Mary-bone,
 They've come and boned your Mary.

The arm that used to take your arm
 Is took to Dr Vyse;
And both my legs are gone to walk
 The hospital at Guy's.

I vowed that you should have my hand,
 But fate gives us denial;
You'll find it there at Dr Bell's
 In spirits and a phial.

As for my feet, the little feet
   You used to call so pretty,
There's one I know, in Bedford Row,
    The t'other's in the City.

I can't tell where my head is gone,
    But Dr Carpue can;
As for my trunk, it's all packed up
    To go by Pickford's van.

I wish you'd go to Mr P.
    And save me such a ride;
I don't half like the outside place,
    They've took for my inside.

The cock it crows – I must be gone!
    My William, we must part!
But I'll be yours in death, altho'
    Sir Astley has my heart.

Don't go to weep upon my grave,
    And think that there I be;
They haven't left an atom there
    Of my anatomie.

THOMAS HOOD (1827)

The poem refers to the practice of robbing graves for use in medical research. Occasionally, as in the famous case of Burke and Hare, murder was used as a short cut in procuring bodies.

The Jackdaw of Rheims

From *The Ingoldsby Legends*

The jackdaw sat on the Cardinal's chair!
Bishop and abbot and prior were there;
    Many a monk and many a friar,
    Many a knight and many a squire,
With a great many more of lesser degree, –
In sooth a goodly company;
And they served the Lord Primate on bended knee,
      Never, I ween,
      Was a prouder seen,
Read of in books, or dreamt of in dreams,
Than the Cardinal Lord Archbishop of Rheims!

      In and out
      Through the motley rout,
That little Jackdaw kept hopping about;
      Here and there,
      Like a dog in a fair,
      Over comfits and cates,
      And dishes and plates,
Cowl and cope and rochet and pall,
Mitre and crozier, he hopped upon all!
      With saucy air,
      He perched on the chair
Where in state the great Lord Cardinal sat;
      And he peered in the face
      Of his Lordship's Grace,
With a satisfied look, as if he would say,
'We two are the greatest here today!'
      And the priests, with awe,
      As such freaks they saw,
Said 'The Devil must be in that little Jackdaw!'

The feast was over, the board was cleared,
The flawns and the custards had all disappeared,

And six little Singing-Boys, – dear little souls!
In nice clean faces and nice white stoles,
    Came in order due,
    Two by two,
Marching that grand refectory through!
A nice little boy held a golden ewer,
Embossed and filled with water as pure
As any that flows between Rhine and Namur,
Which a nice little boy stood ready to catch
In a fine golden hand-basin made to match.
Two nice little boys, rather more grown,
Carried lavender water and eau de Cologne;
And a nice little boy had a nice cake of soap,
Worthy of washing the hands of the Pope.
    One little boy more
    A napkin bore,
Of the best white diaper, fringed with pink,
And a Cardinal's Hat, marked in 'permanent ink'.

The great Lord Cardinal turns at the sight
Of these nice little boys dressed all in white;
    From his finger he draws
    His costly turquoise;
And not thinking sat all about little Jackdaws,
    Deposits it straight
    By the side of his plate,
While the nice little boys on his Eminence wait;
Till, when nobody's dreaming of any such thing,
That little Jackdaw hops off with the ring!

    There's a cry and a shout,
    And a deuce of a rout,
And nobody seems to know what they're about,
But the Monks have their pockets all turned inside out.
    The Friars are kneeling,
    And hunting, and feeling
The carpet, the floor, and the walls and the ceiling.
    The Cardinal drew
    Off each plum-coloured shoe,
And left his red stockings exposed to the view;

He peeps and he feels
In the toes and the heels;
They turn up the dishes, – they turn up the plates, –
They take up the poker and poke out the grates,
– They turn up the rugs,
They examine the mugs: –
But no! – no such thing; –
They can't find THE RING!
And the Abbot declared that, 'when no one had
twigged it,
Some rascal or other had popped in and prigged it!'

The Cardinal rose with a dignified look.
He called for his candle, his bell and his book!
In holy anger and pious grief,
He solemnly cursed that rascally thief!
He cursed him at board, he cursed him in bed,
From the sole of his foot to the crown of his head;
He cursed him in sleeping, that every night
He should dream of the devil, and wake in a fright;
He cursed him in eating, he cursed him in drinking,
He cursed him in coughing, in sneezing and winking;
He cursed him in sitting, in standing, in lying;
He cursed him in walking, in riding, in flying,
He cursed him in living, he cursed him in dying! –
Never was heard such as terrible curse!
But what gave rise
To no little surprise,
Nobody seemed one penny the worse!

The day was gone,
The night came on,
The Monks and Friars the searched till dawn;
When the Sacristan saw
On crumpled claw,
Come limping a poor little lame Jackdaw!
No longer gay
As on yesterday;
His feathers seemed all to be turned the wrong way; –
His pinions drooped – he could hardly stand, –

His head was as bald as the palm of your hand:
    His eye so dim,
    So wasted each limb,
That, heedless of grammar, they all cried 'THAT'S HIM! –
That's the scamp that has done this scandalous thing!
That's the thief that has got my Lord Cardinal's Ring.'

    The poor little Jackdaw,
    When the Monks he saw,
Feebly gave vent to the ghost of a caw;
And turned his bald head, as much as to say,
'Pray be so good as to walk this way!'
    Slower and slower
    He limped on before,
Till they came to the back of the belfry door,
    Where the first thing they saw,
    Midst the sticks and the straw,
Was the RING in the nest of that little Jackdaw!

Then the great Lord Cardinal called for his book,
And off that terrible curse he took;
    The mute expression
    Served in lieu of confession,
And being thus coupled with full restitution,
The Jackdaw got plenary absolution!
    – When those words were heard,
    That poor little bird
Was changed in a moment, 'twas really absurd.

    He grew sleek and fat;
    In addition to that
A fresh crop of feathers came thick as a mat!
    His tail waggled more
    Even than before;
But no longer it wagged with an impudent air,
No longer he perched on the Cardinal's chair.
    He hopped now about
    With a gait devout;
At Matins, at Vespers, he never was out;
And far from any more pilfering deeds,

He always seemed telling the Confessor's beads.
If anyone lied, – or if anyone swore, –
Or slumbered in prayer-time and happened to snore,
        That good Jackdaw
        Would give a great 'Caw!'
As much as to say 'Don't do so any more!'
While many remarked, as his manners they saw,
That they 'never had known such a pious Jackdaw!'
        He long lived the pride
        Of that country-side,
And at last in the odour of sanctity died;
        When, as words were too faint
        His merits to paint,
The Conclave determined to make him a Saint;
And on newly made Saints and Popes, as you know,
It's the custom at Rome new names to bestow,
So they canonized him by the name of Jim Crow!

                                        R. H. BARHAM (Published 1840)

The Crystal Palace

An Irishman visits the Great Exhibition

With ganial foire
Thransfuse me loyre,
Ye sacred nymphs of Pindus,
The whoile I sing
That wondrous thing
The Palace made o' windows!

Say Paxton, truth,
Thou wondrous youth,
What stroke of art celistial,
What power was lint
Ye to invent
This combination cristial.

O would before
That Thomas Moore,
Loikewoise the late Lord Boyron,
Thim aigles sthrong
Of godloike song
Cast oi on that cast oiron!

And saw thim walls,
And glittering halls
Thim rising slendther columns,
Which I, poor pote,
Could not denote,
No, not in twenty vollums.

My Muse's words
Is like the birds
That roosts beneath the panes there:
Her wings she spoils
'Gainst thim broight toiles,
And cracks her silly brains there.

This Palace tall,
This Cristial Hall,
Which Imperors might covet,
Stands in High Park
Loike Noah's Ark,
A rainbow bint above it.

The towers and fanes,
In other scaynes
The fame of this will undo,
Saint Paul's big doom,
Saint Payther's Room,
And Dublin's proud Rotundo.

'Tis here that roams,
As well becomes
Her dignitee and stations,
Victoria Great,
And houlds in state
The Congress of the Nations.

Her subjects pours
From distant shores,
Her Injians and Canajians;
And also we,
Her kingdoms three,
Attind with our allagiance.

*   *   *

With conscious proide
I stud insoide,
And look'd the World's Great Fair in,
Until me sight
Was dazzled quite,
And couldn't see for starin'.

There's holy saints
And window paintts
By Maydiayval Pugin;
Alhamborough Jones
Did paint the tones
Of yellow and gambouge in.

There's fountains there
And crosses fair;
There's water-gods with urrns:
There's organs three,
To play d'ye see
'God save the Queen,' by turrns.

There's Statues bright
Of marble white,
Of silver and of copper;
And some in zinc,
And some, I think,
That isn't even proper!

There's staym Ingynes,
That stands in lines,
Enormous and amazing,
That squeal and snort
Like whales in sport,
Or elephants a-grazing

*   *   *

Amazed I pass
From glass to glass
Deloighted I survey 'em;
Fresh wondthers grows
Before my nose
In this sublime Musayum!

Look, here's a fan
From far Japan,
A sabre from Damasco;
There's shawls ye get
From far Thibet,
And cotton prints from Glasgow.

There's German flutes,
Marocky boots,
And Naples Macaronies;
Bohaymia
Has sent Bohay;
Polonia her polonies.

There's granite flints
That's quite imminse,
There's sacks of coals and fuels,
There's swords and guns,
And soap in tuns,
And gingerbread and Jewels.

There's taypots there
And cannons rare;
There's coffins filled with roses;
There's canvas tints,
Teeth instruments,
And suits of clothes by MOSES.

There's lashins more
Of things in store,
But thim I don't remimber;
Nor could disclose
Did I compose
From Maytime till Novimber.

Ah JUDY thru!
With eyes so blue,
That you were here to view it!
And could I screw
But tu pound tu
'Tis I would thrait you to it!

So let us raise
Victoria's praise,
And Albert's proud condition,
That takes his ayse
As he surveys
This Cristial Exhibition.

                    WILLIAM MAKEPEACE THACKERAY (1851)

5
RESPONSES TO THE
NATURAL WORLD

My Heart Leaps Up

My heart leaps up when I behold
   A Rainbow in the sky,
So was it when my life began;
So is it now I am a man;
So be it when I shall grow old,
   Or let me die!
The Child is father of the Man;
And I could wish my days to be
Bound each to each by natural piety.

WILLIAM WORDSWORTH (1802)

To Autumn

1

Season of mists and mellow fruitfulness
   Close-bosom'd friend of the maturing sun;
Conspiring with him how to load and bless
   With fruit the vines that round the thatch-eves run;
To bend with apples the moss'd cottage trees,
   And fill all fruits with ripeness to the core;
     To swell the gourd, and plump the hazel shells
   With a sweet kernel, to set budding more,
And still more, later flowers for the bees,
Until they think warm days will never cease,
   For summer has o'erbrimmed their clammy cells.

2

Who hath not seen thee oft amid thy store?
   Sometimes whoever seeks abroad may find
Thee sitting careless on a granary floor,
   Thy hair soft-lifted by the winnowing wind;
Or on a half-reaped furrow sound asleep,
   Drows'd with the fume of poppies, while thy hook
     Spares the next swathe and all its twined flowers:

And sometimes like a gleaner thou dost keep
   Steady thy laden head across a brook;
   Or by a cider press, with patient look,
     Thou watchest the last oozings hours by hours

3

Where are the songs of spring? Ay, where are they?
   Think not of them; thou hast thy music too, –
While barred clouds bloom the soft-dying day,
   And touch the stubble plains with rosy hue;
Then in a wailful choir the small gnats mourn
   Among the river sallows, borne aloft
     Or sinking as the light wind lives or dies;
And full-grown lambs loud bleat from hilly bourn,
     Hedge-crickets sing; and now in treble soft,
     The red-breast whistles from a garden croft,
       And gathering swallows twitter in the skies.

JOHN KEATS (1819)

Ode to a Nightingale

1

My heart aches, and a drowsy numbness pains
   My sense, as though of hemlock I had drunk,
Or emptied some dull opiate to the drains
   One minute past, and Lethe-wards had sunk:
Tis not through envy of thy happy lot
   But being too happy in thine happiness –
     That thou, light winged dryad of the trees,
     In some melodious plot
Of beechen green, and shadows numberless,
     Singest of summer in full throated ease.

2

O, for a draught of vintage! that hath been
   Cooled a long age in the deep delved earth,
Tasting of Flora and the country green,

Dance and Provencal song, and sunburnt mirth!
O for a beaker full of the warm South,
    Full of the true, the blushful Hippocrene,
    With beaded bubbles winking at the brim,
        And purple-stained mouth;
That I might drink and leave the world unseen,
    And with thee fade away into the forest dim.

3

Fade far away, dissolve, and quite forget
    What thou amongst the leaves hast never known,
The weariness, the fever and the fret
    Here, where men sit and hear each other groan;
Where palsy shakes a few last sad gray hairs,
    Where youth grows pale, and spectre-thin, and dies,
        Where but to think is to be full of sorrow
            And leaden-eyed despairs,
Where Beauty cannot keep her lustrous eyes,
    Or new Love pine at them beyond tomorrow.

4

Away! away! for I will fly to thee,
    Not charioted by Bacchus and his pards,
But on the viewless wings of Poesy,
    Though the dull brain perplexes and retards:
Already with thee! Tender is the night,
    And haply the Queen-Moon is on her throne,
        Clustered around by all her starry Fays;
            But here there is no light,
Save what from heaven is with the breezes blown
    Through verdurous glooms and winding mossy ways.

5

I cannot see what flowers are at my feet,
    Nor what soft incense hangs upon the boughs,
But, in embalmed darkness, guess each sweet
    Wherewith the seasonable month endows
The grass, the thicket and the fruit-tree wild;
    White hawthorn, and the pastoral eglantine;
        Fast fading violets covered up in leaves;
            And mid-May's eldest child,

The coming musk-rose, full of dewy wine,
   The murmurous haunt of flies on summer eves.

6

Darkling I listen; and for many a time
   I have been half in love with easeful Death,
Called him soft names in many a mused rhyme,
   To take into the air my quiet breath
Now more than ever seems it rich to die,
   To cease upon the midnight with no pain,
     While thou art pouring forth thy soul abroad
      In such an ecstasy!
Still wouldst thou sing, and I have ears in vain –
   To thy high requiem become a sod.

7

Thou wast not born for death, immortal Bird!
   No hungry generations tread thee down;
The voice I hear this passing night was heard
   In ancient days by emperor and clown;
Perhaps the selfsame song that found a path
   Through the sad heart of Ruth, when, sick for home,
     She stood in tears amid the alien corn;
      The same that oft-times hath
Charmed magic casements, opening on the foam
   Of perilous seas, in faery lands forlorn.

8

Forlorn! the very word is like a bell
   To toll me back from thee to my sole self!
Adieu! the fancy cannot cheat so well
   As she is famed to do, deceiving elf.
Adieu! adieu! thy plaintive anthem fades
   Past the near meadows, over the still stream,
     Up the hill side; and now 'tis buried deep
      In the next valley glades:
Was it a vision, or a waking dream?
Fled is that music:– Do I wake or sleep?

                   JOHN KEATS (1819)

Ode to the West Wind

1

O wild West Wind, thou breath of Autumn's being,
Thou from whose unseen presence the leaves dead
Are driven, like ghosts from an enchanter fleeing,

Yellow and black and pale and hectic red,
Pestilence stricken multitudes: O thou,
Who chariotest to their dark wintry bed

The winged seeds, where they lie cold and low,
Each like a corpse within its grave until
Thine azure sister of the Spring shall blow

Her chariot o'er the dreaming earth, and fill
(Driving sweet buds like flocks to feed in air)
With living hues and odours plain and hill:

Wild spirit which art moving everywhere;
Destroyer and preserver; hear, oh, hear!

2

Thou on whose stream, mid the steep sky's commotion,
Loose clouds like earth's decaying leaves are shed,
Shook from the tangled boughs of Heaven and Ocean,

Angels of rain and lightning there are spread
On the blue surface of thine aery surge,
Like the bright hair uplifted from the head

Of some bright Maenad, even from the dim verge
Of the horizon to the zenith's height:
The locks of the approaching storm. Thou dirge

Of the dying year, to which this closing night
Will be the dome of a vast sepulchre,
Vaulted with all thy congregated might

Of vapours, from whose solid atmosphere
Black rain, and fire, and hail will burst: oh, hear!

3

Thou who didst waken from his summer dreams
The blue Mediterranean, where he lay,
Lulled by the coil of his crystalline streams,

Beside a pumice isle in Baiae's bay,
And saw in sleep old palaces and towers
Quivering within the waves intenser day,

All overgrown with azure moss and flowers
So sweet the sense faints picturing them! Thou
For whose path the Atlantic's level powers

Cleave themselves into chasms, while far below
The sea-blooms and the oozy woods which wear
The sapless foliage of the ocean, know

Thy voice and suddenly grow gray with fear,
And tremble, and despoil themselves: oh, hear!

4

If I were a dead leaf thou mightest bear;
If I were a swift cloud to fly with thee;
A wave to pant beneath thy power, and share

The impulse of thy strength, only less free
Than thou, O uncontrollable! If even
I were as in my boyhood, and could be

The comrade of thy wanderings over Heaven,
As then, when to outstrip thy skyey speed
Scarce seemed a vision; I would ne'er have striven

As thus with thee in prayer in my sore need.
Oh, lift me as a wave, a leaf, a cloud!
I fall upon the thorns of life! I bleed!

A heavy weight of hours has chained and bowed
One too like thee, tameless and swift and proud.

5

Make me thy lyre, even as the forest is:
What if my leaves are falling like its own!
The tumult of thy mighty harmonies

Will take from both a deep autumnal tone,
Sweet though in sadness. Be thou, Spirit fierce,
My spirit! Be thou me, impetuous one!

Drive my dead thoughts over the universe
Like withered leaves to quicken a new birth!
And, by the incantation of this verse,

Scatter, as from an unextinguished hearth,
Ashes and sparks, my words among mankind!
Be through my lips to unawakened earth

The trumpet of a prophecy! O Wind,
If Winter comes, can Spring be far behind?

PERCY BYSSHE SHELLEY (1819)

To a Sky-Lark

Hail to thee, blithe Spirit!
    Bird thou never wert –
That from Heaven, or near it,
    Pourest thy full heart
In profuse strains of unpremeditated art.

Higher still and higher
    From the earth thou springest
Like a cloud of fire;
    The blue deep thou wingest,
And singing still dost soar, and soaring ever singest.

In the golden lightning
    Of the sunken Sun –
O'er which clouds are brightning,
    Thou dost float and run;
Like an unbodied joy whose race is just begun.

The pale purple even
    Melts around thy flight,
Like a star of Heaven
    In the broad day-light.
Thou art unseen, – but yet I hear thy shrill delight,

Keen as are the arrows
    Of that silver sphere,
Whose intense lamp narrows
    In the white dawn clear
Until we hardly see – we feel that it is there.

All the earth and air
    With thy voice is loud,
As when Night is bare
    From one lonely cloud
The moon rains out her beams – and Heaven is
    overflowed.

What thou art we know not;
　What is most like thee?
From rainbow clouds there flow not
　Drops so bright to see
As from thy presence showers a rain of melody.

Like a Poet hidden
　In the light of thought,
Singing hymns unbidden,
　Till the world is wrought
To sympathy with hopes and fears it heeded not;

Like a high-born maiden
　In a palace tower,
Soothing her love-laden
　Soul in secret hour,
With music sweet as love – which overflows her bower:

Like a glow-worm golden
　In a dell of dew,
Scattering unbeholden
　Its aerial hue
Among the flowers and grass which screen it from the
　view:

Like a rose embowered
　In its own green leaves –
By warm winds deflowered –
　Till the scent it gives
Makes faint with too much sweet those heavy winged
　thieves:

Sound of vernal showers
　On the tinkling grass,
Rain awakened flowers
　All that ever was
Joyous and clear and fresh, thy music doth surpass.

Teach us, Sprite or Bird,
    What sweet thoughts are thine;
I have never heard
    Praise of love or wine
That panted forth a flood of rapture so divine.

Chorus Hymeneal
    Or triumphal chaunt
Matched with thine would be all
    But an empty vaunt,
A thing wherein we feel there is some hidden want.

What objects are the fountains
    Of thy happy strain?
What fields or waves or mountains?
    What shapes of sky or plain?
What love of thine own kind? what ignorance of pain?

With thy clear keen joyance
    Languor cannot be–
Shadow of annoyance
    Never came near thee;
Thou lovest – but ne'er knew love's sad satiety.

Waking or asleep,
    Thou of death must deem
Things more true and deep
    Than we mortals dream
Or how could thy notes flow in such a chrystal stream?

We look before and after,
    And pine for what is not–
Our sincerest laughter
    With some pain is fraught–
Our sweetest songs are those that tell of saddest thought.

Yet if we could scorn
    Hate and pride and fear;
If we were things born
    Not to shed a tear,
I know not how thy joy we ever should come near.

Better than all measures
    Of delightful sound–
Better than all treasures
    That in books are found–
Thy skill to poet were, thou Scorner of the ground!

Teach me half the gladness
    That thy brain must know,
Such harmonious madness
    From my lips would flow
The world should listen then, as I am listening now.

PERCY BYSSHE SHELLEY (1820)

Hark! 'Tis the Thrush

Hark! 'Tis the Thrush, undaunted, undeprest
By twilight premature of cloud and rain;
Nor does that roaring wind deaden his strain
Who carols thinking of his Love and nest,
And seems, as more incited, still more blest.
Thanks; thou hast snapped a fireside Prisoner's chain,
Exulting Warbler! eased a fretted brain,
And in a moment charmed my cares to rest.
Yes, I will forth, bold Bird! and front the blast,
That we may sing together, if thou wilt,
So loud, so clear, my Partner through life's day,
Mute in her nest love-chosen if not love-built,
Like thine, shall gladden, as in sessions past,
Thrilled by loose snatches of the social Lay.

WILLIAM WORDSWORTH (1838)

The Blackbird

O blackbird! sing me something well:
   While all the neighbours shoot thee round
   I keep smooth plats of fruitful ground
Where thou may'st warble, eat and dwell.

The espaliers and the standards all
   Are thine; the range of lawn and park;
   The unnetted black-hearts ripen dark,
All thine against the garden wall.

Yet, tho' I spared thee all the spring,
   Thy sole delight is, sitting still,
   With that gold dagger of thy bill
To fret the summer jenneting.*

A golden bill! the silver tongue
   Cold February loved is dry:
   Plenty corrupts the melody
That made thee famous once, when young:

And in the sultry garden squares,
   Now thy flute-notes are changed to coarse,
   I hear thee not at all, or hoarse
As when a hawker hawks his wares.

Take warning! he that will not sing
   While yon sun prospers in the blue,
   Shall sing for want, ere leaves are new,
Caught in the frozen palms of Spring.

                  ALFRED LORD TENNYSON (Published 1832)

   * A jenneting is a kind of early apple

Song

1

A spirit haunts the year's last hours,
Dwelling amid these yellowing bowers
        To himself he talks;
For at eventide, listening earnestly,
At his work you may hear him sob and sigh
        In the walks;
            Earthward he boweth the heavy stalks
Of the mouldering flowers:
        Heavily hangs the broad sunflower
            Over its grave i' the earth so chilly;
        Heavily hangs the hollyhock,
            Heavily hangs the tiger-lily.

2

The air is damp and hushed and close
As a sick man's room when he taketh repose
        An hour before death
My very heart faints and my whole soul grieves
At the moist rich smell of the rotting leaves,
        And the breath
            Of the fading edges of box beneath,
And the year's last rose.
        Heavily hangs the broad sunflower
            Over its grave in the earth so chilly;
        Heavily hangs the hollyhock,
            Heavily hangs the tiger-lily.

ALFRED LORD TENNYSON (c.1833)

A Walk at Sunset

When insect wings are glistening in the beam
   Of the low sun, and mountain tops are bright,
Oh, let me by the crystal valley-stream
   Wander amid the mild and mellow light;
And, while the woodthrush pipes his evening lay,
Give me one lonely hour to hymn the setting day.

Oh, sun! that o'er the western mountains now
   Go'st down in glory! ever beautiful
And blessed is thy radiance, whether thou
   Colorest the eastern heaven and night-mist cool,
Till the bright day-star vanish, or on high
Climbest and streamest thy white splendors from mid-sky.

Yet loveliest are thy setting smiles, and fair,
   Fairest of all that earth beholds, the hues
That live among the clouds, and flush the air,
   Lingering and deepening at the hour of dews.
Then softest gales are breathed, and softest heard
The plaining voice of streams, and pensive note of bird.

They who here roamed, of yore, the forest wide,
   Felt, by such charm, their simple bosoms won;
They deemed their quivered warrior, when he died,
   Went to bright isles beneath the setting sun;
Where winds are aye at peace, and skies are fair,
And purple-skirted clouds curtain the crimson air.

So, with the glories of the dying day,
   Its thousand trembling lights and changing hues,
The memory of the brave who passed away
   Tenderly mingled; – fitting hour to muse
On such grave theme, and sweet the dream that shed
Brightness and beauty round the destiny of the dead.

For ages, on the silent forests here,
　　Thy beams did fall before the red man came
　To dwell beneath them; in their shade the deer
　　Fed, and feared not the arrow's deadly aim.
Nor tree was felled in all that world of woods,
Save by the beaver's tooth, or winds or rush of floods.

　Then came the hunter tribes, and thou didst look,
　　For ages, on their deeds in the hard chase,
　And well-fought wars; green sod and silver brook
　　Took the first stain of blood; before thy face
The warrior generations came and passed,
And glory was laid up for many an age to last.

　Now they are gone, gone as thy setting blaze
　　Goes down the west, while night is pressing on,
　And with them the old tale of better days,
　　And trophies of remembered power, are gone.
Yon field that gives the harvest, where the plough,
Strikes the white bone, is all that tells their story now.

　I stand upon their ashes in thy beam,
　　The offspring of another race, I stand
　Beside a stream they loved, this valley-stream;
　　And where the night-fire of the quivered band
Showed the gray oak by fire, and war-song rung,
I teach the quiet shades the strains of this new tongue.

　Farewell! but thou shalt come again – thy light
　　Must shine on other changes, and behold
　　The place of the thronged city still as night –
　　States fallen – new empires built upon the old –
But never shalt thou see these realms again
Darkened by boundless groves, and roamed by savage men.

WILLIAM CULLEN BRYANT (1821)

The Prairies

These are the Gardens of the Desert, these
The unshorn fields, boundless and beautiful,
And fresh as the young earth, ere man had sinned –
The prairies. I behold them for the first,
And my heart swells, while the dilated sight
Takes in the encircling vastness. Lo! they stretch
In airy undulations, far away,
As if the ocean, in his gentlest swell,
Stood still, with all his rounded billows fixed,
And motionless for ever. – Motionless? –
No – they are all unchained again. The clouds
Sweep over with their shadows, and beneath
The surface rolls and fluctuates to the eye;
Dark hollows seem to glide along and chase
The sunny ridges. Breezes of the South!
Who toss the golden and the flame-like flowers,
And pass the prairie-hawk that, poised on high,
Flaps his broad wings, yet moves not – ye have played
Among the palms of Mexico and vines
Of Texas, and have crossed the limpid brooks
That from the fountains of Sonora glide
Into the calm Pacific – have ye fanned
A nobler or a lovelier scene than this?
Man hath no part in all this glorious work:
The hand that built the firmament hath heaved
And smoothed these verdant swells, and sown their slopes
With herbage, planted them with island groves,
And hedged them round with forests. Fitting floor
For this magnificent temple of the sky –
With flowers whose glory and whose multitude
Rival the constellations! The great heavens
Seem to stoop down upon the scene in love,–
A nearer vault, and of a tenderer blue,
Than that which bends above the eastern hills.

    As o'er the verdant waste I guide my steed,
Among the high rank grass that sweeps his sides,

The hollow beating of his footstep seems
A sacrilegious sound. I think of those
Upon whose rest he tramples. Are they here –
The dead of other days! – and did the dust
Of these fair solitudes once stir with life
And burn with passion? Let the mighty mounds
That overlook the rivers, or that rise
In the dim forest crowded with old oaks,
Answer. A race that long has passed away,
Built them; – a disciplined and populous race
Heaped, with long toil, the earth, while yet the Greek
Was hewing the Pentelicus to forms
Of symmetry, and rearing on its rock
The glittering Parthenon. These ample fields
Nourished their harvests, here their herds were fed,
When haply by their stalls the bison lowed,
And bowed his maned shoulder to the yoke.
All day this desert murmured with their toils,
Till twilight blushed and lovers walked and wooed
In a forgotten language, and old tunes,
From instruments of unremembered form,
Gave the soft winds a voice. The red man came –
The roaming hunter tribes, warlike and fierce,
And the mound builders vanished from the earth.
The solitude of centuries untold
Has settled where they dwelt. The prairie wolf
Hunts in their meadows, and his fresh dug den
Yawns by my path. The gopher mines the ground
Where stood their swarming cities. All is gone –
All – save the piles of earth that hold their bones –
The platforms where they worshipped unknown gods –
The barriers which they builded from the soil
To keep the foe at bay – till o'er the walls
The wild beleaguerers broke, and, one by one,
The strongholds of the plain were forced and heaped
With corpses. The brown vultures of the wood
Flocked to those vast uncovered sepulchres,
And sat, unscared and silent, at their feast.
Haply some solitary fugitive,
Lurking in marsh and forest, till the sense

Of desolation and of fear became
Bitterer than death, yielded himself to die.
Man's better nature triumphed then. Kind words
Welcomed and soothed him; the rude conquerors
Seated the captive with their chiefs; he chose
A bride among their maidens, and at length
Seemed to forget, – yet ne'er forgot, – the wife
Of his first love, and her sweet little ones,
Butchered, amidst their shrieks, with all his race.

Thus change the forms of being. Thus arise
Races of living things, glorious in strength,
And perish, as the quickening breath of God
Fills them, or is withdrawn. The red man, too,
Has left the blooming wilds he ranged so long,
And nearer to the Rocky Mountains sought
A wilder hunting ground. The beaver builds
No longer by these streams, but far away,
On waters whose blue surface ne'er gave back
The white man's face – among Missouri's springs
And pools whose issues swells the Oregon –
He rears his little Venice. In these plains
The bison feeds no more. Twice twenty leagues
Beyond remotest smoke of hunter's camp,
Roams the majestic brute, in herds that shake
The earth with thundering steps – yet here I meet
His ancient footprints stamped beside the pool.

Still this great solitude is quick with life.
Myriads of insects, gaudy as the flowers
They flutter over, gentle quadrupeds,
And birds that scarce have learned the fear of man,
Are here, and sliding reptiles of the ground,
Startlingly beautiful. The graceful deer
Bounds to the wood at my approach. The bee,
A more adventurous colonist than man,
With whom he came across the eastern deep,
Fills the savannahs with his murmurings,
And hides his sweets, as in the golden age,

Within the hollow oak. I listen long
To his domestic hum, and think I hear
The sound of that advancing multitude
Which soon shall fill these deserts. From the ground
Comes up the laugh of children, the soft voice
Of maidens, and the sweet and solemn hymn
Of Sabbath worshippers. The low of herds
Blends with the rustling of the heavy grain
Over the dark brown furrows. All at once
A fresher wind sweeps by and breaks my dream
And I am in the wilderness alone.

WILLIAM CULLEN BRYANT (1833)

The poem above refers to a belief that an older civilisation was
responsible for burial mounds found in Illinois, which Bryant was
visiting. The poem was of course written before the great migration
of settlers westward and the decimation of the Indian tribes and the
buffalo on which they depended. The previous poem shows more
sympathy for the Indians themselves.

Lines Composed in a Wood on a Windy Day

My soul is awakened, my spirit is soaring,
And carried aloft on the wings of the breeze;
For above and around me, the wild wind is roaring
Arousing to rapture the earth and the seas.

The long withered grass in the sunshine is glancing,
The bare trees are tossing their branches on high;
The dead leaves beneath them are merrily dancing,
The white clouds are scudding across the blue sky.

I wish I could see how the ocean is lashing
The foam of its billows in whirlwinds of spray,
I wish I could see how its proud waves are dashing
And hear the wild roar of their thunder today!

ANNE BRONTË (1842)

Home Thoughts, from Abroad

1

Oh to be in England,
Now that April's there,
And whoever wakes in England
Sees some morning, unaware,
That the lowest boughs and the brushwood sheaf
Round the elm-bole are in tiny leaf,
While the chaffinch sings on the orchard bough
In England – now!

And after April, when May follows,
And the whitethroat builds, and all the swallows!
Hark where my blossomed pear-tree in the hedge
Leans to the field and scatters on the clover
Blossoms and dewdrops – at the bent spray's edge –
That's the wise thrush; he sings each song twice over,
Lest you think he should never recapture
The first fine careless rapture

And, though the fields look rough with hoary dew,
All will be gay when noontide wakes anew
The buttercups, the little children's dower
– Far brighter than this gaudy melon-flower!

ROBERT BROWNING (1845)

The Snow Storm

Announced by all the trumpets of the sky
Arrives the snow, and, driving o'er the fields,
Seems nowhere to alight: the whited air
Hides hills and woods, the river, and the heaven,
And veils the farmhouse at the garden's end.
The sled and traveller stopped, the courier's feet
Delayed, all friends shut out, the housemates sit
Around the radiant fireplace, enclosed
In a tumultuous privacy of storm.

Come see the north wind's masonry.
Out of an unseen quarry evermore
Furnished with tile, the fierce artificer
Curves his white bastions with projected roof
Round every windward stake, or tree, or door.
Speeding, the myriad handed, his wild work
So fanciful, so savage, nought cares he
For number or proportion. Mockingly
On coop or kennel he hangs Parian wreaths;
A swan-like form invests the hidden thorn;
Fills up the farmer's lane from wall to wall,
Maugre the farmer's sighs; and, at the gate,
A tapering turret overtops the work.
And, when his hours are numbered, and the world
Is all his own, retiring, as he were not,
Leaves, when the sun appears, astonished Art
To mimic in slow structures, stone by stone,
Built in an age, the mad wind's night-work,
The frolic architecture of the snow.

RALPH WALDO EMERSON (1846)

Clock a Clay

In the cowslip's peeps I lie
Hidden from the buzzing fly
While green grass beneath me lies
Pearled wi' dew like fishes' eyes
Here I lie a clock a clay
Waiting for the time o' day.

While grassy forests quake surprise
And the wild wood sobs and sighs
My gold home rocks as like to fall
On its pillar green and tall
When the pattering rain drives by
Clock a clay keeps warm and dry.

Day by day and night by night
All the week I hide from sight
In the cowslips peeps I lie
In rain and dew still warm and dry
Day and night and night and day
Red black spotted clock a clay

My home it shakes in wind and showers
Pale green pillar topped wi' flowers
Bending at the wild wind's breath
Till I touch the grass beneath
Here I live lone clock a clay
Watching for the time of day

JOHN CLARE (c. 1848)

Cowslips, once a commoner flower in England than now, are small-flowered, rich yellow relatives of the primrose. The peeps are the individual flowers, which grow in clusters. The clock a clay is the familiar black spotted red ladybird beetle, whose song here echoes in its first line Ariel's well-known song in Shakespeare's *Tempest*.

The Eagle

Fragment

He clasps the crag with crooked hands;
Close to the sun in lonely lands,
Ring'd with the azure world he stands.

The wrinkled sea beneath him crawls;
He watches from his mountain walls,
And, like a thunderbolt, he falls.

ALFRED, LORD TENNYSON (1851)

'De Gustibus – '

1

Your ghost will walk, you lover of trees,
    (If our loves remain)
    In an English lane,
By a cornfield-side a-flutter with poppies,
Hark, those two in the hazel coppice –
A boy, and a girl, if the good fates please,
    Making love, say, –
    The happier they!
Draw yourself up from the light of the moon,
And let them pass, as they will too soon,
    With the bean-flowers' boon,
    And the blackbird's tune,
    And May, and June!

2

What I love best in all the world
Is a castle, precipice-encurled,
In a gash of the wind grieved Apennine,
Or look for me, old fellow of mine,
(If I get my head from out of the mouth
O' the grave, and loose my spirit's bands,
And come again to the land of lands) –

In a sea-side house to the farther South,
Where the baked cicala dies of drouth,
And one sharp tree – 'tis a cypress – stands,
By the many hundred years red-rusted,
Rough iron-spiked, ripe fruit o'er-crusted,
My sentinel to guard the sands
To the water's edge. For what expands
Before the house, but the great opaque
Blue breadth of sea without a break?
While, in the house, for ever crumbles
Some fragment of the frescoed walls,
From blisters where a scorpion sprawls

A girl bare-footed brings and tumbles
Down on the table green-flesh melons,
And says there's news today – the king
Was shot at, touched in the liver-wing,
Goes with his Bourbon arm in a sling:
She hopes they have not caught the felons,
  Italy, my Italy!
Queen Mary's saying serves for me –
  (When fortune's malice
  Lost her – Calais) –
Open my heart and you will see
Graved inside of it, 'Italy.'
Such lovers old are I and she:
So it always was, so shall ever be!

      ROBERT BROWNING (*c*.1855)

The Lark Ascending

He rises and begins to round,
He drops the silver chain of sound,
On many links without a break,
In chirrup, whistle, slur and shake,
All intervolved and spreading wide,
Like water-dimples down a tide
Where ripple ripple overcurls
And eddy into eddy whirls;
A press of hurried notes that run
So fleet they scarce are more than one,
Yet changingly the trills repeat
And linger ringing while they fleet,
Sweet to the quick o' the ear and dear
To her beyond the handmaid ear,
Who sits beside our inner springs,
To often dry for this he brings,
Which seems the very jet of earth

At sight of sun, her music's mirth,
As up he wings the spiral stair,
A song of light, and pierces air
With fountain ardour, fountain play,
To reach the shining tops of day,
And drink in everything discerned
An ecstasy to music turned,
Impelled by what his happy bill
Disperses; drinking, showering still,
Unthinking save that he may give
His voice the outlet, there to live
Renewed in endless notes of glee,
So thirsty of his voice is he,
For all to hear and all to know
That he is joy, awake, aglow,
The tumult of the heart to hear
Through pureness filtered crystal clear,
And know the pleasure, sprinkled bright
By simple singing of delight,
Shrill, unreflective, unrestrained,
Rapt, ringing, on the jet sustained
Without a break, without a fall,
Sweet silvery, sheer lyrical,
Perennial, quavering up the chord
Like myriad dews of sunny sward
That trembling into fulness shine,
And sparkle dropping argentine;
Such wooing as the ear receives
From zephyr caught in choric leaves
Of aspens when their chattering net
Is flushed to white with shivers wet;
And such the water spirit's chime
On mountain heights in morning's prime,
Too freshly sweet to seem excess,
Too animate to need a stress;
But wider over many heads
The starry voice ascending spreads,
Awakening, as it waxes thin,
The best in us to him akin;
And every face to watch him raised,

Puts on the light of children praised,
So rich our human pleasure pipes,
Though nought be promised from the seas,
But only a soft-ruffling breeze
Sweep glittering on a still content,
Serenity in ravishment.

For singing till his heaven fills,
'Tis love of earth that he instils,
And ever winging up and up,
Our valley is his golden cup,
And he the wine which overflows
To lift us with him as he goes:
The woods, the brooks, the sheep and kine,
He is, the hills, the human line,
The meadows green, the fallows brown,
The dreams of labour in the town;
He sings the sap, the quickened veins;
The wedding song of sun and rains
He is, the dance of children, thanks
Of sowers, shouts of primrose banks,
And eyes of violets while they breathe;
All these the circling song will wreath,
And you shall hear the herb and tree,
The better heart of man shall see,
Shall feel celestially, as long
As you crave nothing but the song.

Was never voice of ours could say
Our inmost in the sweetest way,
Like yonder voice aloft, and link
All hearers in the song they drink.

Our wisdom speaks from failing blood,
Our passion is too full in flood,
We want the key of his wild note,
Of truthful in a truthful throat,
The song seraphically free
Of taint of personality,
So pure that it salutes the suns

The voice of one for millions,
In whom the millions rejoice
For giving their one spirit voice.

Yet men have we, whom we revere,
Now names, and men still housing here,
Whose lives by many a battle-dint
Defaced, and grinding wheels on flint,
Yield substance, though they sing not, sweet
For song our highest heaven to greet:
Whom heavenly singing gives us new,
Enspheres them brilliant in our blue,
From firmest base to farthest leap,
Because their love of earth is deep,
And they are warriors in accord
With life to serve and pass reward,
So touching purest, and so heard
In the brain's reflex of yon bird:
Wherefore their soul in me or mine,
Through self-forgetfulness divine,
In them, that song aloft maintains,
To fill the sky and thrill the plains
With showerings drawn from human stores,
As he to silence nearer soars,
Extends the world at wings and dome,
More spacious making more our home,
Till lost on his aerial rings
In light, and then the fancy sings.

GEORGE MEREDITH (1862)

A Bird came down the Walk

A bird came down the walk –
He did not know I saw –
He bit an angleworm in halves
And ate the fellow, raw,

And then he drank a dew
From a convenient grass
And then hopped sidewise to the wall
To let a beetle pass.

He glanced with rapid eyes
That hurried all abroad,
They looked like frightened beads, I thought.
He stirred his velvet head

Like one in danger, cautious,
I offered him a crumb
And he unrolled his feathers
And rowed him softer home

Than oars divide the ocean,
Too silver for a seam,
Or butterflies, off banks of noon
Leap, plashless, as they swim.

EMILY DICKINSON (*c.* 1862)

There's a Certain Slant of Light

There's a certain slant of light
On winter afternoons
That oppresses – like the weight
Of cathedral tunes

Heavenly hurt it gives us –
We can find no scar
But internal difference
Where the meanings are

None may teach it anything
'Tis the seal despair –
An imperial affliction
Sent us of the air

When it comes, the landscape listens
Shadows hold their breath
When it goes, 'tis like the distance
On the look of death.

EMILY DICKINSON (c. 1861)

A Narrow Fellow

A narrow fellow in the grass
Occasionally rides;
You may have met him – did you not
His notice sudden is.

The grass divides as with a comb,
A spotted shaft is seen;
And then it closes at your feet
And opens further on.

He likes a boggy acre
A floor too cool for corn, –
Yet, when a child and barefoot,
I more than once at noon

Have passed, I thought, a whip lash
Unbraiding in the sun, –
When stooping to secure it
It wrinkled and was gone.

Several of Nature's people
I know, and they know me;
I feel for them a transport
Of cordiality,

But never met this fellow
Attended, or alone
Without a tighter breathing
And zero at the bone.

EMILY DICKINSON (*c.* 1865)

The Bat is Dun

The bat is dun, with wrinkled wings
Like fallow article,
And not a song pervade his lips,
Or none perceptible.

His small umbrella quaintly halved
Describing in the air
An arc alike inscrutable,–
Elate philosopher!

Deputed from what firmament
Of what astute abode,
Empowered with what malevolence
Auspiciously withheld.

To his adroit Creator
Ascribe no less the praise;
Beneficent, believe me,
His eccentricities.

EMILY DICKINSON (*c.* 1876)

The Windhover

To Christ Our Lord

I caught this morning morning's minion, king-
    dom of daylight's dauphin, dapple-dawn drawn Falcon, in
        his riding
    Of the rolling level underneath him steady air, and
        striding
High there, how he hung upon the rein of a wimpling wing
In his ecstasy, then off, off forth on swing,
    As a skate's heel sweeps smooth on a bow-bend: the hurl
        and gliding
    Rebuffed the big wind. My heart in hiding
Stirred for a bird, the achieve of, the mastery of the thing!

Brute beauty and valour and act, oh, air, pride, plume, here
    Buckle! AND the fire that breaks from thee then, a billion
    Time told lovelier, more dangerous, O my chevalier!

No wonder of it: shéer plód makes plough down sillion
    Shine, and blue bleak embers, ah my dear,
    Fall, gall themselves and gash gold-vermilion.

GERARD MANLEY HOPKINS (1877)

The windhover is the kestrel, still a common falcon, often seen hunting alongside motorways. Seen hovering against the sun it is easy to understand how, with its outstretched wings, it reminded Hopkins of Christ on the Cross.

Binsey Poplars

My aspens dear, whose airy cages quelled,
Quelled or quenched in leaves the leaping sun,
All felled, felled, are all felled;
Of a fresh and following folded rank
      Not spared, not one
      That dandled and sandalled
Shadow that swam or sank
On meadow and river and wind-wandering
      weed-winding bank.

O if we but knew what we do
      When we delve or hew –
Hack and rack the growing green!
      Since country is so tender
To touch, her being so slender
That, like this sleek and seeing ball
But a prick will make no eye at all,
Where we, even where we mean
      To mend her we end her,
      When we hew or delve:

After-comers cannot guess the beauty been.
  Ten or twelve, only ten or twelve
Strokes of havoc unselve
  The sweet especial scene,
  Rural scene, a rural scene,
  Sweet especial rural scene

                  GERARD MANLEY HOPKINS (1879)

La Fuite de la Lune

To outer senses there is peace,
A dreamy peace on either hand;
Deep silence in the shadowy land,
Deep silence where the shadows cease,

Save for a cry that echoes shrill
From some lone bird disconsolate,
A corncrake calling to its mate,
The answer from the misty hill.

And suddenly the moon withdraws
Her sickle from the lightening skies
And to her sombre cavern flies
Wrapped in a veil of yellow gauze.

OSCAR WILDE (1881)

Inversnaid

This darksome burn, horseback brown.
Its rollrock highroad roaring down,
In coop and in comb the fleece of his foam
Flutes and low to the lake falls home.

A wind-puff bonnet of fáwn-fróth
Turns and twindles over the broth
Of a pool so pitchblack, fell frowning,
It rounds and rounds Despair to drowning.

Degged with dew, dappled with dew
Are the groins of the braes that the brook treads
    through,
Wiry heathpacks, flitches of fern,
And the beadbonny ash that sits over the burn.

What would the world be, once bereft
Of wet and of wildness? Let them be left,
O let them be left, wildness and wet;
Long live the weeds and the wilderness yet.

GERARD MANLEY HOPKINS (1885)

Night of Frost in May

With splendour of a silver day,
A frosted night had opened May;
And on that plumed and armoured night,
As one close temple hove our wood,
Its border leafage virgin white.
Remote down air an owl hallooed.
The black twig dropped without a twirl;
The bud in jewelled grasp was nipped;
The brown leaf cracked a scorching curl;
A crystal off the green leaf slipped.
Across the tracks of rimy tan,
Some busy thread at whiles would shoot;
A limping minnow-rillet ran,
To hang upon an icy foot.

In this shrill hush of quietude,
The ear conceived a severing cry.
Almost it let the sound elude,
When chuckles three, a warble shy,
From hazels of the garden came,
Near by the crimson-windowed farm,
They laid the trance on breath and frame,
A prelude of the passion-charm.

Then soon was heard, not sooner heard
Than answered, doubled, trebled, more,
Voice of an Eden in the bird,
Renewing with his pipe of four
The sob: a troubled Eden, rich
In throb of heart: unnumbered throats

Flung upward at a fountain's pitch,
The fervour of the four long notes,
That on the fountain's pool subside,
Exult and ruffle and upspring:
Endless the crossing multiplied
Of silver and of golden string.
There chimed a bubbled underbrew
With witch-wild spray of vocal dew.

It seemed a single harper swept
Our wild wood's inner chords and waked
A spirit that for yearning ached
Ere men desired and joyed or wept.
Or now a legion ravishing
Musician rivals did unite
In love of sweetness high to sing
The subtle song that rivals light;

From breast of earth to breast of sky:
And they were secret, they were nigh:
A hand the magic might disperse;
The magic swung my universe.

Yet sharpened breath forbade to dream,
Where all was visionary gleam;
Where Seasons, as with cymbals, clashed;
And feelings, passing joy and woer,
Churned, gurgled, spouted, interflashed,
Nor either was the one we know:
Nor pregnant of the heart contained
In us were they, that griefless plained,
That plaining soared; and through the heart
Struck to one note the wide apart:—
A passion surgent from despair;
A paining bliss in fervid cold;
Off the last vital edge of air,
Leap heavenward of the lofty-souled,
For rapture of a wine of tears;
As had a star among the spheres
Caught up our earth to some mid-height

Of double life to ear and sight,
She giving voice to thought that shines
Keen-brilliant of her deepest mines;
While steely drips the rillet clinked,
And hoar with crust the cowslip swelled.

Then was the lyre of earth beheld,
Then heard by me: it holds me linked;
Across the years to dead-ebb shores
I stand on, my blood-thrill restores.
But would I conjure into me
Those issue notes, I must review
What serious breath the woodland drew;
The low throb of expectancy;
How the white mother-muteness pressed
On leaf and meadow herb; how shook
Nigh speech of mouth, the sparkle crest
Seen spinning on the bracken-crook.

GEORGE MEREDITH (1892)

Loveliest of Trees, the Cherry Now

Loveliest of trees, the cherry now
Is hung with bloom along the bough,
And stands about the woodland ride
Wearing white for Eastertide.

Now of my threescore years and ten,
Twenty will not come again,
And take from seventy springs a score,
It only leaves me fifty more,

And since to look at things in bloom
Fifty springs are little room
About the woodlands I will go
To see the cherry hung with snow.

A. E. HOUSMAN (Published 1896)

6
THE URBAN
SCENE

Composed upon Westminster Bridge

Earth hath not anything to show more fair:
Dull would he be of soul who could pass by
A sight so touching in its majesty:
This City now doth, like a garment, wear
The beauty of the morning, silent, bare,
Ships, towers, domes, theatres and temples lie
Open unto the fields and to the sky;
All bright and glittering in the smokeless air.
Never did sun more beautifully steep,
In his first splendour, valley, rock, or hill:
Ne'er saw I, never felt, a calm so deep!
The river glideth at his own sweet will:
Dear God! the very houses seem asleep;
And all that mighty heart is lying still!

WILLIAM WORDSWORTH (1802)

Wordsworth in London

And first the look and aspect of the place
The broad highway appearance, as it strikes
On Strangers of all ages, the quick dance
Of colours, lights and forms, the Babel din,
The endless stream of men and moving things,
From hour to hour the illimitable walk
Still among streets with clouds and sky above,
The wealth, the bustle and the eagerness,
The glittering Chariots with their pamper'd Steeds,
Stalls, Barrows, Porters; midway in the Street
The Scavenger, who begs with hat in hand,
The labouring Hackney Coaches, the rash speed
Of Coaches travelling far, whirl'd on with horn
Loud blowing, and the sturdy Drayman's Team
Ascending from some Alley of the Thames
And striking right across the crowded Strand
Till the fore-horse veer round with punctual skill:

Here, there and everywhere a weary throng,
The Comers and the Goers face to face,
Face after face; the string of dazzling Wares,
Shop after Shop, with Symbols, blazon'd Names,
And all the Tradesman's honours overhead;
Here, fronts of houses, like a title-page
With letters huge inscribed from top to toe;
Stationed above the door, like guardian Saints,
There, allegoric shapes, female or male,
Or physiognomies of real men,
Land-Warriors, Kings or Admirals of the Sea,
Boyle, Shakspear, Newton, or the attractive head
Of some Scotch doctor, famous in his day.

    Meanwhile the roar continues, till at length,
Escaped as from an enemy we turn
Abruptly into some sequester'd nook
Still as a shelter'd place when winds blow loud:
At leisure thence, through tracts of thin resort,
We take our way: a raree show is here
With Children gather'd round; another Street
Presents a pack of dancing Dogs,
Or Dromedary, with an antic pair
Of Monkies on his back, a minstrel band
Of Savoyards, or, single and alone,
An English Ballad-singer. Private Courts
Gloomy as Coffins, and unsightly Lanes
Thrill'd by some female Vendor's scream, belike
The very shrillest of all London Cries
May then entangle us awhile,
Conducted through those Labyrinths unawares
To privileg'd Regions and inviolate
Where from their airy lodges studious Lawyers
Look out on waters, walks and gardens green.

    Thence back into the throng, until we reach,
Following the tide that slackens by degrees,
Some half-frequented scene where wider Streets
Bring straggling breezes of suburban air;
Here files of ballads dangle from dead walls,

Advertisements of giant-size, from high
Press forward in all colours of the sight;
These, bold in conscious merit; lower down
That, fronted with a most imposing word,
Is, peradventure one in masquerade.
As on the broadening Causeway we advance,
Behold a Face turn'd up towards us, strong
In lineaments, and red with over-toil;
'Tis one perhaps already met elsewhere,
A travelling Cripple, by the trunk cut short,
And stumping with his arms: in Sailor's garb
Another lies at length beside a range
Of written characters with chalk inscrib'd
Upon the smooth flat stones: the Nurse is here,
The Bachelor that loves to sun himself,
The military Idler, and the Dame,
That fieldward takes her walk in decency.

Now homeward through the thickening hubbub, where
See among less distinguishable shapes,
The Italian with his frame of Images
Upon his head; with Basket at his waist
The Jew; the stately and slow moving Turk
With freight of slippers piled beneath his arm.
Briefly, we find, if tired of random sights
And haply to that search our thoughts should turn,
Among the crowd, conspicuous less or more,
As we proceed, all specimens of Man
Through all the colours which the earth bestows,
And every character of form and face,
The Swede, the Russian; from the genial South,
The Frenchman and the Spaniard; from remote
America the hunter-Indian; Moors,
Malays, Lascars, the Tartar and Chinese,
And Negro Ladies in white muslin gowns . . .

from THE PRELUDE, Book 7 (1805)

A City Song

Go look into the City's face,
  That spreadeth over tens of miles;
Go wander through the Merchant place
  Of ledger lore and countless piles.

From palace halls to cellar floors
  In broad highway and narrow street;
From beggars' dens to princes' doors
  Go look and note what ye shall meet.

Close pent and grim, the God of Gain
  Dwells there within his home of stone;
Content with kennel and with chain;
  So that he gnaw a golden bone.

Ah! gloomy are the Winter days
  That close around the traffic mart;
And short-lived are the Summer rays
  That close around the City's heart.

Yet dear, old Nature, fresh and fair,
  Has worshippers for ever true,
For ever fond, and even there
  We see her sweet smile peeping through.

Mark the dim windows ye shall pass,
  And see the petted myrtle here;
While there, upraised in tinted glass,
  The curling hyacinths appear.

The gay geranium, in its pride,
  Looks out to kiss the scanty gleam;
And rosebud nurslings, by its side,
  Are gently brought to share the beam.

Hands, with their daily bread to gain,
  May oft be seen, at twilight hour,

Decking their dingy garret pane
    With wreathing stem or sickly flower.

Smile not to see the broken cup,
    With dusty mould and starting seed;
The one who fills it renders up
    An offering that Heaven may heed.

Look kindly on the housecrop patch,
    Reared by the sinful or the poor;
Spurn not the humblest, who would snatch
    Sparks from the Beautiful or pure.

For not 'all evil' is the one
    Who fondly twines some dwindling leaves,
Now to the life-stream of the sun,
    Then to the raindrops from the eves.

A spark of something goodly still
    Lurks in a bosom while it yields
An instinct love on smoky sills,
    And seeks to call up woods and fields.

A pleasant sight it is to see
    The spirit of Creation haunt
The City paths in some old tree,
    Where butterflies and rooks may flaunt.

Though Toil and Dust may hem us round,
    And drink the freshness of our Life;
Some primal trace will yet be found –
    Some olive-branches in the strife.

The babe will smile at these fair things,
    And strive to catch the types of light;
Telling how faithfully man clings
    To Nature's mystery and might.

Oh! let us look with grateful eye
    On branch and bloom within a City;

They seem, we know not how or why,
    To cheer us like a minstrel's ditty.

They tell of something which defies
    The lust of Wealth and dread of Death –
They point to brighter, bluer skies,
    And whisper with a seraph's breath.

Though mean they seem, though weak they be;
    Yet do they hold our mortal leaven;
And while we see the flower and tree,
    The City yet is nigh to Heaven.

ELIZA COOK (c. 1850)

In a London Drawing Room

The sky is cloudy, yellowed by the smoke.
For view there are the houses opposite
Cutting the sky with one long line of wall
Like solid fog; far as the eye can stretch
Monotony of surface and of form
Without a break to hang a guess upon.
No bird can make a shadow as it flies,
For all is shadow, as in ways o'erhung
By thickest canvass, where the golden rays
Are clothed in hemp. No figure lingering
Pauses to feed the hunger of the eye
Or rest a little on the lap of life.
All hurry on and look upon the ground,
Or glance unmarking at the passers by.
The wheels are hurrying too, cabs, carriages
All closed in multiplied identity.
The world seems one huge prison house and court
Where men are punished at the slightest cost,
With lowest rate of colour, warmth and joy.

GEORGE ELIOT (MARY ANN EVANS) (1865)

Coming up Oxford Street: Evening

The sun from the west glares back,
And the sun from the watered track,
And the sun from the sheets of glass,
And the sun from each window brass;
Sun-mirrorings, too, brighten
From show-cases beneath
The laughing eyes and teeth
Of ladies who rouge and whiten,
And the same warm god explores
Panels and chinks of doors;
Problems with chymic bottles
Profound as Aristotles
He solves, and with good cause,
Having been ere man was.
Also he dazzles the pupils of one who walks west,
A city clerk, with eyes not of the best,
Who sees no escape to the very verge of his days
From the rut of Oxford Street into open ways;
And he goes along with head and eyes flagging folorn,
Empty of interest in things, and wondering why he was born.

THOMAS HARDY (1872)

Symphony in Yellow

An omnibus across the bridge
  Crawls like a yellow butterfly,
  And, here and there, a passer-by
Shows like a little restless midge.

Big barges full of yellow hay
  Are moved against the shadowy wharf,
  And, like a yellow silken scarf
The thick fog hangs along the quay.

The yellow leaves begin to fade
   And flutter from the Temple elms,
   And at my feet the pale green Thames
Lies like a rod of rippled jade.

OSCAR WILDE (1889)

Impression du Matin

The Thames nocturne of blue and gold
   Changed to a Harmony in grey:
   A barge with ochre-coloured hay
Dropped from the wharf: and chill and cold

The yellow fog came creeping down
   The bridges, till the houses' walls
   Seemed changed to shadows and St Paul's
Loomed like a bubble o'er the town.

Then suddenly arose the clang
   Of waking life; the streets were stirred
   With country wagons; and a bird
Flew to the glistening roofs and sang.

But one pale woman all alone,
   The daylight kissing her wan hair,
   Loitered beneath the gaslamps' flare,
With lips of flame and heart of stone.

OSCAR WILDE (1889)

A London Plane Tree

Green is the plane tree in the square,
   The other trees are brown;
They droop and pine for country air;
   The plane tree loves the town.

Here, from my garret-pane, I mark
   The plane-tree bud and blow,
Shed her recuperative bark,
   And spread her shade below.

Among her branches, in and out,
　　The city breezes play;
The dun fog wraps her round about;
　　Above, the smoke curls grey.

Others the country take for choice,
　　And hold the town in scorn;
But she has listened to the voice
　　On city breezes born.

AMY LEVY (1889)

Ballade of an Omnibus

Some men to carriages aspire;
On some the costly hansoms wait;
Some seek a fly, on job or hire;
Some mount the trotting steed, elate.
I envy not the rich and great,
A wandering minstrel, poor and free,
I am contented with my fate –
An omnibus suffices me.

In winter days of rain and mire
I find within a corner strait
The 'busmen know me and my lyre
From Brompton to the Bull and Gate.
When summer comes, I mount in state
The topmost summit, whence I see
Croesus look up, compassionate –
An omnibus suffices me.

I mark, untroubled by desire,
Lucullus' phaeton and its freight.
The scene whereof I cannot tire
The human tale of love and hate,
The city pageant, early and late
Unfolds itself, rolls by to be
A pleasure, deep and delicate.
An omnibus suffices me.

Princess, your splendour you require,
I my simplicity; agree
Neither to late lower or higher.
An omnibus suffices me.

AMY LEVY (1889)

Ballade of a Special Edition

He comes: I hear him up the street –
  Bird of ill omen, flapping wide
The pinion of a printed sheet,
  His hoarse note scares the eventide.
Of slaughter, theft and suicide
  He is the herald and the friend;
Now he vociferates with pride –
  A double murder in Mile End.

A hanging to his soul is sweet;
  His gloating fancy's fain to bide
Where human freighted vessels meet,
  And misdirected trains collide.
With shocking accidents supplied,
  He tramps the town from end to end.
How often have we heard it cried –
  A double murder in Mile End.

War loves he; victory or defeat,
  So there be loss on either side.
His tale of horrors incomplete,
  Imagination's aid is tried.
Since no distinguished man has died,
  And since the Fates, relenting, send
No great catastrophe, he's spied
  This double murder in Mile End.

Fiend, get thee gone! no more repeat
  Those sounds which do mine ears offend,
It is apocryphal, you cheat,
  Your double murder in Mile End.

AMY LEVY (1889)

7
VIEWS OF
CHILDHOOD

Ode: Intimations of Immortality from Recollections of Early Childhood

The Child is Father of the Man
And I could wish to be
Bound each to each by natural piety.

1

There was a time when meadow, grove and stream,
The earth and every common sight,
    To me did seem
  Apparelled in celestial light,
The glory and the freshness of a dream.
It is not now as it hath been of yore; –
    Turn wheresoe'er I may,
    By night or day,
The things which I have seen, I now can see no more.

2

    The Rainbow comes and goes,
    And lovely is the Rose,
    The Moon doth with delight
    Look round her when the heavens are bare,
    Waters on a starry night
Are beautiful and fair;
  The sunshine is a glorious birth,
  But yet I know, where'er I go
That there has past away a glory from the earth.

3

Now, while the birds thus sing a joyous song,
  And while the young lambs bound
    As to the tabor's sound.
To me alone there came a thought of grief:
A timely utterance gave that thought relief,
    And I again am strong:
The cataracts blow their trumpets from the steep;
No more shall grief of mine the season wrong;

I hear the echoes through the mountains throng,
The winds come to me from the fields of sleep,
    And all the earth is gay;
     Land and sea
    Give themselves up to jollity,
   And, with the heart of May
    Doth every Beast keep holiday; –
     Thou Child of Joy,
Shout round me, let me hear thy shouts, thou happy
   Shepherd Boy!

4

Ye blessed Creatures, I have heard thy call
    Ye to each other make; I see
The Heavens laugh with you in your jubilee;
  My heart is at your festival,
    My head hath its coronal,
The fulness of your bliss, I feel – I feel it all.
   O evil day, if I were sullen
  While Earth is herself adorning,
   This sweet May morning,
  And the Children are culling
    On every side
  In a thousand valleys, far and wide,
  Fresh flowers, while the sun shines warm,
And the Babe leaps up on his Mother's arm; –
  I hear, I hear, with joy I hear!
  But there's a Tree, of many, one
A single Field which I have looked upon,
Both of them speak of something that is gone:
  The Pansy at my feet
  Doth the same tale repeat:
Whither is fled the visionary gleam?
Where is it now, the glory and the dream?

5

Our birth is but a sleep, and a forgetting:
This soul that rises with us, our lifes star
    Hath had elsewhere its setting,

And cometh from afar;
Not in entire forgetfulness,
And not in utter nakedness,
But trailing clouds of glory do we come
From God who is our home:
Heaven lies about us in our infancy!
Shades of the prison house begin to close
Upon the growing Boy
But he beholds the light and whence it flows
He sees it in his joy;
The Youth, who daily farther from the east
Must travel, still is Nature's Priest,
And by the vision splendid
Is on his way attended;
At length the Man perceives it die away,
And fade into the light of common day.

6

Earth fills her lap with pleasures of her own;
Yearnings she hath in her own natural kind,
And, even with something of a Mother's mind,
And no unworthy aim,
The homely Nurse doth all he can
To make her Foster-child, her Inmate Man,
Forget the glories he hath known
And that imperial palace whence he came.

7

Behold the Child among his new-born blisses,
A six years' Darling of a pigmy size!
See, where mid work of his own hand he lies,
Fretted by sallies of his mother's kisses,
With light upon him from his father's eyes!
See, at his feet, some little plan or chart,
Some fragment from his dream of human life,
Shaped by himself with newly-learned art;
A wedding or a festival,
A mourning or a funeral
And this hath now his heart,
And unto this he frames his song:

Then will he fit his tongue
To dialogues of business, love or strife;
But it will not be long
Ere this be thrown aside,
And with new joy and pride
The little Actor cons another part;
Filling from time to time his 'humorous stage'
With all the Persons, down to palsied Age,
That Life brings with her in her equipage;
As if his whole vocation
Were endless imitation.

8

Thou, whose exterior semblance doth belie
Thy Soul's immensity;
Thou best Philosopher, who yet dost keep
Thy heritage, thou Eye among the blind,
That, deaf and silent, read'st the eternal deep,
Haunted for ever by the eternal mind, –
Mighty Prophet! Seer blest!
On whom those truths do rest,
Which we are toiling all our lives to find,
In darkness lost, the darkness of the grave;
Thou, over whom thy Immortality
Broods like the Day, a Master o'er a Slave,
A Presence which is yet not to be put by;
Thou little Child, yet glorious in the might
Of heaven-born freedom on thy being's height,
Why with such earnest pains dost thou provoke
The years to bring the inevitable yoke,
Thus blindly, with thy blessedness at strife?
Full soon thy Souls shall have her earthly freight
And custom lie upon thee with a weight,
Heavy as frost, and deep almost as life!

9

O joy! that in our embers
Is something that doth live,
That nature yet remembers

What was so fugitive!
The thought of our past years in me doth breed
Perpetual benediction; not indeed
For that which is most worthy to be blest;
Delight and liberty, the simple creed
Of Childhood, whether busy or at rest,
With new-fledged hope still fluttering in his breast: –
    Not for these I raise
    The song of thanks and praise;
  But for those obstinate questionings
  Of sense and outward things,
  Fallings from us, vanishings;
  Blank misgivings of a Creature
Moving about in worlds not realised,
High instincts before which our mortal Nature
Did tremble like a guilty Thing surprised:
    But, for those first affections,
    Those shadowy recollections,
  Which, be they what they may,
Are yet the fountain-light of all our day,
Are yet a master light of all our seeing;
Uphold us, cherish, and have power to make
Our noisy years seem moments in the being
Of the eternal Silence; truths that wake,
      To perish never;
Which neither listlessness, nor mad endeavour,
      Nor Man nor Boy,
Nor all that is at enmity with joy,
Can utterly abolish or destroy.
  Hence, in a season of calm weather
    Though inland far we be,
Our Souls have sight of that immortal sea
    Which brought us hither,
  Can, in a moment travel thither,
And see the Children sport upon the shore,
And hear the mighty waters rolling, evermore.

10

Then sing, ye Birds, sing, sing a joyous song!
   And let the young Lambs bound
   As to the tabor's sound!
We in thought will join your throng,
   Ye that pipe and ye that play,
   Ye that through your hearts today
   Feel the gladness of the May!
What though the radiance which was once so bright
Be now for ever taken from my sight,
  Though nothing can bring back the hour
Of splendour in the grass, of glory in the flower;
   We will grieve not, rather find
   Strength in what remains behind;
   In the primal sympathy
   Which having been must ever be;
   In the soothing thoughts that spring
   Out of human suffering;
   In the faith that looks through death,
In years that bring the philosophic mind.

11

And O ye Fountains, Meadows, Hills and Groves,
Forebode not any severing of our loves!
Yet in my heart of hearts I feel your might;
I only have relinquished one delight
To live beneath your more habitual sway.
I love the Brooks which down their channels fret,
Even more than when I tripped lightly as they;
The innocent brightness of a new-born Day
   Is lovely yet;
The Clouds that gather round the setting sun
Do take a sober colouring from an eye
That hath kept watch o'er man's mortality;
Another race hath been, and other palms are won.
Thanks to the human heart by which we live,
Thanks to its tenderness, its joys and fears,
To me the meanest flower that blows can give
Thoughts that do often lie too deep for tears.

WILLIAM WORDSWORTH (1804)

Wordsworth's Boyhood

Fair seed-time had my soul, and I grew up
Fostered alike by beauty and by fear;
Much favour'd by my birthplace, and no less
In that beloved Vale to which ere long
I was transplanted. Well I call to mind
('Twas at an early age, ere I had seen
Nine summers) when upon the mountain slope
The frost and breath of frosty wind had snapped
The last autumnal crocus, 'twas my joy
To wander half the night among the Cliffs
And the smooth Hollows, where the woodcocks ran
Along the open turf. In thought and wish
That time, my shoulder all with springes hung,
I was a fell destroyer. On the heights
Scudding away from snare to snare, I plied
My anxious visitation, hurrying on,
Still hurrying, hurrying onward; moon and stars
Were shining o'er my head; I was alone,
And seemed to be a trouble to the peace
That was among them. Sometimes it befel
In these night-wanderings, that a strong desire
O'erpower'd my better reason, and the bird
Which was the product of another's toil
Became my prey; and when the deed was done
I heard among the solitary hills
Low breathings coming after me, and sounds
Of undistinguishable motion, steps
Almost as silent as the turf they trod.
Nor less in springtime when on southern banks
The shining sun had from his knot of leaves
Decoy'd the primrose flower, and when the Vales
And woods were warm, was I a plunderer then
In the high places, on the lonesome peaks
Where'er, among the mountains and the winds,
The Mother Bird had built her lodge. Though mean
My object, and inglorious, yet the end
Was not ignoble. Oh! when I have hung

Above the raven's nest, by knots of grass
And half-inch fissures in the slippery rock
But ill-sustained, and almost, as it seemed,
Suspended by the blast which blew amain,
Shouldering the naked crag; Oh! at that time,
With what strange utterance did the loud dry wind
Blow through my ears! The sky seemed not a sky
Of earth, and with what motion mov'd the clouds!

    The mind of Man is fram'd even like the breath
And harmony of music. There is a dark
Invisible workmanship that reconciles
Discordant elements, and makes them move
In one society. Ah me! that all
The terrors, all the early miseries,
Regrets, vexations, lassitudes, that all
The thoughts and feelings which have been infus'd
Into my mind, should ever have made up
The calm existence that is mine when I
Am worthy of myself! Praise to the end!
Thanks likewise for the means! But I believe
That Nature, oftentimes, when she would frame
A favour'd Being, from his earliest dawn
Of infancy doth open out the clouds,
As at the touch of lightning, seeking him,
With gentlest visitation; not the less,
Though haply aiming at the self-same end,
Does it delight her sometimes to employ
Severer interventions, ministry
More palpable, and so she dealt with me.

    One evening (surely I was led by her)
I went alone into a Shepherd's Boat,
A Skiff that to a Willow tree was tied
Within a rocky Cave, its usual home.
'Twas by the shores of Patterdale, a Vale
Wherein I was a stranger, thither come
A School-boy Traveller, at the Holidays.
Forth rambled from the Village Inn alone
No sooner had I sight of this small Skiff,

Discover'd thus by unexpected chance,
Than I unloos'd her tether and embarked.
The moon was up, the Lake was shining clear
Among the hoary mountains; from the Shore
I push'd, and struck the oars and struck again
In cadence, and my little Boat mov'd on
Even like a Man who walks with stately step,
Though bent on speed. It was an act of stealth
And troubl'd pleasure; not without the voice
Of mountain echoes did my Boat move on,
Leaving behind her still on either side
Small circles glittering idly in the moon,
Until they melted all into one track
Of sparkling light. A rocky Steep uprose
Above the Caverns of the Willow tree,
And now, as suited one who proudly row'd
With his best skill, I fix'd a steady view
Upon the top of that same craggy ridge,
The bound of the horizon, for behind
Was nothing but the stars and the grey sky.
She was an elfin Pinnace; lustily
I dipp'd my oars into the silent Lake,
And as I rose upon the stroke, my Boat
Went heaving through the water like a Swan;
When from behind that craggy Steep, till then
The bound of the horizon, a huge Cliff,
As if with voluntary power instinct,
Uprear'd its head. I struck and struck again,
And growing still in stature, the huge Cliff
Rose up between me and the stars, and still,
With measur'd motion, like a living thing,
Strode after me. With trembling hands I turn'd,
And through the silent water made my way
Back to the Cavern of the Willow tree.
There, in her mooring-place, I left my Bark,
And through the meadows homeward went, with grave
And serious thoughts; and after I had seen
That spectacle, for many days, my brain
Work'd with a dim and undetermin'd sense
Of unknown modes of being; in my thoughts

There was a darkness, call it solitude,
Or blank desertion, no familiar shapes
Of hourly objects, images of trees
Of sea or sky, no colours of green fields;
But huge and mighty Forms that do not live
Like living men mov'd slowly through my mind
By day, and were the trouble of my dreams.

    Wisdom and Spirit of the universe!
Thou Soul that art the Eternity of Thought
That giv'st to forms and images a breath
And everlasting motion! not in vain,
By day or starlight thus from my first dawn
Of Childhood didst thou intertwine for me
The passions that build up our human Soul,
Not with the mean and vulgar works of Man,
But with high objects, with enduring things,
With life and nature, purifying thus
The elements of feeling and of thought,
And sanctifying, by such discipline,
Both pain and fear, until we recognize
A grandeur in the beatings of the heart.

    Nor was this fellowship vouchsaf'd to me
With stinted kindness. In November days,
When vapours, rolling down the valleys, made
A lonely scene more lonesome; among woods
At noon, and 'mid the calm of summer nights,
When by the margin of the trembling Lake,
Beneath the gloomy hills I lonesome went
In solitude, such intercourse was mine;
'Twas mine among the fields both day and night,
And by the waters all the summer long.

    And in the frosty season, when the sun
Was set, and visible for many a mile
The cottage windows through the twilight blaz'd,
I heeded not the summons:– happy time
It was indeed for all of us; to me
It was a time of rapture: clear and loud

The village clock toll'd six; I wheel'd about,
Proud and exulting, like an untired horse,
That cares not for its home, – all shod with steel
We hiss'd along the polish'd ice, in games
Confederate, imitative of the chace
And woodland pleasures, the resounding horn,
The Pack loud bellowing, and the hunted hare.
So through the darkness and the cold we flew,
And not a voice was idle; with the din,
Meanwhile, the precipices rang aloud,
The leafy trees and every icy crag
Tinkled like iron, while the distant hills
Into the tumult sent an alien sound
Of melancholy, not unnoticed, while the stars,
Eastward, were sparkling clear, and in the west
The orange sky of evening died away.

Not seldom from the uproar I retired
Into a silent bay, or sportively
Glanced sideway, leaving the tumultuous throng,
To cut across the reflex of a star
That gleamed upon the ice; and oftentimes
When we had given our bodies to the wind,
And all the shadowy banks, on either side,
Came sweeping through the darkness, spinning still
The rapid line of motion; then at once
Have I, reclining back upon my heels,
Stopp'd short, yet still the solitary Cliffs
Wheel'd by me, even as if the earth had roll'd
With visible motion her diurnal round;
Behind me did they stretch in solemn train
Feebler and feebler, and I stood and watched
Till all was tranquil as a dreamless sleep.

Ye presences of Nature, in the sky
Or on the earth! Ye Visions of the hills!
And Souls of lonely places! can I think
A vulgar hope was yours when Ye employ'd
Such ministry, when Ye through many a year
Haunting me thus amidst my boyish sports,

On caves and trees, upon the woods and hills,
Impress'd upon all forms the characters
Of danger or desire, and thus did make
The surface of the universal earth
With triumph, and delight, and hope, and fear,
Work, like a sea?
                    Not uselessly employ'd,
I might pursue this theme through every change
Of exercise and play, to which the year
Did summon us in its delightful round.

  We were a noisy crew, the sun in heaven
Beheld not vales more beautiful than ours,
Nor saw a race in happiness and joy
More worthy of the ground where they were sown.
I would record with no reluctant voice
The woods of autumn and their hazel bowers
With milk-white clusters hung; the rod and line,
True symbol of the foolishness of hope,
Which with its strong enchantment led us on
By rocks and pools, shut out from every star
All the green summer, to folorn cascades
Among the windings of the mountain brooks.
– Unfading recollections! at this hour
The heart is almost mine with which I felt
From some hill-top, on sunny afternoons
The Kite high up among the fleecy clouds
Pull at its rein, like an impatient Courser,
Or from the meadows sent, on gusty days,
Beheld her breast the wind, then suddenly
Dash'd headlong; and rejected by the storm.

                    from THE PRELUDE, Book 1, Lines 305–524 (1805)

I Remember, I Remember

I remember, I remember,
The house where I was born,
The little window where the sun
Came peeping in at morn;
He never came a wink too soon,
Nor brought too long a day,
But now I often wish the night,
Had borne my breath away!

I remember, I remember,
The roses, red and white,
The vi'lets, and the lily-cups,
The flowers made of light!
The lilacs where the robin built,
And where my brother set
The laburnum on his birthday, –
The tree is living yet!

I remember, I remember,
Where I was used to swing,
And thought the air must rush as fresh
To swallows on the wing;
My spirit grew in feathers then,
That is so heavy now,
And summer pools could hardly cool
The fever on my brow!

I remember, I remember,
The fir trees, dark and high;
I used to think their slender tops
Were close against the sky:
It was a childish ignorance,
But now 'tis little joy,
To know I'm farther off from heaven,
Than when I was a boy.

THOMAS HOOD (1827)

A Parental Ode to my Son,
aged three years and five months

Thou happy, happy elf!
(But stop, – first let me kiss away that tear)
      Thou tiny image of myself
(My love, he's poking peas into his ear!)
      Thou merry, laughing sprite,
      With spirits feather-light,
Untouched by sorrow and unsoil'd by sin –
(Good heavens, the child is swallowing a pin!)

      Thou little tricksy Puck!
With antic toys so funnily bestuck,
Light as the singing bird that wings the air –
(The door! The door! he'll tumble down the stair!)
      Thou darling of thy sire!
(Why, Jane, he'll set his pinafore afire!)
      Thou imp of mirth and joy!
In love's dear chain so bright and strong a link,
Thou idol of thy parents – (Drat the boy!
      There goes my ink!)

      Thou cherub – but of earth
Fit playfellow for Fays, by moonlight pale,
      In harmless sport and mirth,
(That dog will bite him if he pulls its tail!)
Thou human humming bee, extracting honey
From every blossom in the world that blows,
   Singing in Youth's Elysium ever sunny –
(Another tumble! – That's his precious nose!)

      Thy father's pride and hope!
(He'll break the mirror with that skipping rope!)
With pure heart newly stamped from Nature's mint –
      (Where *did* he learn that squint?)
      Thou young, domestic dove!
(He'll have that jug off, with another shove!)

Dear nursling of the hymeneal nest!
(Are those torn clothes his best?)
  Little epitome of man!
(He'll climb upon the table; that's his plan!)
Touch'd with the beauteous tints of dawning life –
  (He's got a knife!)

  Thou enviable being
No storms, no clouds, in thy blue sky foreseeing,
  Play on, play on,
  My elfin John!
Toss the light ball, – bestride the stick –
(I knew so many cakes would make him sick!)
With fancies buoyant as the thistledown,
Prompting the face grotesque, and antic brisk,
  With many a lamb-like frisk –
(He's got the scissors, snipping at your gown!)

  Thou pretty, opening rose!
(Go to your mother, child, and wipe your nose!)
Balmy, and breathing music like the South,
(He really brings my heart into my mouth!)
Fresh as the morning, brilliant as its star, –
(I wish that window had an iron bar!)
Bold as the hawk, yet gentle as the dove –
  (I'll tell you what, my love,
I cannot write unless he's sent above!)

THOMAS HOOD (c. 1838)

Rustic Childhood

No city primness train'd my feet
To strut in childhood through the street,
But freedom let them loose to tread
The yellow cowslip's downcast head;
Or climb, above the twining hop
And ivy to the elm tree's top;
Where southern airs of blue-sky'd day
Breath'd o'er the daisy and the may.
    I knew you young, and love you now,
      O shining grass, and shady bough.

Far off from town, where splendour tries
To draw the looks of gather'd eyes,
And clocks, unheeded, fail to warn
The loud-tongued party of the morn,
I spent in woodland shades my day
In cheerful work or happy play,
And slept at night where rustling leaves
Threw moonlight shadows o'er my eaves.
    I knew you young, and love you now,
      O shining grass and shady bough.

Or in the grassy drove by ranks
Of white stemmed ashes or by banks
Of narrow lanes, in-winding round
The hedgy sides of shelving ground;
Where low-shot light struck in to end
Again at some cool-shaded bend,
Where we might see through darkleav'd boughs
The evening light on green hill-brows.
I knew you young, and love you now,
    O shining grass, and shady bough.

Or on the hillock where I lay
At rest on some bright holyday;
When short noon-shadows lay below
The thorn in blossom white as snow;
And warm air bent the glistening tops

Of bushes in the lowland copse,
Before the blue hills swelling high
And far against the southern sky.
    I knew you young, and love you now,
    O shining grass and shady bough.

WILLIAM BARNES (c.1846)

The Old Mill-Stream

Beautiful streamlet, how precious to me
Was the green-swarded paradise watered by thee;
I dream of thee still, as thou wert in my youth,
Thy meanderings haunt me with freshness and truth.

I had heard of full many a river of fame,
With its wide rolling flood, and its classical name;
But the Thames of Old England the Tiber of Rome,
Could not peer with the mill-streamlet close to my home.

Full well I remember the gravelly spot,
Where I slyly repaired, though I knew I should not;
Where I stood with my handful of pebbles to make
That formation of fancy, a duck and a drake.

How severe was the scolding, how heavy the threat
When my pinafore hung on me, dirty and wet;
How heedlessly silent I stood to be told
Of the danger of drowning, the risk of a cold!

'Now mark!' cried a mother, 'the mischief done there
Is unbearable – go to that stream if you dare!'
But I sped to that stream like a frolicsome colt,
For I knew that her thunder-cloud carried no bolt.

Though puzzled with longitude, adverb and noun,
Till my forehead was sunk in a studious frown;
Yet that stream was a Lethe that swept from my soul
The grammar, the globes, and my tutor's control.

I wonder if still the young anglers begin,
As I did, with willow-wand, packthread, and pin;
When I threw in my line with expectancy high
As to perch in my basket and eels in a pie:

When I watched every bubble that broke on a weed,
Yet found I caught nothing but lily and reed;
Till time and discernment began to instil
The manoeuvres of Walton with infinite skill.

Full soon I discovered the birch-shadowed place
That harboured the trout and the silver-backed dace;
Where the coming of night found me blest and content,
With my patience unworn and my fishing-rod bent.

How fresh were the flags on the stone-studded ridge,
That rudely supported the narrow oak bridge;
And that bridge, oh! how boldly and safely I ran
On the thin plank that now I should timidly scan.

I traversed it often at fall of the night
When the clouds of December shut out the moon's light;
A mother might tremble, but I never did;
For my footing was sure, though the pale stars were hid.

When the breath of stern winter had fettered the tide,
What joy to career on its feet-warming slide;
With mirth in each eye, an bright health on each cheek,
While the gale in our faces came piercing and bleak.

The snow-flakes fell thick on our wind-roughened curls,
But we laughed as we shook off the feathery pearls;
And the running, the tripping, the pull and the haul
Had a glorious end in the slip and the sprawl.

*   *   *   *   *

What pleasure it was to spring forth in the sun,
When the school door was oped, and our lessons were
     done,
When 'Where shall we play?' was the doubt and the call,
And 'Down by the mill-stream', was echoed by all.

When tired of childhood's rude boisterous pranks,
We pulled the tall rushes that grew on its banks;
And, busily quiet, we sat ourselves down
To weave the rough basket, or plait the light crown.

I remember the launch of our fairy-built ship,
How we set her white sails, pulled her anchor atrip;
Till mischievous hands, working hard at the craft
Turned the ship to a boat, and the boat to a raft.

The first of my doggerel breathings was there, –
'Twas the hope of a poet, 'An Ode To Despair,'
I won't vouch for its metre, its sense, or its rhyme,
But I know that I then thought it truly sublime.

Beautiful streamlet! I dream of thee still;
Of thy pouring cascade, and the tic-tacing mill;
Thou livest in memory and wilt not depart,
For thy waters seem blent with the streams of my heart.

Home of my youth! if I go to thee now,
None can remember my voice or my brow;
None can remember the sunny-faced child,
That played by the water-mill joyous and wild.

The aged, who laid their thin hands on my head,
To smooth my dark shining curls, rest with the dead;
The young who partook of my sports and my glee,
Can see naught but a wandering stranger in me.

Beautiful streamlet! I sought thee again,
But the changes that marked thee awakened deep pain;
Desolation had reigned; thou wert not as of yore –
Home of my Childhood, I'll see thee no more!

ELIZA COOK (Mid-century)

I Met a King this Afternoon!

I met a king this afternoon!
He had not on a crown indeed,
A little palmleaf hat was all,
And he was barefoot, I'm afraid!

But sure I am he ermine wore
Beneath his faded jacket's blue
And sure I am, the crest he wore
Within that jacket's pocket too!

For 'twas too stately for an earl,
A marquis would not go so grand!
'Twas possibly a Czar petite –
A Pope or something of that kind!

If I might tell you of a horse
My freckled monarch held the rein,
Doubtless an estimable beast,
But not at all disposed to run!

And such a wagon! While I live
Dare I presume to see
Another such a vehicle
As then transported me!

Two other ragged princes
His royal state partook!
Doubtless the first excursion
Those sovereigns ever took!

I question if the royal coach
Round which the Footmen wait
Has the significance on high
Of this barefoot estate!

EMILY DICKINSON (*c.* 1860)

They Shut Me Up in Prose

They shut me up in prose,
As when a little girl
They put me in the closet
Because they liked me 'still'.

Still! Could themself have peeped
And seen my brain go round,
They might as well have lodged a bird
For treason in the pound.

Himself has but to will,
And easy as a star
Look down upon captivity
And laugh – No more have I!

EMILY DICKINSON (*c.* 1862)

The Toys

My little son, who looked from thoughtful eyes
And moved and spoke in grown-up thoughtful wise,
Having my law the seventh time disobeyed,
I struck him, and dismissed
With hard words, and unkissed,
His Mother, who was patient, being dead.
Then, fearing that his grief should hinder sleep,
I visited his bed,
But found him slumbering deep,
With darkened eyelids, and their lashes yet
From his late sobbing wet.
And I with moan
Kissing away his tears, left others of my own;
For on a table, drawn beside his head,
He had put, within his reach,
A box of counters and a red-veined stone,
A piece of glass abraded by the beach

And six or seven shells,
A bottle with bluebells
And two French copper coins, ranged there with
    careful art,
To comfort his sad heart.

So when that night I prayed
To God, I wept and said:
Are, when at last we lie with tranced breath,
Not vexing Thee in death,
And Thou rememberest of what joys
We made our joys,
How weakly understood,
Thy great commanded good,
Then fatherly, not less
Than I whom Thou hast moulded from the clay,
Thou'lt leave thy wrath and say,
'I will be sorry for their childishness.'

                COVENTRY PATMORE (*c.* 1862)

Brother and Sister

1

I cannot choose but think upon the time
When our two lives grew like two buds that kiss
At lightest thrill from the bee's swinging chime,
Because the one so near the other is.

He was the elder, and a little man
Of forty inches, bound to show no dread,
And I the girl that puppy-like now ran,
Now lagged behind my brother's larger tread.

I held him wise, and when he talked to me
Of snakes and birds, and which God loved the best,
I thought his knowledge marked the boundary
Where men grew blind, though angels knew the rest.

    If he said 'Hush!' I tried to hold my breath;
    Wherever he said 'Come!' I stepped in faith.

2

Long years have left their writing on my brow,
But yet the freshness and the dew-fed beam
Of those young mornings are about me now,
When we two wandered toward the far-off stream

With rod and line. Our basket held a store
Baked for us only, and I thought with joy
That I should have my share, though he had more,
Because he was the elder and a boy.

The firmaments of daisies since to me
Have had those mornings in their opening eyes,
The bunched cowslip's pale transparency
Carries that sunshine of sweet memories,

   And wild rose branches take their finest scent
   From those blest hours of infantine content.

3

Our mother bade us keep the trodden ways,
Stroked down my tippet, set my brother's frill,
Then, with the benediction of her gaze
Clung to us lessening, and pursued us still

Across the homestead to the rookery elms,
Whose tall old trunks had each a grassy mound,
So rich for us, we counted them as realms
With varied products: here were earth-nuts found,

And here the Lady-fingers in deep shade;
Here sloping toward the Moat the rushes grew,
The large to split for pith, the small to braid;
While over all the dark rooks cawing flew,

   And made a happy strange solemnity
   A deep-toned chant from life unknown to me.

4

Our meadow-path had memorable spots:
One where it bridges a tiny rivulet,
Deep hid my tangled blue Forget-me-nots;
And all along the waving grasses met

My little palm, or nodded to my cheek,
When flowers with upturned faces gazing drew
My wonder downward, seeming all to speak
With eyes of souls that dumbly heard and knew.

Then came the copse, where wild things rushed unseen,
And black-scathed grass betrayed the past abode
Of mystic gypsies, who still lurked between
Me and each hidden distance of the road.

    A gipsy once had startled me at play,
    Blotting with her dark smile my sunny day.

5

Thus rambling, we were schooled in deepest lore,
And learned the meanings that gave words a soul,
The fear, the love, the primal passionate store,
Whose shaping impulses make manhood whole.

Those hours were seed to all my after good;
My infant gladness, through eye, ear, and touch
Took easily as warmth a various food
To nourish the sweet skill of loving much.

For who in age shall roam the earth and find
Reasons for loving that will strike out love
With sudden rod from the hard year-pressed mind?
Were reasons sown as thick as stars above,

    'Tis love must see them, as the eye sees light:
    Day is but number to the darkened sight.

6

Our brown canal was endless to my thought;
And on its banks I sat in dreamy peace,
Unknowing how the good I loved was wrought,
Untroubled by the fear that it would cease.

Slowly the barges floated into view
Rounding a grassy hill to me sublime
With some Unknown beyond it, whither flew
The parting cuckoo toward a fresh spring time.

The wide-arched bridge, the scented elder flowers,
The wondrous watery rings that die too soon,
The echoes of the quarry, the still hours
With white robe sweeping on the shadeless noon

  Were but my growing self, are part of me,
  My present Past, my root of piety.

7

Those long days measured by my little feet
Had chronicles which yield me many a text;
Where irony still finds an image meet
Of full-grown judgements in this world perplext.

One day, my brother left me in high charge,
To mind the rod, while he went seeking bait,
And bade me, when I saw a nearing barge,
Snatch out the line, lest he should come too late.

Proud of the task, I watched with all my might
For one whole minute, till my eyes grew wide,
Till earth and sky took on a strange new light
And seemed a dream-world floating on some tide –

  A fair pavilioned boat, for me alone,
  Bearing me onward through the vast unknown.

8

But sudden came the barge's pitch-black prow,
Nearer and angrier came my brother's cry,
And all my soul was quivering fear, when lo!
Upon the imperilled line, suspended high,

A silver perch! My guilt that won the prey,
Now turned to merit, had a guerdon rich
Of hugs and praises, and made merry play,
Until my triumph reached its highest pitch

When all at home were told the wondrous feat,
And how the little sister had fished well.
In secret, though my fortune tasted sweet,
I wondered why this happiness befell.

   'The little lass had luck,' the gardener said:
   And so I learned, luck was with glory wed.

9

We had the self-same world enlarged for each
By loving difference of girl and boy:
The fruit that hung on high beyond my reach
He plucked for me, and oft he must employ

A measuring glance to guide my tiny shoe,
Where lay firm stepping stones, or call to mind
'This thing I like my sister may not do,
For she is little, and I must be kind.'

Thus boyish Will the nobler mastery learned
Where inward wisdom over impulse reigns,
Widening its life with separate life discerned,
A Like unlike, a Self that self restrains.

   His years with others must the sweeter be
   For those brief days he spent in loving me.

10

His sorrow was my sorrow, and his joy
Sent little leaps and laughs through all my frame;
My doll seemed lifeless and no girlish toy
Had any reason when my brother came.

I knelt with him at marbles, marked his fling
Cut the ringed stem and make the apple drop,
Or watched him winding close the spiral string
That looped the orbits of the humming top.

Grasped by such fellowship my vagrant thought
Ceased with dream-fruit dream-wishes to fulfil;
My aery-picturing fantasy was taught
Subjection to the harder, truer skill

   That seeks with deeds to grave a thought-tracked line,
   And by 'What is,' 'What will be' to define.

11

School parted us; we never found again
That childish world where our two spirits mingled
Like scents from varying roses that remain
One sweetness nor can evermore be singled.

Yet the twin habit of that early time
Lingered for long about the heart and tongue:
We had been natives of one happy clime,
And its dear accent to our utterance clung.

Till the dire years whose awful name is Change
Had grasped our souls still yearning in divorce,
And, pitiless, shaped them in two forms that range
Two elements which sever their life's course.

   But were another childhood-world my share,
   I would be born a little sister there.

GEORGE ELIOT (MARY ANN EVANS) (1869)

Written about her relationship with her estranged brother Isaac: a
relationship that inspired her novel *The Mill on the Floss*.

From all the Jails

From all the jails the boys and girls
Ecstatically leap, –
Beloved only afternoon
That prison doesn't keep

They storm the earth and stun the air,
A mob of solid bliss –
Alas! that frowns should lie in wait –
For such a foe as this!

EMILY DICKINSON (c. 1881)

Spring and Fall to a Young Child

Márgarét, are you gríeving
Over Goldengrove unleaving?
Leáves, líke the things of man you
With your fresh thoughts care for, can you?
Áh! Ás the heart grows older
It will come to such sights colder
By and by, nor spare a sigh
Though thoughts of wanworld leafmeal lie;
And yet you *will* weep and know why.
Now no matter, child, the name:
Sórrow's spríngs áre the same.
Nor mouth had, no, nor mind expressed
What heart heard of, ghost guessed:
It is the blight man was born for,
It is Margaret you mourn for.

GERARD MANLEY HOPKINS (1880)

8
THOUGHTS & MEMORIES
OF DEATH

Surprised by Joy

Surprised by joy, impatient as the Wind,
I turned to share the transport – Oh! with whom
But thee deep buried in the silent tomb,
That spot which no vicissitude can find?
Love, faithful love recalled thee to my mind –
But how could I forget thee? Through what power
Even for the least division of an hour,
Have I been so beguil'd as to be blind
To my most grievous loss! That thought's return
Was the worst pang that sorrow ever bore,
Save one, one only, when I stood forlorn,
Knowing my heart's best treasure was no more;
That neither present time, nor years unborn
Could to my sight that heavenly face restore.

WILLIAM WORDSWORTH (1813–14)

from Adonais

36

Our Adonais has drunk poison – oh
What deaf and viperous murderer could crown
Life's early cup with such a draught of woe?
The nameless worm would now itself disown;
It felt, yet could escape the magic tone
Whose prelude held all envy hate and wrong,
But what was howling in one breast alone,
Silent with expectation of the song,
Whose master's hand is cold, whose silver lyre unstrung.

37

Live thou, whose infamy is not thy fame!
Live! fear no heavier chastisement from me,
Thou noteless blot on a remembered name!
But be thyself, and know thyself to be!
And ever at thy season be thou free

To spill the venom when thy fangs o'erflow;
Remorse and self-contempt shall cling to thee;
Hot shame shall burn upon thy sacred brow,
And like a beaten hound tremble thou shalt – as now.

38

Nor let us weep that our delight is fled
Far from these carrion kites that scream below;
He wakes or sleeps with the enduring dead;
Thou canst not soar where he is sitting now. –
Dust to the dust, but the pure spirit shall flow
Back to the burning fountain whence it came,
A portion of the Eternal, which must glow
Through time and change, unquenchably the same,
Whilst thy cold embers choke the sordid heart of shame.

39

Peace, peace! he is not dead, he doth not sleep –
He hath awakened from the dream of life –
'Tis we who, lost in stormy visions, keep
With phantoms an unprofitable strife,
And, in mad trance, strike with our spirit's knife
Invulnerable nothings. – We decay
Like corpses in a charnel; fear and grief
Convulse us and consume us day by day,
And cold hopes swarm like worms within our living clay.

40

He has outsoared the shadow of our night;
Envy and calumny and hate and pain,
And that unrest which men miscall delight,
Can touch him not and torture not again;
From the contagion of the world's slow stain
He is secure, and now can never mourn
A heart grown cold, a head grown gray in vain;
Nor, when the spirit's self has ceased to burn,
With sparkless ashes load an unlamented urn.

41

He lives, he wakes – 'tis death is dead, not he;
Mourn not for Adonais. – Thou young dawn,
Turn all thy dew to splendour, for from thee
The spirit thou lamentest is not gone;
Ye caverns and ye forests, cease to moan!
Cease, ye faint flowers and fountains, and thou Air,
Which like a mourning veil thy scarf hadst thrown
O'er the abandoned Earth, now leave it bare
Even to the joyous stars which smile on its despair!

42

He is made one with Nature: there is heard
His voice in all her music, from the moan
Of thunder, to the song of night's sweet bird;
He is a presence to be felt and known
In darkness and in light, from herb and stone,
Spreading itself where'er that Power may move
Which has withdrawn his being to its own;
Which wields the world with never-wearied love,
Sustains it from beneath, and kindles it above.

43

He is a portion of the loveliness
Which once he made more lovely: he doth bear
His part, while the one Spirit's plastic stress
Sweeps through the dull dense world, compelling there
All new successions to the forms they wear;
Torturing th' unwilling dross that checks its flight
To its own likeness, as each mass may bear;
And bursting in its beauty and its might
From trees and beasts and men into the Heaven's light.

44

The splendours of the firmament of time
May be eclipsed, but are extinguished not;
Like stars to their appointed height they climb,
And death is a low mist which cannot blot
The brightness it may veil. When lofty thought
Lift a young heart above its mortal lair,

And love and life contend in it for what
Shall be its earthly doom, the dead live there
And move like winds of light on dark and stormy air.

45

The inheritors of unfulfilled renown
Rose from their thrones, built beyond mortal thought,
Far in the unapparent. Chatterton
Rose pale,– his solemn agony had not
Yet faded from him; Sidney, as he fought
And as he fell and as he lived and loved
Sublimely mild, a Spirit without spot,
Arose; and Lucan, by his death approved;
Oblivion as they rose shrank like a thing reproved.*

46

And many more, whose names on earth are dark,
But whose transmitted effluence cannot die
So long as fire outlives the parent spark,
Rose, robed in dazzling immortality.
'Thou art become as one of us,' they cry,
'It was for thee yon kingless sphere has long
Swung blind in unascended majesty,
Silent along amid an Heaven of Song.
Assume thy winged throne, thou Vesper of our throng!'

47

Who mourns for Adonais? Oh, come forth,
Fond wretch! and know thyself and him aright.
Clasp with thy panting soul the pendulous Earth;
As from a centre, dart thy spirit's light
Beyond all worlds, until its spacious might
Satiate the void circumference: then shrink
Even to a point within our day and night;
And keep thy heart light lest it make thee sink
When hope has kindled hope, and lured thee to the brink.

---

* Chatterton, Sidney and Lucan were all poets who died young,
Thomas Chatterton, known for his medieval pastiches, by suicide
(1770), Sir Philip Sidney of wounds at the Battle of Zutphen (1586) and
Lucan as a victim of the tyranny of the Roman Emperor Nero in 65 AD.

48

Or go to Rome, which is the sepulchre,
Oh, not of him, but of our joy: 'tis nought
That ages empires and religions there
Lie buried in the ravage they have wrought;
For such as he can lend, – they borrow not
Glory from those who made the world their prey;
And he is gathered to the kings of thought
Who waged contention with their time's decay,
And of the past are all that cannot pass away.

49

Go thou to Rome, – at once the Paradise,
The grave, the city, and the wilderness;
And where its wrecks like shattered mountains rise,
And flowering weeds, and fragrant copses dress
The bones of desolation's nakedness
Pass, till the spirit of the spot shall lead
Thy footsteps to a slope of green access
Where, like an infant's smile, over the dead
A light of laughing flowers along the grass is spread.;

50

And gray walls moulder round, on which dull Time
Feeds, like slow fire upon a hoary brand;
And one keen pyramid with wedge sublime,
Pavilioning the dust of him who planned
This refuge for his memory, doth stand
Like flame transformed to marble; and, beneath,
A field is spread, on which a newer band
Have pitched in Heaven's smile their camp of death,
Welcoming him we lose with scarce extinguished breath.

51

Here pause: these graves are all too young as yet
To have outgrown the sorrow which consigned
Its charge to each; and if the seal is set,
Here, on one fountain of a mourning mind,
Break it not thou! too surely shalt thou find

Thine own well full, if thou returnest home,
Of tears and gall. From the world's bitter wind
Seek shelter in the shadow of the tomb.
What Adonais is, why fear we to become?

52

The One remains, the many change and pass;
Heaven's light forever shines, Earth's shadows fly;
Life, like a dome of many-coloured glass,
Stains the white radiance of Eternity,
Until Death tramples it to fragments. – Die,
If thou wouldst be with that which thou dost seek!
Follow where all is fled! – Rome's azure sky,
Flowers, ruins, statues, music, words, are weak
The glory they transfuse with fitting truth to speak.

53

Why linger, why turn back, why shrink, my Heart?
Thy hopes are gone before: from all things here
They have departed; thou shouldst now depart!
A light is passed from the revolving year,
And man, and woman; and what still is dear
Attracts to crush, repels to make thee wither.
The soft sky smiles, – the low wind whispers near:
'Tis Adonais calls! oh hasten thither,
No more let Life divide what Death can join together.

54

That Light whose smile kindles the Universe,
That Beauty in which all things work and move,
That Benediction which the eclipsing Curse
Of birth can quench not, that sustaining Love
Which through the web of being blindly wove
By man and beast and earth and land and sea,
Burns bright or dim, as each are mirrors of
The fire for which all thirst; now beams on me,
Consuming the last clouds of cold mortality.

55

The breath whose might I have invoked in song
Descends on me; my spirit's bark is driven
Far from the shore, far from the trembling throng
Whose sails were never to the tempest given;
The massy earth and sphered skies are riven!
I am borne darkly, fearfully afar;
Whilst, burning through the inmost veil of Heaven,
The soul of Adonais, like a star,
Beacons from the abode where the Eternal are.

(PERCY BYSSHE SHELLEY)

Shelley is here mourning, in the style of the grand Classical elegy imitated by Milton before him, the death of John Keats from tuberculosis in 1821. The 'poison' referred to is the hostility of influential critics whose reviews were thought to have hastened the young poet's death. Keats was buried in the Protestant cemetery in Rome, not long after the death of Shelley's young son William. The last stanzas uncannily anticipate Shelley's own death from drowning at sea in a storm which overwhelmed his yacht in July 1822.

The Old Arm-chair

I love it, I love it; and who shall dare
To chide me for loving that old Arm-chair?
I've treasured it long as a sainted prize;
I've bedewed it with tears and embalmed it with sighs;
'Tis bound with a thousand bands to my heart;
Not a tie will break, not a link will start.
Would ye learn the spell? a mother sat there;
And a sacred thing is that old Arm-chair.

In Childhood's hour I lingered near
The hallowed seat with listening ear;
And gentle words that mother would give;
To fit me to die and teach me to live.
She told me shame would never betide,
With truth for my creed and God for my guide;
She taught me to lisp my earliest prayer;
As I knelt beside that old Arm-chair.

I sat and watched her many a day,
When her eye grew dim, and her locks were grey;
And I almost worshipped her when she smiled,
And turned from her Bible to bless her child,
Years rolled on; but the last one sped:
I learned how much the heart can bear,
When I saw her die in that old Arm-chair.

'Tis past, 'tis past, but I gaze on it now
With quivering breath and throbbing brow;
'Twas there she nursed me, 'twas there she died;
And Memory flows with lava tide,
Say it is folly, and deems me weak,
While the scalding drops start down my cheek;
But I love it, I love it, and cannot tear
My soul from a mother's old Arm-chair.

ELIZA COOK (1836)

One of the most popular poems of the century.

Night

I love the silent hour of night,
  For blissful dreams may then arise,
Revealing to my charmed sight
  What may not bless my waking eyes.

And then a voice may meet my ear,
  That death has silenced long ago;
And hope and rapture may appear
  Instead of solitude and woe.

Cold in the grave for years has lain
  The form it was my bliss to see;
And only dreams can bring again
  The darling of my heart to me.

ANNE BRONTE (1845)

Hamatreya

Minott, Lee, Willard, Hosmer, Meriam, Flint
Possessed the land which rendered to their toil
Hay, corn, roots, hemp, flax, apples and wood.
Each of these landlords walked amidst his farm,
Saying, ' 'Tis mine, my children's and my name's:
How sweet the west wind sounds in my own trees!
How graceful climb those shadows on my hill!
I fancy these pure waters and the flags
Know me, as does my dog: we sympathize;
And, I affirm, my actions smack of the soil.'
Where are these men? Asleep beneath their grounds;
And strangers, fond as they, their furrows plough.
Earth laughs in flowers, to see her boastful boys
Earth-proud, proud of the earth which is not theirs;
Who steer the plough, but cannot steer their feet
Clear of the grave.
They added ridge to valley; brook to pond,

And sighed for all that bounded their domain.
'This suits me for a pasture; that's my park;
We must have clay, lime, gravel, granite-ledge,
And misty lowland, where to go for peat.
The land is well, – lies fairly to the south.
'Tis good, when you have crossed the sea and back,
To find the sitfast acres where you left them.'
Ah! The hot owner sees not Death, who adds
Him to his land, a lump of mould the more.
Hear what the Earth says –

EARTH-SONG

'Mine and yours;
Mine, not yours.
Earth endures;
Stars abide–
Shine down in the old sea;
Old are the shores;
But where are old men?
I who have seen much,
Such have I never seen.

'The lawyer's deed
Ran sure,
In tail,
To them and to their heirs
Who shall succeed,
Without fail,
Forevermore.

'Here is the land,
Shaggy with wood.
With its old valley,
Mound and flood.
But the heritors?
Fled like the flood's foam,–
The lawyer and the laws,
And the kingdom,
Clean swept herefrom.

'They called me theirs,
Who so controlled me;
Yet every one
Wished to stay, and is gone.
How am I theirs,
If they cannot hold me,
But I hold them?'
When I heard the Earth-song,
I was no longer brave.
My avarice cooled
Like lust in the chill of the grave.

RALPH WALDO EMERSON (Published 1846)

Hamatreya (Maitreya) is a future incarnation of Buddha who will bring peace and enlightment.

from *In Memoriam A. H. H.*

Strong Son of God, Immortal Love,
    Whom we that have not seen thy face,
    By faith and faith alone embrace,
Believing where we cannot prove;

Thine are these orbs of light and shade;
    Thou madest Life in man and brute;
    Thou madest Death, and lo, thy foot
Is on the skull which thou hast made.

Thou wilt not leave us in the dust;
    Thou madest man, he knows not why,
    He thinks he was not made to die,
But thou hast made him; thou art just.

Thou seemest human and divine,
    The highest, holiest manhood, thou;
    Our wills are ours, we know not how;
Our wills are ours, to make them thine.

Our little systems have their day,
    They have their day and cease to be;
    They are but broken lights of thee,
And thou, O Lord, art more than they.

We have but faith; we cannot know;
    For knowledge is of things we see;
    And yet we trust it comes from thee,
A beam in darkness: let it grow.

Let knowledge grow from more to more,
    But more of reverence in us dwell;
    That mind and soul, according well,
May make one music, as before

But vaster. We are fools and slight;
    We mock thee when we do not fear;
    But help thy foolish ones to bear;
Help thy vain worlds to bear thy light.

Forgive what seemed my sin in me;
    What seemed my worth since I began;
    For merit lives from man to man,
And not from man, O Lord, to thee.

Forgive my sin for one removed,
    Thy creature whom I found so fair.
    I trust he lives in thee, and there,
I find him worthier to be loved.

Forgive these wild and wandering cries,
    Confusions of a wasted youth;
    Forgive them where they fail in truth,
And in thy wisdom make me wise.

1

I held it truth, with him who sings
    To one clear harp, in diverse tones,
    That men may rise on stepping-stones
Of their dead selves to higher things.

But who shall so forecast the years
    And find in loss a gain to match?

Or reach a hand thro' time to catch
The far-off interest of tears?

Let Love clasp Grief, lest both be drown'd,
    Let darkness keep her raven gloss:
    Ah sweeter to be struck by loss,
To dance with death, to beat the ground,

Than that the victor Hours should scorn
    The long result of love and boast,
    'Behold the man that lov'd and lost,
But all he was is overworn.'

2

Old Yew, which graspest at the stones,
    Which name the ever-lying dead,
    Thy fibres net the dreamless head,
Thy roots are wrapt about the bones.

The seasons bring the flower again
    And bring the firstling to the flock;
    And in the dusk of thee, the clock
Beats out the little lives of men.

O not for thee the glow, the bloom,
    Who changest not in any gale,
    Nor branding summer suns avail
To touch thy thousand years of gloom;

And gazing on thee, sullen tree
    Sick for thy stubborn hardihood,
    I seem to fail from out my blood
And grow incorporate into thee.

7

Dark house, by which once more I stand
    Here, in the long unlovely street,
    Doors, where my heart was used to beat
So quickly, waiting for a hand,

A hand that can be clasped no more –
    Behold me, for I cannot sleep,

And like a guilty thing I creep
At earliest morning to the door.

He is not here, but far away
   The noise of life begins again
   And ghastly through the drizzling rain
On the bald street breaks the blank day.

11

Calm is the morn without a sound,
   Calm as to suit a calmer grief,
   And only thro' the faded leaf
The chestnut pattering to the ground:

Calm and deep peace on this high wold,
   And on these dews that drench the furze
   And all the silvery gossamers
That twinkle into green and gold:

Calm and still light on yon great plain
   That sweeps with all its autumn bowers,
   And crowded farms and lessening towers,
To mingle with the bounding main;

Calm and deep peace in this wide air,
   These leaves that redden to the fall;
   And in my heart, if calm at all,
If any calm, a calm despair:

Calm on the seas, and silver sleep,
   And waves that sway themselves in rest,
   And dead calm in that noble breast
Which heaves but with the heaving deep.

14

If one should bring me this report,
   That thou hadst touch'd the land today,
   And I went down unto the quay,
And found thee lying in the port;

And standing, muffled round with woe,
   Should see thy passengers in rank

Come stepping lightly down the plank,
And beckoning unto those they know;

And if along with these should come
   The man I held as half-divine;
   Should strike a sudden hand in mine,
And ask a thousand things of home;

And I should tell him all my pain,
   And how my life had droop'd of late,
   And he should sorrow o'er my state
And marvel what possess'd my brain;

And I perceiv'd no touch of change,
   No hint of death in all his frame,
   But found him all in all the same,
I should not feel it to be strange.

                    15

Tonight the winds begin to rise
   And roar from yonder dropping day:
   The last red leaf is whirl'd away;
The rooks are blown about the skies;

The forest crack'd, the waters curl'd,
   The cattle huddled on the lea;
   And wildly dash'd on tower and tree
The sunbeam strikes along the world:

And but for fancies, which aver
   That all thy motions gently pass
   Athwart a pane of molten glass,
I scarce could brook the strain and stir

That makes the barren branches loud;
   And but for fear it is not so,
   The wild unrest that lives on woe
Would dote and pore on yonder cloud

That rises upward ever higher,
   And upward drags a labouring breast,
   And topples round the dreary West,
A looming bastion fringed with fire.

27

I envy not in any moods
   The captive void of noble rage,
   The linnet born within the cage,
That never knew the summer woods:

I envy not the beast that takes
   His license in the field of time,
   Unfetter'd by the sense of crime,
To whom a conscience never wakes;

Nor what may count itself as blest,
   The heart that never plighted troth
   But stagnates in the weeds of sloth;
Nor any want-begotten rest.

I hold it true, whate'er befall;
   I feel it when I sorrow most;
   'Tis better to have lov'd and lost
Than never to have lov'd at all.

34

My own dim life should teach me this,
   That life should live for evermore,
   Else earth is darkness at the core,
And dust and ashes all that is;

This round of green, this orb of flame,
   Fantastic beauty; such as lurks
   In some wild Poet, when he works
Without a conscience or an aim.

What then were God to such as I?
   'Twere hardly worth my while to choose
   Of things all mortal, or to use
A little patience, ere I die;

'Twere best at once to sink to peace,
   Like birds the charming serpent draws,
   To drop head foremost in the jaws
Of vacant darkness and to cease.

48

If these brief lays, of Sorrow born,
　　Were taken to be such as closed
　　Grave doubts and answers here proposed,
Then these were such as men might scorn;

Her care is not to part and prove;
　　She takes, when harsher moods remit,
　　What slender shade of doubt may flit,
And makes it vassal unto love.:

And hence, indeed, she sports with words
　　But better serves a wholesome law,
　　And holds it sin and shame to draw
The deeper measure from the chords:

Nor dare she trust a larger lay,
　　But, rather, loosens from the lip
　　Short swallow-flights of song that dip
Their wings in tears and skim away.

50

Be near me when my light is low,
　　When the blood creeps, and the nerves prick
　　And tingle; and the heart is sick,
And all the wheels of Being slow.

Be near me when the sensuous frame
　　Is rack'd with pangs that conquer trust;
　　And Time, a maniac scattering dust,
And Life a Fury slinging flame

Be near me when my faith is dry,
　　And men, the flies of latter spring,
That lay their eggs, and sting and sing
　　And weave their petty cells and die.

Be near me when I fade away,
　　To point the term of human life
　　And on the low dark verge of life
The twilight of eternal day.

54

O yet we trust that somehow good
 Will be the final end of ill,
 To pangs of nature, sins of will
Defects of doubt and taints of blood;

That nothing walks with aimless feet;
 That not one life shall be destroy'd,
 Or cast as rubbish to the void,
When God hath made the pile complete;

That not a worm is cloven in vain;
 That not a moth with vain desire
 Is shrivell'd in a fruitless fire,
Or but subserves another's gain.

Behold, we know not anything;
 I can but trust that good shall fall
 At last – far off – at last, to all,
And every winter change to spring.

So runs my dream: but what am I?
 An infant crying in the night:
 An infant crying for the light:
And with no language but a cry.

55

The wish, that of the living whole
 No life may fail beyond the grave,
 Derives it not from what we have
The likest God within the soul?

Are God and Nature then at strife,
 That Nature lends such evil dreams?
 So careful of the type she seems,
So careless of the single life:

That I, considering everywhere
 Her secret meaning in her deeds,
 And finding that of fifty seeds
She often brings but one to bear,

I falter where I firmly trod,
    And falling with my weight of cares
    Upon the great world's altar stairs
That slope through darkness up to God,

I stretch lame hands of faith, and grope,
    And gather dust and chaff, and call
    To what I feel is Lord of all,
And faintly trust the larger hope.

56

'So careful of the type?', but no,
    From scarped cliff, and quarried stone
    She cries, 'A thousand types are gone:
I care for nothing, all shall go.

'Thou makest thine appeal to me:
    I bring to life, I bring to death:
    The spirit does but mean the breath:
I know no more.' And he, shall he,

Man, her last work, who seem'd so fair,
    Such splendid purpose in his eyes,
    Who roll'd the psalm to wintry skies,
Who built him fanes of fruitless prayer,

Who trusted God was love indeed
    And love Creation's final law –
    Though Nature, red in tooth and claw
With ravine, shrieked against his creed –

Who loved, who suffered countless ills,
    Who battled for the True, the Just,
    Be blown about the desert dust,
Or sealed within the iron hills?

No more? A monster then, a dream,
    A discord. Dragons of the prime,
    That tare each other in their slime,
Were mellow music, match'd with him.

O life as futile then, as frail!
    O, for thy voice to soothe and bless!

What hope of answer or redress?
Behind the veil, behind the veil.

64

Dost thou look back on what hath been
  As some divinely gifted man,
  Whose life in low estate began
And on a simple village green;

Who breaks his birth's invidious bar,
  And grasps the skirts of happy chance,
  And breasts the blows of circumstance,
And grapples with his evil star;

Who makes by force his merit known
  And lives to clutch the golden keys.
  To mould a mighty state's decrees,
And shape the whisper of the throne;

And moving still to higher and higher,
  Becomes on Fortune's crowning slope
  The pillar of a people's hope,
The centre of a world's desire;

Yet feels, as in a pensive dream,
  When all his active powers are still,
  A distant dearness in the hill,
A secret sweetness in the stream,

The limit of his narrower fate
  While yet beside its vocal springs
  He play'd at counsellors and kings
With one that was his earliest mate;

Who ploughs with pain his native lea
  And reaps the labour of his hands,
  Or in the furrow musing stands:
'Does my old friend remember me?'

67

When on my bed the moonlight falls,
    I know that in thy place of rest
    By that broad water of the west
There comes a glory on the walls:

Thy marble bright in dark appears,
    As slowly steals a silver flame
    Along the letters of thy name,
And o'er the number of thy years.

The mystic glory swims away;
    From off my bed the moonlight dies;
    And, closing eaves of wearied eyes,
I sleep till dusk is dipt in gray,

And then I know the mist is drawn
    A lucid veil from coast to coast,
    And in the dark church, like a ghost
Thy tablet glimmers to the dawn.

74

As sometimes in a dead man's face,
    To those that watch it more and more,
    A likeness, hardly seen before,
Comes out, to someone of his race:

So, dearest, now thy brows are cold,
    I see thee what thou art, and know
    Thy likeness to the wise below,
Thy kindred with the great of old.

But there is more than I can see,
    And what I see I leave unsaid,
    Nor speak it knowing Death has made
His darkness beautiful with thee.

91

When rosy plumelets tuft the larch,
    And rarely pipes the mounted thrush;
    Or underneath the barren bush
Flits by the sea-blue bird of March;

Come, wear the form by which I know
   Thy spirit in time among thy peers;
   The hope of unaccomplish'd years
Be large and lucid round thy brow.

When summer's hourly mellowing change
   May breathe, with many roses sweet,
   Upon the thousand waves of wheat
That ripple round the lonely grange;

Come; not in watches of the night
   But where the sunbeam broodeth warm,
   Come, beauteous in thine after form,
And like a finer light in light.

101

Unwatch'd the garden bough shall sway,
   The tender blossoms flutter down,
   Unlov'd that beech will gather brown,
The maple burn itself away;

Unloved the sunflower, shining fair,
   Ray round with flames her disk of seed,
   And many a rose carnation feed
With summer spice the humming air:

Unlov'd by many a sandy bar,
   The brook shall babble down the plain,
   At noon, or when the lesser wain
Is twisting round the polar star;

Uncared for, gird the windy grove,
   And flood the haunts of hern and crake;
   Or into silver arrows break
The sailing moon in creek and cove;

Till from the garden and the child
   A fresh association blow
   And year by year the landscape grow
Familiar to the stranger's child;

As year by year the labourer tills
   His wonted glebe, or lops the glades;

And year by year our memory fades
From all the circle of the hills.

106

Ring out, wild bells, to the wild sky,
    The flying clouds, the frosty light:
    The year is dying in the night;
Ring out, wild bells, and let him die.

Ring out the old, ring in the new,
    Ring, happy bells, across the snow:
    The year is going, let him go;
Ring out the false, ring in the true.

Ring out the grief that saps the mind,
    For those that here we see no more,
    Ring out the feud of rich and poor,
Ring in redress to all mankind.

Ring out a slowly dying cause,
    And ancient forms of party strife;
    Ring in the nobler forms of life,
With sweeter manners, purer laws.

Ring out the want, the care, the sin,
    The faithless coldness of the times;
    Ring out, ring out my mournful rhymes
But ring the fuller minstrel in.

Ring out false pride in place and blood;
    The civic slander and the spite;
    Ring in the love of truth and right,
Ring in the common love of good.

Ring out old shapes of foul disease;
    Ring out the narrowing lust of gold;
    Ring out the thousand wars of old,
Ring in the thousand years of peace.

Ring in the valiant man and free,
    The larger heart, the kindlier hand;
    Ring out the darkness of the land,
Ring in the Christ that is to be.

119

Doors, where my heart was used to beat
   So quickly, not as one who weeps
   I come once more; the city sleeps;
I smell the meadow in the street;

I hear the chirp of birds; I see
   Betwixt the black fronts long withdrawn
   A light-blue lane of early dawn,
And think of early days and thee,

And bless thee, for thy lips are bland,
   And bright the friendship of thine eye;
   And in my thoughts, with scarce a sigh,
I take the pressure of thy hand.

123

There rolls the deep where grew the tree
   O earth, what changes thou hast seen!
   There where the long street roars hath been
The stillness of the central sea.

The hills are shadows and they flow
   From form to form, and nothing stands;
   They melt like mist, the solid lands,
Like clouds they shape themselves and go.

But in my spirit will I dwell,
   And dream my dream, and hold it true,
   For tho' my lips may breathe adieu,
I cannot think the thing farewell.

127

And all is well, though faith and form
   Be sundered in the night of fear:
   Well roars the storm to those that hear
A deeper voice across the storm,

Proclaiming social truth shall spread,
   And justice, ev'n tho' thrice again
   The red fool-fury of the Seine
Should pile her barricades with dead.

But ill for him that wears a crown,
    And him, the lazar in his rags;
    They tremble, the sustaining crags;
The spires of ice are toppled down,

And molten up, and roar in flood;
    The fortress crashes from on high,
    The brute earth lightens to the sky,
And the great Aeon sinks in blood.

And compass'd by the fires of Hell;
    While thou, dear spirit, happy star
    O'erlook the tumult from afar
And smilest, knowing all is well.

ALFRED, LORD TENNYSON (1833–50)

A. H. H. was Tennyson's beloved Cambridge friend Arthur Henry
Hallam, who died suddenly at the age of twenty-two in 1833.

How many times these low feet staggered

How many times these low feet staggered,
Only the soldered mouth can tell!
Try! can you stir the awful rivet?
Try! can you lift the hasps of steel?

Stroke the cool forehead, hot so often,
Lift, if you can, the listless hair;
Handle the adamantine fingers
Never a thimble more shall wear.

Buzz the dull flies on the chamber window;
Brave shines the sun through the freckled pane;
Fearless the cobweb swings from the ceiling –
Indolent housewife, in daisies lain!

EMILY DICKINSON (c. 1860)

Lines written by a Death-Bed

Yes, now the longing is o'erpast,
Which, dogg'd by fear and fought by shame,
Shook her weak bosom day and night,
Consum'd her beauty like a flame,
And dimm'd it like the desert blast.
And though the curtains hide her face,
Yet were it lifted to the light
The sweet expression of her brow
Would charm the gazer, till his thought
Eras'd the ravages of time,
Fill'd up the hollow cheek, and brought
A freshness back as of her prime –
So healing is her quiet now.
So perfectly the lines express
A placid, settled loveliness;
Her youngest rival's freshest grace.

But ah, though peace indeed is here,
And ease from shame, and rest from fear;
Though nothing can dismarble now
The smoothness of that limpid brow;
Yet is a calm like this, in truth,
The crowning end of life and youth?
And when this boon rewards the dead,
Are all debts paid, has all been said?
And is the heart of youth so light,
Its step so firm, its eye so bright,
Because on its hot brow there blows
A wind of promise and repose
From the far grave to which it goes?

Because it has the hope to come
One day to harbour in the tomb?
Ah no, the bliss youth dreams is one
For daylight, for the cheerful sun,
For feeling nerves and living breath –
Youth dreams a bliss on this side death.

It dreams a rest, if not more deep,
More grateful than this marble sleep.
It hears a voice within it tell –
'Calm's not life's crown, though calm is well.'
'Tis all perhaps which man acquires;
But 'tis not what our youth desires.

MATTHEW ARNOLD (1852)

In the Valley of Cauteretz

All along the valley, stream that flashest white,
Deepening thy voice with the deepening of the night,
All along the valley where thy waters flow,
I walked with one I loved two and thirty years ago.
All along the valley while I walked today,
The two and thirty years were a mist that rolls away;
For all along the valley, down thy rocky bed,
Thy living voice to me was as the voice of the dead,
And all along the valley, by rock and cave and tree,
The voice of the dead was a living voice to me.

ALFRED, LORD TENNYSON (1864)

The Wife a-Lost

Since I noo mwore do zee your feäce,
    Up stears or down below,
I'll zit me in this lwonesome pleäce,
    Where flat-bough'd beech do grow:
Below the beeches' bough, my love,
    Where you did never come,
And I don't look to meet ye now,
    As I do look at hwome.

Since you noo mwore be at my side,
    In walks in zummer het,
I'll go alwone where mist do ride,

Drough trees a-drippèn wet:
Below the rain-wet bough, my love,
   Where you did never come,
An' I don't grieve to miss ye now,
   As I do grieve at hwome.

Since now bezide my dinner-bwoard
   Your vaice do never sound,
I'll eat the bit I can avword,
   A-vield upon the ground;
Below the darksome bough, my love,
   Where you did never dine,
An' I don't grieve to miss ye now,
   As I at hwome do pine.

Since I do miss your vaice an' feäce
   In prayer at eventide,
I'll pray wi' woone sad vaice vor greäce
   To goo where you do bide;
Above the tree an' bough, my love,
   Where you be gone avore;
An' be a-waitèn vor me now,
   To come vor evermwore.

WILLIAM BARNES (1859)

O Lyric Love

O Lyric Love, half-angel and half-bird
And all a wonder and a wild desire,—
Boldest of hearts that ever braved the sun,
Took sanctuary within the holiest blue,
And sang a kindred soul out to his face, —
Yet human at the red-ripe of the heart —
When the first summons from the darkling earth
Reached thee amid thy chambers, blanched their blue,
And bared them of the glory — to drop down,
To toil for man, to suffer or to die, —
This is the same voice; can thy soul know change?

Hail then, and hearken from the realms of help!
Never may I commence my song, my due
To God who best taught song by gift of thee,
Except with bent head and beseeching hand –
That still, despite the distance and the dark,
What was, again may be; some interchange
Of grace, some splendour once thy very thought,
Some benediction, anciently thy smile:
Never conclude, but raising hand and head
Thither where eyes, that cannot reach, yet yearn
For all hope, all sustainment, all reward,
Their utmost up and on – so blessing back
In those thy realms of help, that heaven thy home,
Some whiteness which, I judge, thy face makes proud,
Some wanness where, I think, thy foot may fall.

ROBERT BROWNING (1865)

From *The Ring and the Book,* lines 1391–416; Elizabeth Barrett Browning had died in 1861.

When Lilacs Last in the Dooryard Bloomed

1

When lilacs last in the dooryard bloomed,
And the great star early droop'd in the western sky, in the
    night,
I mourn'd, and yet shall mourn with ever-returning spring.

Ever returning spring, trinity sure to me you bring,
Lilac blooming perennial and drooping star in the west,
And thought of him I love.

2

O powerful western fallen star!
O shades of night – O moody, tearful night!
O great star disappear'd – O the black murk that hides
    the star!
O cruel hands that hold me powerless – O helpless soul
    of me!
O harsh surrounding cloud that will not free my soul.

3

In the dooryard fronting an old farmhouse near the white-
    wash'd palings,
Stands the lilac-bush tall-growing with heart-shaped leaves
    of rich green,
With many a pointed blossom rising delicate, with the
    perfume strong I love,
With every leaf a miracle – and from this bush in the
    dooryard,
With delicate color'd blossoms and heart-shaped leaves of
    rich green,
A sprig with its flowers I break.

4

In the swamp in secluded recesses,
A shy and hidden bird is warbling a song.

Solitary the thrush,
The hermit withdrawn to himself, avoiding the settlements,
Sings by himself a song.

Song of the bleeding throat,
Death's outlet song of life, (for well dear brother I know
If thou wast not granted to sing thou would'st surely die.)

5

Over the breast of the spring, the land and cities,
Amid lanes and through old woods, where lately the violets
    peeped from the ground, spotting the gray debris,
Amid the grass in the fields each side of the lanes, passing
    the endless grass,
Passing the yellow-speared wheat, every grain from its
    shroud in the dark-brown fields uprisen,

Passing the apple-tree blows of white and pink in the
    orchards,
Carrying a corpse to where it shall rest in the grave
Night and day journeys a coffin.

6

Coffin that passes through lanes and streets,
Through day and night with the great cloud darkening
    the land,
With the pomp of the inloop'd flags with the cities draped
    in black,
With the show of the States themselves as of crape-veiled
    women standing,
With processions long and winding and the flambeaus of the
    night,
With the countless torches lit, with the silent sea of faces
    and the unbared heads,
With the waiting depot, the arriving coffin, and the sombre
    faces,
With dirges through the night, with the thousand voices
    rising strong and solemn,

With all the mournful voices of the dirges pour'd around the
    coffin,
The dim lit churches and the shuddering organs – where
    amid these you journey,
With the tolling tolling bells' perpetual clang,
Here, coffin that slowly passes,
I give you my sprig of lilac.

7

(Nor for you, for one alone
Blossoms and branches green to coffins all I bring,
For fresh as the morning, thus would I chant a song for
    you O sane and sacred death.
All over bouquets of roses,
O death, I cover you over with roses and early lilies.
But mostly and now the lilac that blooms the first,
Copious I break, I break the sprigs from the bushes,
With loaded arms I come, pouring for you,
For you and the coffins all of you, O death.)

8

O western orb sailing the heaven
Now I know what you must have meant a month since I
    walk'd,
As I walk'd in silence the transparent shadowy night
As I saw you had something to tell as you bent to me night
    after night,
As you droop'd from the sky low down as if to my side,
    (while the other stars all look'd on,)
As we wander'd together the solemn night, (for something I
    know not what kept me from sleep,)
As the night advanced, and I saw on the rim of the west how
    full you were of woe,
As I stood on the rising ground in the breeze in the cool
    transparent night,
As I watch'd where you pass'd and was lost in the
    netherward black of the night,
As my soul in its trouble dissatisfied sank, as where you, sad
    orb,
Concluded dropt in the night, and was gone.

9

Sing on there in the swamp,
O singer, bashful and tender, I hear your notes, I hear your
    call,
I hear, I come presently, I understand you,
But a moment I linger, for the lustrous star has detained me,
The star my departing comrade holds and detains me.

10

O how shall I warble myself for the dead one there I loved?
And how shall I deck my song for the large sweet soul that
    has gone?
And what shall my perfume be for the grave of him I love?

Sea-winds blown from east and west,
Blown from the Eastern sea and blown from the Western sea,
    till there on the prairies meeting,
These and with these and the breath of my chant,
I'll perfume the grave of him I love.

11

O what shall I hang on the chamber walls?
And what shall the pictures be that I hang on the walls,
To adorn the burial-house of him I love?

Pictures of growing spring and farms and homes,
With the Fourth-month eve at sundown and gray smoke
    lucid and bright,
With floods of the yellow gold of the gorgeous, indolent
    sinking sun, burning, expanding the air,
With the fresh green herbage underfoot, and the pale green
    leaves of the trees prolific,
In the distance the flowing glaze, the breast of the river, with
    a wind-dapple here and there,

With ranging hills on the banks, with many a line against
    the sky, and shadows,
And the city with dwellings so dense, and stacks of
    chimneys,
And all the scenes of life and the workshops, and the
    workmen, homeward returning.

12

Lo, body and soul – this land,
My own Manhattan with spires, and the sparkling and
    hurrying tides, and the ships,
The varied and ample land, the South and the North in the
    light, Ohio's shores and flashing Missouri,
And ever the far-spreading prairies cover'd with grass and
    corn.
Lo, the most excellent sun, so calm and haughty,
The violet and purple morn with just-felt breezes,
The gentle soft-born measureless light,
The miracle spreading bathing all, the fulfill'd noon,
The coming eve delicious, the welcome night and the stars,
Over my cities shining all, enveloping man and land.

13

Sing on, sing on, you gray-brown bird,
Sing from the swamps, the recesses, pour your chant from
    the bushes,
Limitless out of the dusk, out of the cedars and pines.

Sing on, dearest brother, warble your reedy song,
Loud human song, with voice of uttermost woe.

O liquid and free and tender!
O wild and loose to my soul! – O wondrous singer!
You only I hear – yet the star holds me, (but will soon
    depart,)
Yet the lilac with mastering odor holds me.

14

Now while I sat in the day and look'd forth
In the close of the day with its light and the fields of spring,
    and the farmers preparing their crops
In the large unconscious scenery of my land with its lakes
    and forests,
In the heavenly aerial beauty, (after the perturb'd winds and
    the storms,)
Under the arching heavens of the afternoon swift passing,
    and the voices of children and women,

The many moving sea-tides, and I saw the ships how they
    sail'd,
And the summer approaching with richness, and the fields
    all busy with labor,
And the infinite separate houses, how they all went on, each
    with its meals and minutia of daily usages,
And the streets how their throbbings throbb'd, and the cities
    pent – lo, then and there,
Falling upon them all and among them all, enveloping me
    with the rest,
Appear'd the cloud, appear'd the long black trail,
And I knew death, its thought, and the sacred knowledge of
    death.

Then with the knowledge of death as walking one side of
    me,
And the thought of death close-walking the other side of me,
And I in the middle as with companions, and as holding the
    hands of companions,
I fled forth to the hiding receiving night that talks not,
Down to the shores of the water, the path by the swamp in
    the dimness,
To the solemn shadowy cedars and ghostly pines so still.

And the singer so shy to the rest receiv'd me,
The gray-brown bird I know receiv'd us comrades three,
And he sang the carol of death, and a verse for him I love.

And the charm of the carol rapt me,
As I held as if by their hands my comrades in the night,
And the voice of my spirit tallied the song of the bird.

Come lovely and soothing death
Undulate round the world, serenely arriving, arriving,
In the day, in the night, to all, to each,
Sooner or later, delicate death.

Prais'd be the fathomless universe,
For life and joy, and for objects and knowledge curious,
And for love, sweet love – but praise! praise! praise!
For the sure enwinding arms of cool-enfolding death.

Dark mother always gliding near with soft feet,
Have none chanted for thee a chant of fullest welcome?
Then I chant it for thee, I glorify thee above all,
I bring thee a song that when thou must indeed come, come
*   unfalteringly.*

Approach, strong deliveress,
When it is so, when thou hast taken them I joyously sing the
*   dead,*
Lost in the loving floating ocean of thee,
Laved in the flood of thy bliss, O death.

From me to thee glad serenades,
Dances for thee I propose saluting thee, adornments and feasting
*   for thee,*
And the sights of the open landscape and the high-spread sky are
*   fitting,*
And life and the fields, and the huge and thoughtful night.

The night in silence under many a star,
The ocean shore and the husky whispering wave whose voice I
*   know,*
And the soul turning to thee O vast and well-veil'd death,
And the body gratefully nestling close to thee.

Over the tree-tops I float thee a song,
Over the rising and the sinking waves, over the myriad fields and
*   the prairies wide,*
Over the dense-packed cities all, and the teeming wharves and
*   ways,*
I float this carol with joy, with joy to thee O death.

15

To the tally of my soul
Loud and strong kept up the gray-brown bird,
With pure deliberate tones spreading filling the night.

Loud in the pines and the cedars dim,
Clear in the freshness moist and the swamp-perfume,
And I with my comrades there in the night.

While my sight that was bound in my eyes unclosed,
As to long panoramas of visions.

And I saw askant the armies,
I saw as in noiseless dreams hundreds of battle-flags,
Borne through the smoke of the battles and pierc'd with
    missiles I saw them,
And carried hither and yon through the smoke, and torn and
    bloody,
And at last but a few shreds left on the staffs, (and all in
    silence,)
And the staffs all splinter'd and broken.

I saw battle-corpses, myriads of them,
And the white skeletons of young men I saw them,
I saw the debris and debris of all the slain soldiers of the war,
But I saw they were not as was thought,
They themselves were fully at rest, they suffer'd not,
The living remained and suffer'd, the mother suffer'd,
And the wife and the child and the musing comrade
    suffer'd,
And the armies that remain'd suffer'd.

16

Passing the vision, passing the night,
Passing, unloosing the hold of my comrades' hands,
Passing the song of the hermit bird and the tallying song of
    my soul,
Victorious song, death's outlet song, yet varying ever-altering
    song,
As low and wailing, yet clear the notes, rising and falling,
    flooding the night,
Sadly sinking and fainting, as warning and warning, and yet
    again bustling with joy,
Covering the earth and filling the spread of the heaven,
As that powerful psalm of the night I heard from recesses,
Passing, I leave thee lilac with heart-shaped leaves,
I leave thee there in the dooryard, blooming, returning with
    spring.
I cease from my song for thee,
From my gaze on thee in the west, fronting the west,
    communing with thee,
O comrade lustrous with silver face in the night.

Yet each to keep and all, retrievements out of the night,
The song, the wondrous chant of the gray-brown bird,
And the tallying chant, the echo arous'd in my soul,
With the lustrous and drooping star with the countenance
    full of woe,
With the holders holding my hand nearing the call of the
    bird,
Comrades mine and I in the midst, and the memory ever to
    keep, for the dead I lov'd so well,
For the sweetest, wisest soul of all my days and lands – and
    this for his dear sake,
Lilac and star and bird twined with the chant of my soul,
There in the fragrant pines, and the cedars dark and dim.

                                    WALT WHITMAN (1865)

Abraham Lincoln was assassinated in Washington DC in April 1865,
and his coffin was taken slowly back to his home town in Illinois for
burial.

The Last Night that She Lived

The last night that she lived
It was a common night
Except the dying – this to us
Made nature different.

We noticed smallest things –
Things overlooked before
By this great light upon our minds
Italicized, as 'twere.

That others could exist
While she must finish quite,
A jealousy for her arose
So nearly infinite.

We waited while she passed;
It was a narrow time.
Too jostled were our souls to speak;
At length the notice came.

She mentioned, and forgot;
Then lightly as a reed
Bent to the water, struggled scarce,
Consented, and was dead.

And we, we placed the hair,
And drew the head erect;
And then an awful leisure was
Our faith to regulate.

EMILY DICKINSON (1866)

Parted

Farewell to one now silenced quite,
Sent out of hearing, out of sight,—
  My friend of friends, whom I shall miss,
  He is not banished, though, for this,—
Nor he, nor sadness, nor delight.

Though I shall talk with him no more,
A low voice sounds upon the shore.
  He must not watch my resting place
  But who shall drive a mournful face
From the sad winds about my door?

I shall not hear his voice complain,
But who shall stop the patient rain?
  His tears must not disturb my heart,
  But who shall change the years and part
The world from every thought of pain?

Although my life is left so dim,
The morning crowns the mountain rim;
  Joy is not gone from summer skies,
  Nor innocence from children's eyes,
And all these things are part of him.

He is not banished, for the showers
Yet wake this green warm earth of ours.
  How can the summer not be sweet?
  I shall not have him at my feet,
And yet my feet are on the flowers.

ALICE MEYNELL (Published 1875)

Felix Randal

Felix Randal the farrier, O he is dead then? my duty all ended,
Who have watched his mould of man, big-boned and hardy-
  handsome
Pining, pining, till time when reason rambled in it and some
Fatal four disorders, fleshed there, all contended?

Sickness broke him. Impatient, he cursed at first, but mended
Being anointed and all; though a heavenlier heart began some
Months earlier, since I had our sweet reprieve and ransom
Tendered to him. Ah well, God rest him all road ever he
  offended!

This seeing the sick endears us to them to us, us it endears,
My tongue had taught thee comfort, touch had quenched thy
  tears,
Thy tears that touched my heart, child, Felix, poor Felix Randal;

How far from then forethought of, all thy more boisterous years,
When thou at the random grim forge, powerful amidst peers,
Didst fettle for the great grey drayhorse his bright and battering
  sandal!

GERARD MANLEY HOPKINS (1880)

Contradictions

Now, even, I cannot think it true,
My friend, that there is no more you.
Almost as soon were no more I,
Which were of course absurdity!

Your place is bare, you are not seen,
Your grave, I'm told, is growing green;
And both for you and me, you know,
There's no Above and no Below.
That you are dead must be inferred,
And yet my thought rejects the word.

AMY LEVY (Published 1889)

Thoughts of Phena

At news of her death

Not a line of writing have I
        Not a thread of her hair,
No mark of her late time as dame in her dwelling, whereby
        I may picture her there;
        And in vain do I urge my unsight
        To conceive my lost prize
At her close, whom I knew, when her dreams were
    upbrimming with light,
        And with laughter her eyes.

What scenes spread around her last days,
        Sad, shining, or dim?
Did her gifts, and compassions enray and enarch her
    sweet ways
        With an aureate nimb?
        Or did life-light decline from her years,
        And mischances control
Her full day-star; unease or regret, or forebodings or fears
        Disenoble her soul?

Thus I do but the phantom retain
        Of the maiden of yore
As my relic; yet haply the best of her – fined in my brain
        It may be the more
        That no line of her writing have I,
        Nor a thread of her hair,
No mark of her late time as dame in her dwelling, whereby
        I may picture her there.

THOMAS HARDY (1890)

'Phena' – Tryphena Sparks – was Hardy's early love.

9
VARIETIES OF LOVE
& ITS AFTERMATH

She was a Phantom of delight

She was a Phantom of delight
When first she gleam'd upon my sight;
A lovely Apparition, sent
To be a moment's ornament;
Her eyes as stars of Twilight fair;
Like Twilight's, too, her dusky hair;
But all things else about her drawn
From May-time and the cheerful dawn;
A dancing Shape, an Image gay,
To haunt, to startle, and way-lay.

I saw her upon nearer view,
A Spirit, yet a Woman too!
Her household motions light and free,
And steps of virgin-liberty;
A countenance in which did meet
Sweet records, promises as sweet;
A Creature not too bright or good
For human nature's daily food;
For transient sorrows, simple wiles,
Praise, blame, love, kisses, tears, and smiles.

And now I see with eye serene
The very pulse of the machine;
A Being breathing thoughtful breath,
A Traveller between life and death;
The reason firm, the temperate will,
Endurance, foresight, strength, and skill;
A perfect Woman, nobly planned,
To warn, to comfort, and command;
And yet a Spirit still, and bright
With something of angelic light.

WILLIAM WORDSWORTH (1770–1850)

She was a Phantom of Delight

She was a Phantom of delight,
When first she gleam'd upon my sight;
A lovely apparition sent
To be a moment's ornament;
Her eyes as stars of Twilight fair;
Like Twilight too her dusky hair;
From all things else about her drawn;
From May-time and the cheerful Dawn;
A dancing Shape, an Image gay,
To haunt, to startle and way-lay.

I saw her upon nearer view,
A Spirit, yet a Woman too;
Her household motions light and free,
And steps of virgin-liberty;
A countenance in which did meet
Sweet records, promises as sweet;
A Creature not too bright or good
For human nature's daily food;
For transient sorrows, simple wiles,
Praise, blame, love, kisses, tears and smiles.

And now I see, with eye serene,
The very pulse of the machine;
A Being breathing thoughtful breath,
A Traveller between life and death;
The reason firm, the temperate will,
Endurance, foresight, strength, and skill;
A perfect Woman, nobly planned,
To warn, to comfort, and command;
And yet as Spirit still, and bright
With something of angelic light.

WILLIAM WORDSWORTH (1804)

The First Kiss of Love

Away with your fictions of flimsy romance
    Those tissues of folly which folly has wove
Give me the mild beam of the soul breathing glance,
    Or the rapture which dwells on the first kiss of love.

Ye rhymers whose bosoms with phantasy glow,
    Whose pastoral passions are made for the grove,
From what blest inspiration your sonnets would flow
    Could you ever have tasted the first kiss of love.

If Apollo should e'er his assistance refuse,
    Or the Nine be disposed from your service to rove,
Invoke them no more, bid adieu to the muse,
    And try the effect of the first kiss of love.

I hate you, you cold compositions of art!
    Though prudes may condemn me and bigots reprove,
I court the effusions that spring from the heart,
    Which throbs with delight to the first kiss of love.

Your shepherds, your flocks, those fantastical themes,
    Perhaps may amuse, yet they never can move:
Arcadia displays but a region of dreams:
    What are visions like these to the first kiss of love?

O cease to affirm that man, since his birth,
    From Adam till now has with wretchedness strove,
Some portion of Paradise still is on earth,
    And Eden revives in the first kiss of love.

When age chills the blood, when our pleasures are past –
    For years fleet away with the wings of the dove –
The dearest remembrance will still be the last,
    Our sweetest memorial the first kiss of love.

GEORGE GORDON, LORD BYRON (Published 1807)

When We Two Parted

When we two parted
    In silence and tears
Half broken hearted
    To sever for years,
Pale grew thy cheek and cold
    Colder thy kiss;
Truly that hour foretold
    Sorrow to this.

The dew of the morning
    Sunk chill on my brow –
It felt like the warning
    Of what I feel now.
Thy vows are all broken,
    And light is thy fame:
I hear thy name spoken,
    And share in its shame.

They name thee before me,
    A knell to mine ear;
A shudder come o'er me –
    Why wert thou so dear?
They know not I knew thee,
    Who knew thee too well; –
Long, long shall I rue thee,
    Too deeply to tell.

In secret we met –
    In silence I grieve,
That thy heart could forget,
    Thy spirit deceive.
If I should meet thee,
    After long years,
How should I greet thee?
    With silence and tears.

GEORGE GORDON, LORD BYRON (1815)

So we'll go no more a-roving

So we'll go no more a-roving
    So late into the night
Though the heart be still as loving
    And the moon be still as bright.

For the sword outwears its sheath
    And the soul wears out its breast
And the heart must pause to breathe
    And love itself have rest.

Though the night was made for loving
    And the day returns too soon,
Yet we'll go no more a-roving,
    By the light of the moon.

                    GEORGE GORDON, LORD BYRON (1817)

Sonnet written on a Blank Page in Shakespeare's Poems facing 'A Lover's Complaint'

Bright star! would I were steadfast as thou art!
Not in lone splendour hung aloft the night
And watching, with eternal lids apart,
Like nature's patient, sleepless eremite,
The moving waters at their priestlike task
Of pure ablution round earth's human shores,
Or gazing on the new soft fallen mask
Of snow upon the mountains and the moors:
    No – yet still steadfast, still unchangeable,
Pillowed upon my fair love's ripening breast,
To feel forever its soft fall and swell,
Awake for ever in a sweet unrest,
Still, still to hear her tender-taken breath
And so live ever – or else swoon to death.

                    JOHN KEATS (1819)

from *Don Juan*

Donna Julia, married to the fifty-year-old Don Alfonso,
has fallen in love with the sixteen-year-old Juan.

54

'Twas on the sixth of June, about the hour
   Of half-past six – perhaps still nearer seven –
When Julia sate within as pretty a bower
   As e'er held houri in that heathenish heaven
Described by Mahomet and Anacreon Moore,*
   To whom the lyre and laurels have been given,
With all the trophies of triumphant song –
He won them well, and may he wear them long!

55

She sate, but not alone; I know not well
   How this same interview had taken place,
And, even if I knew, I should not tell–
   People should hold their tongues in any case;
No matter how or why the thing befell,
   But there were she and Juan, face to face–
When two such faces are so, 'twould be wise,
But very difficult, to shut their eyes.

56

How beautiful she look'd! Her conscious heart
   Glow'd in her cheek, and yet she felt no wrong,
Oh Love! how perfect is thy mystic art,
   Strengthening the weak, and trampling on the strong!
How self-deceitful is the sagest part
   Of mortals whom thy lure has led along!
The precipice she stood on was immense,
So was her creed in her own innocence.

---

* Anacreon Moore was Byron's friend, the poet Tom Moore, who
translated the Greek love poet, Anachreon.

57

She thought of her own strength and Juan's youth,
    And of the folly of all prudish fears,
Victorious virtue and domestic truth,
    And then of Don Alfonso's fifty years:
I wish these last had not occurr'd, in sooth,
    Because that number rarely much endears,
And through all climes, the snowy and the sunny,
Sounds ill in love, whate'er it may in money.

58

When people say, 'I've told you *fifty* times,'
    They mean to scold, and very often do;
When poets say, 'I've written *fifty* rhymes,'
    They make you dread that they'll recite them too;
In gangs of *fifty*, thieves commit their crimes;
    At *fifty* love for love is rare, 'tis true,
But then, no doubt, it equally as true is,
A good deal may be bought for *fifty* Louis.*

59

Julia had honour, virtue, truth and love
    For Don Alfonso, and she inly swore,
By all the powers below to powers above,
    She never would disgrace the ring she wore,
Nor leave a wish which wisdom might reprove;
    And, while she ponder'd this, besides much more,
One hand on Juan's carelessly was thrown,
Quite by mistake – she thought it was her own;

60

Unconsciously, she leant upon the other,
    Which play'd within the tangles of her hair;
And to contend with thoughts she could not smother
    She seem'd, by the distraction of her air.
'Twas surely very wrong of Juan's mother
    To leave together this imprudent pair,
She, who for many years had watch'd her son so –
I'm very certain *mine* would not have done so.

* Louis were valuable gold coins.

61

The hand which still held Juan's by degrees
   Gently, but palpably, confirm'd its grasp,
As if it said, 'Detain me if you please';
   Yet there's no doubt she only meant to clasp
His fingers with a pure Platonic squeeze;
   She would have shrunk as from a toad or asp,
Had she imagined such a thing could rouse
A feeling dangerous to a prudent spouse.

62

I cannot know what Juan thought of this,
   But what he did, is much what you would do;
His young lip thank'd it with a grateful kiss,
   And then, abash'd at its own joy, withdrew
In deep despair, lest he had done amiss, –
   Love is so very timid, when 'tis new:
She blush'd, and frown'd not, but she strove to speak
And held her tongue, her voice was grown so weak.

63

The sun set, and up rose the yellow moon:
   The devil's in the moon for mischief; they
Who call her CHASTE, methinks began too soon
   Their nomenclature; there is not a day,
The longest, not the twenty-first of June,
   Sees half the business in a wicked way
On which three single hours of moonshine smile –
And then she looks so modest all the while.

64

There is a dangerous silence in that hour,
   A stillness which leaves room for the full soul
To open all itself, without the power
   Of calling wholly back its self control;
The silver light which, hallowing tree and tower,
   Sheds beauty and deep softness o'er the whole
Breathes also to the heart, and o'er it throws
A loving languor, which is not repose.

65

And Julia sate with Juan, half embraced
 And half retiring from the glowing arm,
Which trembled like the bosom where 'twas placed;
 Yet still she must have thought there was no harm,
Or else 'twere easy to withdraw her waist;
 But then the situation had its charm,
And then – God knows what next – I can't go on;
I'm almost sorry that I e'er begun.

66

Oh, Plato! Plato! you have paved the way,
 With your confounded fantasies, to more
Immoral conduct by the fancied sway
 Your system feigns o'er the controlless core
Of human hearts, than all the long array
 Of poets and romancers:– you're a bore,
A charlatan, a coxcomb – and have been,
At best no better than a go-between.

67

And Julia's voice was lost, except in sighs,
 Until too late for useful conversation;
The tears were gushing from her gentle eyes,
 I wish, indeed, they had not had occasion;
But who, alas! can love and then be wise?
 Not that remorse did not oppose temptation;
A little while she strove, and much repented,
And whispering 'I will ne'er consent' – consented.

GEORGE GORDON, LORD BYRON (c. 1819)

Believe me if all those endearing young charms

Believe me if all those endearing young charms
    Which I gaze on so fondly today,
Were to fade by tomorrow, and fleet in my arms
    Like fairy gifts fading away,
Thou woulds't still be adored, as this moment thou art
    Let thy loveliness fade as it will,
And around the fair ruin each wish of my heart
    Would entwine itself verdantly still.

It is not while beauty and youth are thine own,
    And thy cheeks unprofaned by a tear
That the fervour and faith of a soul can be known,
    To which Time will but make thee more dear;
No the heart that has truly loved never forgets,
    But as truly loves on to the close,
As the sunflower turns on her god, when he sets,
    The same look which he turned as he rose.

THOMAS MOORE

Porphyria's Lover

The rain set early in tonight,
    The sullen wind was soon awake,
It tore the elm-tops down for spite,
    And did its worst to vex the lake;
I listened with heart fit to break
    When glided in Porphyria; straight
She shut the cold out and the storm,
    And kneeled and made the cheerless grate
Blaze up, and all the cottage warm;
    Which done, she rose, and from her form
Withdrew the dripping cloak and shawl,
    And laid her soiled gloves by, untied
Her hat and let the damp hair fall,

And, last, she sat down by my side
    And called me. When no voice replied,
She put my arm about her waist
    And made her smooth white shoulder bare
And all her yellow hair displaced,
    And, stooping, made my cheek lie there,
    And spread o'er all her yellow hair,
Murmuring how she loved me – she,
    Too weak, for all her heart's endeavour,
To set its struggling passion free
    From pride, and vainer ties dissever,
    And give herself to me for ever.
But passion sometimes would prevail,
    Nor could to-night's gay feast restrain
A sudden thought of one so pale
    For love of her, and all in vain;
    So she was come through wind and rain.
Be sure I looked up at her eyes
    Happy and proud; at last I knew
Porphyria worshipped me; surprise
    Made my heart swell, and still it grew,
    While I debated what to do.
That moment she was mine, mine, fair,
    Perfectly pure and good: I found
A thing to do, and all her hair
    In one long yellow string I wound
    Three times her little throat around
And strangled her. No pain felt she;
    I am quite sure she felt no pain.
As a shut bud that holds a bee,
    I warily oped her eyes: again
    Laughed the blue eyes without a stain.
And I untightened next the tress
    About her neck; her cheek once more
Blushed bright beneath my burning kiss;
    I propped her head up as before,
    Only, this time my shoulder bore
Her head, which droops upon it still:
    The smiling little rosy head,
So glad it has its utmost will,

That all it scorned at once is fled,
    And I, its love, am gained instead!
Porphyria's love: she guessed not how
    Her darling one wish would be heard.
And thus we sit together now,
    And all night long we have not stirred.

ROBERT BROWNING (1834)

from *Sonnets from the Portuguese*

6

Go from me. Yet I feel that I shall stand
Henceforward in thy shadow. Nevermore
Alone upon the threshold of my door
Of individual life, I shall command
The uses of my soul, nor lift my hand
Serenely in the sunshine as before,
Without the sense of that which I forbore –
Thy touch upon the palm. The widest land
Doom takes to part us, leaves thy heart in mine
With pulses that beat double. What I do
And what I dream include thee, as the wine
Must taste of its own grapes. And when I sue
God for myself, he hears that name of thine,
And sees within my eyes the tears of two.

14

If thou must love me, let it be for nought
Except for love's sake only. Do not say
I love her for her smile – her look – her way
Of speaking gently, – for a trick of thought
That falls in well with mine, and certes brought
A sense of pleasant ease on such a day' –
For these things in themselves, beloved, may
Be changed, or change for thee, – and love, so wrought

May be unwrought so. Neither love me for
Thine own dear pity's wiping my cheeks dry, –
A creature might forget to weep, who bore
Thy comfort long, and lose thy love thereby!
But love me for love's sake, that evermore
Thou may'st love on, through love's eternity.

15

Accuse me not, beseech thee, that I wear
Too calm and sad a face in front of thine;
For we two look two ways, and cannot shine
With the same sunlight on our brow and hair.
On me thou lookest with no doubting care,
As on a bee shut in a crystalline;
Since sorrow hath shut me safe in love's divine,
And to spread wing and fly in the outer air
Were most impossible failure, if I strove
To fail so. But I look on thee – on thee –
Beholding, besides love, the end of love,
Hearing oblivion beyond memory;
As one who sits and gazes from above
Over the rivers to the bitter sea.

22

When our two souls stand up erect and strong,
Face to face, silent, drawing nigh and nigher,
Until the lengthening wings break into fire
At either curved point, – what bitter wrong
Can the earth do to us, that we should not long
Be here contented? Think, in mounting higher,
The angels would press on us and aspire
To drop some golden orb of perfect song
Into our deep dear silence. Let us stay
Rather on earth, Beloved, – where the unfit
Contrarious moods of men recoil away
And isolate pure spirits, and permit
A space to stand and love in for a day,
With darkness and the death hour rounding it.

44

Beloved, thou hast brought me many flowers
Plucked in the garden, all the summer through,
And winter, and it seemed as if they grew
In this close room, nor missed the sun and showers.
So, in the like name of that love of ours,
Take back these thoughts which here unfolded too,
And which on warm and cold days I withdrew
From my heart's ground. Indeed those beds and bowers
Be overgrown with bitter weeds and rue,
And wait their weeding; yet, here's eglantine,
Here's ivy! take them, as I used to do
Thy flowers, and keep them where they shall not pine.
Instruct thine eyes to keep their colours true,
And tell thy soul, their roots are left in mine.

ELIZABETH BARRETT BROWNING (1847)

Love Among the Ruins

1

Where the quiet-coloured end of evening smiles,
    Miles and miles
On the solitary pastures where our sheep
    Half-asleep
Tinkle homeward through the twilight, stray or stop
    As they crop –
Was the site once of a city great and gay
    (So they say),
Of our country's very capital, its prince
    Ages since
Held his court in, gathered councils, wielding far
    Peace or war.

2

Now – the country does not even boast a tree
    As you see,
To distinguish slopes of verdure, certain rills
    From the hills

Intersect and give a name to (else they run
    Into one),
Where the domed and daring palace shot its spires
    Up like fires
O'er the hundred-gated circuit of a wall
    Bounding all,
Made of marble, men might march on, nor be pressed,
    Twelve abreast.

3

And such plenty and perfection yet of grass
    Never was!
Such a carpet as, this summertime, o'erspreads
    And embeds
Every vestige of the city, guessed alone,
    Stock or stone –
Where a multitude of men breathed joy or woe
    Long ago;
Lust of glory and that shame alike, the gold
    Bought and sold.

4

Now – the single litttle turret that remains
    On the plains,
By the caper over-rooted, by the gourd
    Overscored,
While the patching houseleek's head of blossoms
  winks
    Through the chinks –
Marks the basement whence a tower in ancient time
    Sprang sublime,
And a burning ring, all round, the chariots traced
    As they raced,
And the monarch and his minions and his dames
    Viewed the games.

5

And I know, while thus the quiet-coloured eve
    Smiles to leave
To their folding, all our many-tinkling fleece
    In such peace,

And the slopes and rills in undistinguished gray
    Melt away –
That a girl with eager eyes and yellow hair
    Waits me there
In the turret whence the charioteers caught soul
    For the goal,
When the king looked, where she looks now,
    breathless, dumb,
      Till I come.

6

But they looked upon the city, every side,
    Far and wide,
All the mountains topped with temples, all the glades'
    Colonnades,
All the causeys, bridges, aqueducts – and then,
    All the men!
When I do come, she will speak not, she will stand,
    Either hand
On my shoulder, give her eyes the first embrace
    Of my face,
Ere we rush, ere we extinguish sight and speech
    Each on each.

7

In one year they sent a million fighters forth
    South and north,
And they built their gods a brazen pillar high
    As the sky,
Yet reserved a thousand chariots in full force –
    Gold, of course.
Oh heart! oh blood that freezes, blood that burns!
    Earth's returns
For whole centuries of folly, noise and sin!
    Shut them in,
With their triumphs and their glories and the rest!
    Love is best.

ROBERT BROWNING (1853)

By the Fireside

1

How well I know what I mean to do
   When the long dark autumn evenings come;
And where, my soul, is thy pleasant hue?
   With the music of all thy voices, dumb
In life's November too!

2

I shall be found by the fire, suppose,
   O'er a great wise book, as beseemeth age,
While the shutters flap as the cross-wind blows
   And I turn the page, and I turn the page,
Not verse now, only prose!

3

Till the young ones whisper, finger on lip,
   'There he is at it, deep in Greek;
Now then, or never, out we slip
   To cut from the hazels by the creek
A mainmast for our ship!'

4

I shall be at it indeed, my friends:
   Greek puts already on either side
Such a branch-work as soon extends
   To a vista opening far and wide,
And I pass out where it ends.

5

The outside-frame like your hazel-trees;
   But the inside archway widens fast,
And a rarer sort succeeds to these,
   And we slope to Italy at last
And youth, by green degrees.

6

I follow wherever I am led,
   Knowing so well the leader's hand:
Oh woman-country, wooed, not wed,
   Loved all the more by earth's male-lands,
Laid to their hearts instead!

7

Look at the ruined chapel again
   Half-way up in the Alpine gorge!
Is that a tower I point you plain,
   Or is it a mill, or an iron forge
Breaks solitude in vain?

8

A turn, and we stand in the heart of things;
   The woods are round us, heaped and dim;
From slab to slab how it slips and springs,
   The thread of water, single and slim,
Through the ravage some torrent brings!

9

Does it feed the little lake below?
   That speck of white just on its marge
Is Pella; see, in the evening glow,
   How sharp the silver spear-heads charge
When Alp meets heaven in snow!

10

On the other side is the straight-up rock;
   And a path is kept 'twixt the gorge and it
By boulder stones, where lichens mock
   The marks on a moth, and small ferns fit
Their teeth to the polished block.

11

Oh the sense of the yellow mountain flowers,
   And thorny balls, each three in one,
The chestnuts throw on our path in showers!
   For the drop of the woodland fruit's begun,
These early November hours,

12

That crimson the creeper's leaf across
    Like a splash of blood, intense, abrupt,
O'er a shield else gold from rim to boss,
    And lay it for show on the fairy-cupped
Elf-needled mat of moss,

13

By the rose-fleshed mushrooms, undivulged
    Last evening – nay, in today's first dew
Yon sudden coral nipple bulged,
    Where a freaked fawn-coloured flaky crew
Of toadstools peep indulged.

14

And yonder, at the foot of the fronting ridge
    That takes the turn to a range beyond,
Is the chapel reached by the one-arched bridge
    Where the water is topped in a stagnant pond
Danced over by the midge.

15

The chapel and bridge are of stone alike,
    Blackish grey, and mostly wet;
Cut hemp-stalks steep in the narrow dyke.
    See here again, how the lichens fret
And the roots of the ivy strike!

16

Poor little place, where its one priest comes
    On a *festa* day, if he comes at all,
To the dozen folk from their scattered homes,
    Gathered within that precinct small
By the dozen ways one roams –

17

To drop from the charcoal burners' huts,
    Or climb from the hemp-dressers' low shed,
Leave the grange where the woodman stores his nuts,
    Or the wattled cote where the fowlers spread
Their gear on the rocks bare juts.

18

It has some pretension too, this front,
    With its bit of fresco half-moon-wise
Set over the porch, Art's early wont:
    'Tis *John in the Desert*, I surmise,
But has borne the weather's brunt –

19

Not from the fault of the builder, though,
    For a pent-house properly projects
Where three carved beams make a certain show,
    Dating – good thought of our architect's –
Five, six, nine, he lets you know.

20

And all day long a bird sings there,
    And a stray sheep drinks at the pond at times;
The place is silent and aware;
    It has had its scenes, its joys and crimes,
But that is its own affair.

21

My perfect wife, my Leonor,
    Oh heart, my own, oh eyes, mine too,
Whom else could I look backward for,
    With whom beside should I dare pursue
The path grey heads abhor?

22

For it leads to a crag's sheer edge with them;
    Youth, flowery all the way, there stops –
Not they; age threatens and they contemn,
    Till they reach the gulf wherein youth drops,
One inch from life's safe hem.

23

With me, youth led . . . I will speak now,
    No longer watch you as you sit
Reading by firelight, that great brow
    And the spirit-small hand still propping it,
Mutely, my heart knows how –

24

When, if I think but deep enough,
   You are wont to answer, prompt as rhyme;
And you, too, find, without rebuff,
   Response your soul seeks many a time
Piercing its fine flesh-stuff.

25

My own, confirm me! If I tread
   This path back, is it not in pride
To think how little I dreamed it led
   To an age so blest that, by its side,
Youth seems the waste instead?

26

My own, see where the years conduct!
   At first, 'twas something our two souls
Should mix as mists do; each is sucked
   In each now; on the new stream rolls,
Whatever rocks obstruct.

27

Think, when our one soul understands
   The great Word which makes all things new
When earth breaks up and heaven expands
   How will the change strike me and you
In the house not made with hands?

28

Oh, I must feel you brain prompt mine,
   Your heart anticipate my heart,
You must be just before, in fine,
   See, and make me see, for your part,
New depths of the divine!

29

But who could have expected this
   When we two drew together first
Just for the obvious human bliss,
   To satisfy life's daily thirst
With a thing men seldom miss?

30

Come back with me to the first of all,
    Let us lean and love it over again,
Let us now forget and now recall,
    Break the rosary in a pearly rain,
And gather what we let fall!

31

What did I say? – that a small bird sings
    All day long, save when a brown pair
Of hawks from the wood float with wide wings
    Strained to a bell: 'gainst noon-day glare
You count the streaks and rings.

32

But at afternoon or almost eve
    'Tis better; then the silence grows
To that degree, you half believe
    It must get rid of what it knows,
Its bosom does so heave.

33

Hither we walked then, side by side,
    Arm in arm and cheek to cheek,
And still I questioned, or replied,
    While my heart, convulsed to really speak,
Lay choking in its pride.

34

Silent, the crumbling bridge we cross,
    And pity and praise the chapel sweet,
And care about the fresco's loss,
    And wish for our souls a like retreat,
And wonder at the moss.

35

Stoop and kneel at the settle under,
    Look through the window's grated square:
Nothing to see! For fear of plunder,
    The cross is down and the altar bare,
As if thieves don't fear thunder.

36

We stoop and look in through the grate,
　　See the little porch and the rustic door,
Read duly the dead builder's date;
　　Then cross the bridge that we crossed before,
Take the path again – but wait!

37

One moment, one and infinite!
　　The water slips o'er stock and stone;
The West is tender, hardly bright;
　　How grey at once is the evening grown –
One star, its chrysolite!

38

We two stood there with never a third,
　　But each by each, as each knew well;
The sights we saw and the sounds we heard,
　　The lights and the shades made up a spell
Till the trouble grew and stirred.

39

Oh, the little more and how much it is!
　　And the little less, and what worlds away!
How a sound shall quicken content to bliss,
　　Or a breath suspend the blood's best play,
And life be a proof of this!

40

Had she willed it still had stood the screen
　　So slight, so sure, 'twixt my love and her:
I could fix her face with a guard between,
　　And find her soul as when friends confer,
Friends – lovers that might have been!

41

For my heart had a touch of the woodland-time,
　　Wanting to sleep now over its best.
Shake the whole tree in the summer-prime,
　　But bring to the last leaf no such test!
'Hold the last fast!' runs the rhyme.

42

For a chance to make your little much,
    To gain a lover and lose a friend,
Venture the tree and a myriad such,
    When nothing you mar but the year can mend:
But a last leaf – fear to touch!

43

Yet should it unfasten itself and fall
    Eddying down till it find your face
At some slight wind – best chance of all!
    Be your heart henceforth its dwelling place
You trembled to forestall!

44

Worth how well those dark grey eyes,
    That hair so dark and dear, how worth,
That a man should strive and agonize,
    And taste a veriest hell on earth,
For the hope of such a prize!

45

You might have turned and tried a man,
    Set him a space to weary and wear,
And prove which suited more your plan,
    His best of hope or his worst despair,
Yet end as he began.

46

But you spared me this, like the heart you are,
    And filled my empty heart at a word.
If two lives join, there is oft a scar,
    They are one and one, with a shadowy third;
One near one is too far.

47

A moment after, and hands unseen
    Were hanging the night around us fast;
But we knew that a bar was broken between
    Life and life: we were mixed at last,
In spite of the mortal screen.

48

The forests had done it; there they stood;
   We caught for a moment the powers at play;
They had mingled us so, for once and good,
   Their work was done – we might go or stay;
They relapsed to their ancient mood.

49

How the world is made for each of us!
   How all we perceive and know in it
Tends to some moment's product thus,
   When a soul declares itself – to wit,
By its fruit, the thing it does!

50

Be hate that fruit or love that fruit,
   It forwards the general deed of man,
And each of the Many helps to recruit
   The life of the race by a general plan;
Each living his own, to boot.

51

I am named and known by that moment's feat;
   There took my station and degree;
So grew my own small life complete,
   As nature obtained her best of me –
One born to love you, sweet!

52

And to watch you sink by the fireside now
   Back again, as you mutely sit
Musing by firelight, that great brow
   And the spirit-small hand still propping it,
Yonder, my heart knows how!

53

So, earth has gained by one man the more,
   And the gain of earth must be heaven's gain too;
And the whole is well worth thinking o'er
   When autumn comes, which I mean to do
One day, as I said before.

ROBERT BROWNING (Published 1855)

The Storm

1

Both hollow and hill were as dumb as death,
    While the heavens were moodily changing form.
    And the hush that is herald of creeping storm
Had made heavy the crouch'd land's breath.

2

At the wide-flung casement she stood, full height,
    With her glittering hair tumbled over her back,
    And against the black sky's supernatural black,
Shone her white neck, scornfully white.

3

I could catch not a gleam of her anger'd eyes,
    (She was sullenly watching the storm-cloud roll),
    But I felt they were drawing down into her soul
The thunder that darkened the skies.

4

'And so do we part, then, for ever?' I said,
    'O speak only one word, and I pardon the rest!'
    For sole answer, her white scarf over her breast
She tighten'd, not turning her head.

5

'Ah, must sweet love cruelly play with pain?
    Or,' I groaned, 'Are those blue eyes such deserts of
        blindness
    That, O woman, your heart hath no heed of unkindness
To the man on whose breast it hath lain?'

6

Then alive leapt the lightning. She turn'd in its glare,
    And the tempest had cloth'd her with terror: it clung
    To the folds of her vaporous garments, and hung
In the heaps of her heavy wild hair.

7

One word broke the silence: but one: and it fell
    With the weight of a mountain upon me. Next moment
    All was bellowing thunder, and she from my comment
Was gone ere it ceased. Who can tell

8

How I got to my home in the horrible hills,
    Through black swimmings of storm and burst seams
        of blue rain?
    Sick, I lean'd from the lattice, and dizzy with pain
And listen'd, and heard the loud rills,

9

And look'd, and beheld the red moon low in air,
    Then my heart leapt . . . I felt and foreknew it before
    I heard her light hand on the latch of the door!
When it open'd at last – she was there!

10

Child-like and wistful and sorrow-eyed,
    With the rain in her hair, and the tears on her cheek,
    Down she knelt – all her fair forehead fallen and meek
In the light of the moon – at my side.

11

And she call'd me by every caressing old name
    She of old had invented and chosen for me,
    While she crouch'd at my feet, with her cheek on my
        knee,
Like a wild thing grown suddenly tame.

12

'Twas no vision! This morning, the earth, prest beneath
    Her light foot, keeps the print. 'Twas no vision last
        night!
    For the lily she dropp'd as she went, is yet white,
With the dew on its delicate sheath!

                     'OWEN MEREDITH', LORD LYTTON (1858)

To a Woman

Since all that I can do for thee
Is to do nothing, this my prayer must be;
That thou may'st never guess nor ever see
The all-endured this nothing-done costs me.

'OWEN MEREDITH', LORD LYTTON (1858)

Worn Out

Thy strong arms are round me, love,
My head is on thy breast;
Low words of comfort come from me
Yet my soul has no rest.

For I am but a startled thing
Nor can I ever be
Aught save a bird whose broken wing
Must fly away from thee.

I cannot give to thee the love
I gave so long ago
The love that turned and struck me down
Amid the blinding snow.

I can but give a failing heart
And weary eyes of pain,
A faded mouth that cannot smile
And may not laugh again.

Yet keep thy arms around me, love,
Until I fall asleep;
Then leave me, saying no goodbye
Lest I might wake, and weep.

ELIZABETH SIDDAL (Before 1862)

See Christina Rossetti's poem 'In An Artist's Studio' below.

First Love

I ne'er was struck before that hour,
    With love so sudden and so sweet,
Her face it bloomed like a sweet flower
    And stole my heart away complete.
My face turned pale as deadly pale.
    My legs refused to walk away,
And when she looked, what could I ail?
    My life and all seemed turned to clay.

And then my blood rushed to my face
    And took my eyesight quite away,
The trees and bushes round the place
    Seemed midnight at noonday.
I could not see a single thing,
    Words from my heart did start –
They spoke as chords do from the string,
    And blood burnt round my heart.

Are flowers the winter's choice?
    Is love's bed always snow?
She seemed to hear my silent voice,
    Not love's appeals to know.
I never saw so sweet a face
    As that I stood before.
My heart has left its dwelling place
    And can return no more.

JOHN CLARE (Before 1864)

'No, Thank You, John'

I never said I loved you, John,
    Why will you teaze me day by day,
And wax a weariness to think upon
    With always 'do' and 'pray'.

You know I never loved you, John,
    No fault of mine made me your toast:
Why will you haunt me with a face as wan
    As shows an hour-old ghost?

I day say Meg or Moll would take
    Pity upon you, if you'd ask:
And pray don't remain single for my sake
    Who can't perform that task.

I have no heart? Perhaps I have not;
    But then you're mad to take offence
That I don't give you what I have not got:
    Use your own common sense.

Let bygones be bygones:
    Don't call me false, who owed not to be true:
I'd rather answer 'No' to fifty Johns
    Than answer 'Yes' to you.

Let's mar our pleasant days no more,
    Song birds of passage, days of youth:
Catch at today, forget the days before:
    I'll wink at your untruth.

Let us strike hands as hearty friends;
    No more, nor less; and frienship's good:
Only don't keep in view ulterior ends,
    And points not understood

In open treaty. Rise above
    Quibbles, and shuffling off and on:
Here's friendship for you, if you like; but love, –
    No, thank you, John.

CHRISTINA ROSSETTI (1860)

The Visiting Sea

As the inhastening tide doth roll,
Home from the deep, along the whole
   Wide shining strand and floods the caves,
    – Your love comes filling with happy waves
The open seashore of my soul.

But inland from the seaward spaces,
None knows, not even you the places
   Brimmed at your coming out of sight,
    – The little solitudes of delight
This tide constrains in dim embraces.

You see the happy shore, wave-rimmed
But know not of the quiet dimmed
   Rivers your coming floods and fills,
    The little pools mid happier hills,
My silent rivulets, overbrimmed.

What! I have secrets from you? Yes,
But, visiting Sea, your love doth press
   And reach in further than you know,
    And fills all these; and when you go,
There's loneliness in loneliness.

ALICE MEYNELL (1875)

from *Modern Love*

1

By this he knew she wept with waking eyes:
That, at his hand's light quiver by her head,
The strange low sobs that shook their common bed
Were called into her with a sharp surprise,
And strangled mute, like little gaping snakes,
Dreadfully venomous to him. She lay
Stone-still, and the long darkness flowed away
With muffled pulses. Then, as midnight makes
Her giant heart of Memory and Tears
Drink the pale heart of silence, and so beat
Sleep's heavy measure, they from head to feet
Were moveless, looking through their dead black years,
By vain regret scrawled over the blank wall.
Like sculptured effigies they might be seen
Upon their marriage-bed, the sword between;
Each wishing for the sword that severs all.

7

She issues radiant from her dressing room,
Like one prepared to scale an upper sphere:
– By stirring up a lower, much I fear!
How deftly that oiled barber lays his bloom!
That long-shanked, dapper Cupid with frisked curls,
Can make a woman torturingly fair;
The gold-eyed serpent dwelling in rich hair,
Awakes beneath his magic whisks and twirls.
His art can take the eyes from out my head,
Until I see with eyes of other men;
While deeper knowledge crouches in its den,
And sends a spark up: – is it true we are wed?
Yea! filthiness of body is most vile,
But faithlessness of heart I do hold worse.
The former, it were not so great a curse
To read on the steel mirror of her smile.

8

Yet it was plain she struggled, and that salt
Of righteous feeling made her pitiful.
Poor twisting worm, so queenly beautiful!
Where came the cleft between us? whose the fault?
My tears are on thee, that have rarely dropped
As balm for any bitter wound of mine:
My breast will open for thee at a sign!
But, no: we are two reed pipes, coarsely stopped:
The God once filled them with his mellow breath;
And they were music till he flung them down,
Used! used! Hear now the discord-loving clown
Puff his gross spirit in them, worse than death!
I do not know myself without thee more:
In this unholy battle I grow base;
If the same soul be under the same face,
Speak, and a taste of that old time restore!

17

At dinner she is hostess, I am host.
Was the feast ever cheerfuller? She keeps
The Topic over intellectual deeps
In buoyancy afloat. They see no ghost.
With sparkling surface eyes we play the ball:
It is in truth a most contagious game:
Hiding The Skeleton shall be its name.
Such play as this the devils might appal!
But here's the greater wonder; in that we
Enamoured of an acting none can tire,
Each other like true hypocrites admire;
Warm-lighted looks, Love's ephemerioe,
Shoot gaily o'er the dishes and the wine.
We waken envy at our happy lot.
Fast, sweet and golden, shows the marriage knot.
Dear guests, you now have seen Love's corpse-light shine.

34

Madam would speak with me. So, now it comes.
The Deluge or else fire! She's well; she thanks
My husbandship. Our chain on silence clanks.
Time leers between, above his twiddling thumbs.
Am I quite well? Most excellent in health!
The journals too I diligently peruse.
Vesuvius is expected to give news:
Niagara is no noisier. By stealth
Our eyes dart scrutinizing snakes. She's glad
I'm happy, says her quivering upper-lip.
'And are not you?' 'How could I be?' 'Take ship!
For happiness is somewhere to be had.'
'Nowhere for me!' Her voice is barely heard.
I am not melted, and make no pretence.
With commonplace I freeze her tongue and sense.
Niagara or Vesuvius is deferred.

39

She yields: my Lady in her noblest mood
Has yielded: she, my golden-crowned rose!
The bride of every sense! more sweet than those
Who breathe the violet breath of maidenhood.
O visage of still music in the sky!
Soft moon! I feel thy song, my fairest friend!
True harmony within can apprehend
Dumb harmony without. And hark! 'tis nigh!
Belief has struck the note of sound: a gleam
Of living silver shows me where she shook
Her long white fingers down the shadowy brook,
That sings her song, half waking, half in dream.
What two come here to mar this heavenly tune?
A man is one: the woman bears my name,
And honour. Their hands touch! Am I still tame?
God, what a dancing spectre seems the moon!

40

I bade my Lady think what she might mean.
Know I my meaning, I? Can I love one,
And yet be jealous of another? None
Commits such folly. Terrible Love, I ween,
Has might, even dead, half sighing to upheave
The lightless seas of selfishness amain:
Seas that in a man's heart have no rain
To fall and still them. Peace can I achieve,
By turning to this fountain-source of woe,
This woman, who's to Love as fire to wood?
She breathed the violet breath of maidenhood
Against my kisses once! but I say, No!
The thing is mocked at! Helplessly afloat,
I know not what to do, whereto I strive,
The dread that my old love may be alive,
Has seized my nursling new love by the throat.

45

It is the season of the sweet wild rose,
My Lady's emblem in the heart of me!
So golden-crowned shines she gloriously,
And with that softest dream of blood she glows:
Mild as an evening heaven round Hesper bright!
I pluck the flower, and smell it, and revive
The time when in her eyes I stood alive.
I seem to look upon it out of Night.
Here's Madam, stepping hastily. Her whims
Bid her demand the flower, which I let drop.
As I proceed, I feel her sharply stop,
And crush it under heel with trembling limbs.
She joins me in a cat-like way, and talks
Of company, and even condescends
To utter laughing scandal of old friends.
These are our summer days, and these our walks.

48

Their sense is with their senses all mixed in,
Destroyed by subtleties these women are!
More brain, O Lord, more brain! or we shall mar
Utterly this fair garden we might win.
Behold, I looked for peace, and thought it near.
Our inmost hearts had opened, each to each.
We drank the pure daylight of honest speech.
Alas, that was the fatal draught, I fear.
For when of my lost Lady came the word,
This woman, O this agony of flesh!
Jealous devotion made her break the mesh,
That I might seek this other like a bird.
I do adore the nobleness! despise
The act! She has gone forth, I know not where.
Will the hard world my sentience of her share?
I feet the truth; so let the world surmise.

49

He found her by the ocean's moaning verge,
Nor any wicked change in her discerned;
And she believed his old love had returned,
Which was her exultation and her scourge.
She took his hand, and walked with him, and seemed
The wife he sought, though shadow-like and dry.
She had one terror, lest her heart should sigh,
And tell her loudly she no longer dreamed.
She dared not say, 'This is my breast: look in.'
But there's a strength to help the desperate weak.
That night he learnt how silence best can speak,
The awful things when Pity pleads for Sin.
About the middle of the night her call
Was heard, and he came wondering to the bed.
'Now kiss me, dear! it may be, now!' she said.
Lethe had passed those lips and she knew all.

50

Thus piteously Love closed what he begat:
The union of this ever diverse pair!
These two were rapid falcons in a snare,
Condemned to do the flitting of the bat.
Lovers beneath the shining sky of May,
They wandered once; clear as the dew on flowers;
But they fed not on the advancing hours
Their hearts held craving for the buried day.
Then each applied to each that fatal knife
Deep questioning, which probes to endless dole.
Ah, what a dusty answer gets the soul
When hot for certainties in this our life! –
In tragic hints here see what evermore,
Moves as yonder midnight ocean's force,
Thundering like ramping hosts of warrior horse,
To throw that faint thin line upon the shore!

GEORGE MEREDITH (1862)

This sequence is inspired by Meredith's own unhappy marriage, though his wife died a natural death unlike the 'Madam' of *Modern Love,* whom the poet makes commit suicide by poison (the meaning of 'drinking Lethe', the river of Hades in the Classical Underworld which the dead drank to forget their former lives). The 'Lady' is the mistress of the speaker in the poem. 'Ephemerioe', Sonnet 17, is Greek for 'creatures that last a day'.

I Cannot Live with You

I cannot live with you
It would be life
And life is over there
Behind the shelf

The sexton keeps the key to,
Putting up
Our life, his porcelain,
Like a cup

Discarded of the housewife,
Quaint, or broken
A newer Sevres pleases,
Old ones crack.

I could not die, with you,
For one must wait
To shut the other's gaze down, –
You could not,

And I, could I stand by
And see you freeze
Without my right of frost,
Death's privilege?

Nor could I rise with you,
Because your face
Would put out Jesus',
That new Grace

Grow plain and foreign
On my homesick eye –
Except that you than He
Shone closer by.

They'd judge us – how?
For you served Heaven, you know –
Or sought to:
I could not,

Because you saturated sight,
And I had no more eyes
For sordid excellence
As Paradise

And were you lost, I would be,
Though my name
Rang loudest
On the heavenly fame.

And were you saved,
And I condemned to be
Where you were not
That self were Hell to me

So we must meet apart
You there, I here,
With just the door ajar
That oceans are
And prayer
And that white sustenance,
Despair!

EMILY DICKINSON (*c.* 1862)

The Moon is Distant from the Sea

The moon is distant from the sea,
And yet, with amber hands
She leads him, docile as a boy,
Along appointed sands.

He never misses a degree;
Obedient to her eye
He comes just so far toward the town:
Just so far goes away.

O, Signor, thine, the amber hand
And mine the distant sea, –
Obedient to the least command
Thine eye impose on me.

EMILY DICKINSON (*c.* 1862)

Neutral Tones

We stood by a pond that winter day,
And the sun was white, as though chidden of God,
And a few leaves lay on the starving sod:
   They had fallen from an ash and were gray.

Your eyes on me were as eyes that rove
Over tedious riddles of years ago;
And some words played between us, to and fro,
   On which lost the more by our love.

The smile on your face was the deadest thing
Alive enough to have strength to die;
And a grin of bitterness swept thereby
   Like an ominous bird a-wing . . .

Since then, keen lessons that love deceives,
And wrings with wrong, have shaped to me
Your face, and the God-curst sun, and a tree,
   And a pond edged with grayish leaves.

THOMAS HARDY (1867)

Insomnia

Thin are the night-skirts left behind
　　By daybreak hours that onward creep,
　　And thin, alas! the shred of sleep
That wavers with the spirit's wind:
But in half-dreams that shift and roll
　　And still remember and forget,
My soul this hour has drawn your soul
　　　A litttle nearer yet.

Our lives, most dear, are never near,
　　Our thoughts are never far apart,
　　Though all that draws us heart to heart
Seems fainter now, and now more clear.
Tonight Love claims his full control,
　　And with desire and with regret
My soul, this hour has drawn your soul
　　　A little nearer yet.

Is there a home where heavy earth
　　Melts to bright air that knows no pain,
　　Where water leaves no thirst again
And springing fire is Love's new birth?
If faith long bound to one true goal
　　May there at length its hope beget,
My soul that hour shall draw your soul
　　　For ever nearer yet.

DANTE GABRIEL ROSSETTI (Published 1870)

A Prayer

Since that I may not have
Love on this side the grave,
    Let me imagine Love.
Since not mine is the bliss
Of 'claspt hands and lips that kiss',
    Let me in dreams it prove.
What tho' as the years roll
No soul shall melt to my soul,
    Let me conceive such thing:
Tho' never shall entwine
Loving arms round mine
    Let dreams caresses bring.
To live – it is my doom –
Lonely, as in a tomb,
    This cross on me was laid;
My God, I know not why;
Here in the dark I lie,
    Lonely, yet not afraid.

AMY LEVY (1881)

At a Dinner Party

With fruit and flowers the board is deckt,
    The wine and laughter flow;
I'll not complain – could one expect
    So dull a world to know?

You look across the fruit and flowers,
    My glance your glances find. –
It is our secret, only ours,
    Since all the world is blind.

AMY LEVY (1889)

The Two Trees

Beloved, gaze in thine own heart,
The holy tree is growing there,
From joy the holy branches start,
And all the trembling flowers they bear.
The changing colours of its fruit
Have dowered the stars with merry light;
The surety of its hidden root
Has planted quiet in the night;
The shaking of its leafy head
Has given the waves their melody,
And made my lips and music wed,
Murmuring a wizard song for thee;
There the Loves a circle go,
The flaming circle of our days,
Gyring, spiring to and fro
In those great ignorant leafy ways;
Remembering all that shaken hair
And how the winged sandals dart,
Thine eyes grow full of tender care:
Beloved, gaze in thine own heart.

Gaze no more in the bitter glass
The demons with their subtle guile
Lift up before us when they pass
Or only gaze a little while;
For there a fatal image grows
That the stormy night receives,
Roots half-hidden under snows,
Broken boughs and blackened leaves.
For all things turn to bitterness
In that dim glass the demons hold,
The glass of outer weariness
Made when God slept in times of old.
There, through the broken branches go
The ravens of unresting thought;
Flying, crying, to and fro,
Cruel claw and hungry throat,

Or else they stand and sniff the wind,
And shake their ragged wings, alas!
Thy tender eyes grow all unkind:
Gaze no more in the bitter glass.

WILLIAM BUTLER YEATS (1893)

This poem contains the first appearance of images that were to be very important in Yeats's later, far greater poetry. These poems are inspired by his turbulent relationship with the fervently nationalistic beauty Maud Gonne, whom he met in 1889, and who was his *femme fatale* and inspiration for the rest of his life. Below he compares her impact to that of Helen of Troy, and in the second poem expresses his anguish at her rejection of him for the future Easter Rising hero John MacBride.

The Sorrow of Love

The brawling of a sparrow in the eaves,
The brilliant moon, and all the milky sky,
And all that famous harmony of leaves
Had blotted out man's image and his cry.

A girl arose, that had red mournful lips
And seemed the image of the world in tears,
Doomed like Odysseus and the labouring ships
And proud as Priam, murdered with his peers,

Arose, and on the instant, clamorous eves,
A climbing moon, upon an empty sky,
And all that lamentation of the leaves,
Could but compose man's image and his cry.

WILLIAM BUTLER YEATS (1893)

He Thinks of his Past Greatness
when a Part of the
Constellations of Heaven

I have drunk ale from the Country of the Young
And weep because I know all things now;
I have been a hazel-tree and they hung
The Pilot Star and the Crooked Plough
Among my leaves, in time out of mind:
I became a rush, that horses tread:
I became a man, a hater of the wind,
Knowing one, out of all things alone, that his head,
May not lie on the breast, nor his lips on the hair
Of the woman that he loves, until he dies.
O beast of the wilderness, bird of the air,
Must I endure your amorous cries?

WILLIAM BUTLER YEATS (1899)

10
WARS
ANCIENT &
MODERN

The Destruction of Sennacherib

The Assyrian came down like a wolf on the fold,
And his cohorts were gleaming in purple and gold,
And the sheen of their spears was like stars on the sea
When the blue waves rolls nightly on deep Galilee

Like the leaves of the forest, when Summer is green,
That host with their banners at sunset was seen:
Like the leaves of the forest when Autumn hath blown,
That host on the morrow lay withered and strown

For the Angel of Death spread his wings on the blast,
And breathed in the face of the foe as he passed.;
And the eyes of the sleepers wax'd deadly and chill,
And their hearts but once heav'd and for ever grew still!

And there lay the steed, with his nostril all wide,
But through it there rolled not thee breath of his pride;
And the foam of his gasping lay white on the turf,
And cold as the spray of the rock beating surf.

And there lay the rider, distorted and pale,
With the dew on his brow, and the rust on his mail:
And the tents were all silent, the banners alone,
The lances unlifted, the trumpet unblown.

And the widows of Ashur are loud in their wail,
And the idols are broke in the temples of Baal;
And the might of the Gentile, unsmote by the sword,
Hath melted like snow in the glance of the Lord.

GEORGE GORDON, LORD BYRON (1815)

Sennacherib was a king of Assyria who led an ill-fated attack on Jerusalem in the seventh century BC. The poem, with its stirring rhythms, expresses Byron's feelings about all powerful tyrannies that oppress small nations.

Hohenlinden

On Linden when the sun was low,
All bloodless lay the untrodden snow
And dark as winter was the flow
    Of Iser, rolling rapidly.

But Linden saw another sight,
When the drum beat at dead of night
Commanding fires of death to light
    The darkness of her scenery

By torch and trumpet fast arrayed
Each horseman drew his battle blade
And furious every charger neighed
    To join the dreadful revelry.

Then shook the hills with thunder riven
Then rushed the steed to battle driven
And louder than the bolts of heaven
    Far flashed the red artillery.

But redder yet that light shall glow
On Linden's hills of stained snow;
And bloodier yet the torrent flow
    Of Iser rolling rapidly.

Tis morn, but scarce yon level sun
Can pierce the war-clouds, rolling dun
Where furious Frank and fiery Hun
    Shout in their sulphurous canopy.

The combat deepens. On ye brave
Who rush to glory, or the grave!
Wave, Munich, all thy banners wave,
    And charge with all thy chivalry!

Few, few shall part, where many meet
The snow shall be their winding sheet
And every turf beneath their feet
    Shall be a soldier's sepulchre.

THOMAS CAMPBELL

from *Childe Harold's Pilgrimage*

17

Stop, for thy tread is on an Empire's dust!
An Earthquake's spoil is sepulchred below!
Is the spot marked with no colossal bust?
Nor column trophied for triumphal show?
None; but the moral's truth tells simpler so,
As the ground was before, thus let it be; –
How that red rain hath made the harvest grow!
And is this all the world has gained by thee,
Thou first and last of fields! king-making Victory?

18

And Harold stands upon this place of skulls,
The grave of France, the deadly Waterloo!
How in an hour the power which gave annuls
Its gifts, transferring fame as fleeting too!
In 'pride of place' here last the eagle flew,
Then tore with bloody talon the rent plain,
Pierced by the shaft of banded nations through;
Ambition, life and labours all were vain;
He wears the shatter'd links of the worlds broken chain.

19

Fit retribution! Gaul may champ the bit
And foam in fetters; – but is earth more free?
Did nations combat to make *One* submit;
Or league to teach all kings true sovereignty?
What, shall reviving Thraldom again be
The patch'd up idol of enlighten'd days?
Shall we, who struck the Lion down, shall we
Pay the Wolf homage? proffering lowly gaze
And servile knees to thrones? No; prove before ye praise!

20

If not, o'er one fall'n despot boast no more!
In vain fair cheeks were furrow'd with hot tears

For Europe's flowers long rooted up before
The trampler of her vineyards; in vain years
Of death, depopulation, bondage, fears,
Have all been borne, and broken by the accord
Of roused up millions; all that most endears
Glory, is when the myrtle wreathes a sword
Such as Harmodius drew on Athens' tyrant lord.

21

There was a sound of revelry by night,
And Belgium's capital had gathered then
Her beauty and her Chivalry, and bright
The lamps shone o'er fair women and brave men;
A thousand hearts beat happily, and when
Music arose with its voluptuous swell,
Soft eyes look'd love to eyes which spake again,
And all went merry as a marriage bell;
But hush! hark! a deep sound strikes like a rising knell!

22

Did ye not hear it? — No, 'twas but the wind,
Or the car rattling o'er the stony street;
On with the dance! let joy be unconfined;
No sleep till morn when Youth and Pleasure meet
To chase the glowing Hours with flying feet —
But hark — that heavy sound breaks in once more,
As if the clouds its echo would repeat;
And nearer, clearer, deadlier than before!
Arm! Arm! it is — it is the cannon's opening roar!

23

Within a window'd niche of that high hall
Sate Brunswick's fated chieftain; he did hear
That sound the first amidst the festival,
And caught its tone with Death's prophetic ear;
And when they smiled because he deem'd it near,
His heart more truly knew that peal too well
Which stretche'd his father on a bloody bier,
And roused the vengeance blood alone could quell;
He rush'd into the field, and, foremost fighting, fell.

24

Ah! then and there was hurrying to and fro,
And gathering tears, and tremblings of distress,
And cheeks all pale, which but an hour ago,
Blush'd at the praise of their own loveliness;
And there were sudden partings, such as press
The life from out young hearts, and choking sighs
Which ne'er might be repeated; who could guess
If ever more should meet those mutual eyes,
Since upon night so sweet such awful morn could rise!

25

And there was mounting in hot haste: the steed,
The mustering squadron, and the clattering car,
Went pouring forward with impetuous speed,
And swiftly forming in the ranks of war;
And the deep thunder peal on peal afar;
And near, the beat of the alarming drum
Roused up the soldier ere the morning star;
While throng'd the citizens with terror dumb,
Or whispering, with white lips – 'The foe! they come!
    they come!'

26

And wild and high the 'Camerons gathering' rose!
The war-note of Lochiel, which Albyn's hills
Have heard, and heard, too, have her Saxon foes: –
How in the noon of night that pibroch thrills,
Savage and shrill! But with the breath which fills
Their mountain-pipe, so fill the mountaineers
With the fierce native daring which instils
The stirring memory of a thousand years,
And Evan's, Donald's fame rings in each clansman's ears!

27

And Ardennes waves above them her green leaves,
Dewy with nature's tear-drops as they pass,
Grieving, if aught inanimate e'er grieves,
Over the unreturning brave, – alas!

Ere evening to be trodden like the grass
Which now beneath them, but above shall grow
In its next verdure, when this fiery mass
Of living valour, rolling on the foe
And burning with high hope shall moulder cold and low.

28

Last noon beheld them full of lusty life,
Last eve in Beauty's circle proudly gay,
The midnight brought the signal-sound of strife,
The morn the marshalling in arms, – the day
Battle's magnificently stern array!
The thunder-clouds close o'er it, which when rent
The earth is cover'd thick with other clay,
Which her own clay shall cover, heap'd and pent,
Rider and horse – friend, foe, – in one red burial blent.

GEORGE GORDON, LORD BYRON (1816)

The Burial of Sir John Moore at Corunna

Not a drum was heard, not a funeral note,
    As his corse to the rampart we hurried;
Not a soldier discharged his farewell shot
    O'er the grave where our hero was buried.

We buried him darkly at dead of night,
    The sods with our bayonets turning;
By the struggling moonbeam's misty light
    And the lantern dimly burning.

No useless coffin enclosed his breast,
    Not in sheet or in shroud we wound him;
But he lay like a warrior taking his rest,
    With his martial cloak around him.

Few and short were the prayers we said,
    And we spoke not a word of sorrow;
But we steadfastly gazed on the face that was dead,
    And we bitterly thought of the morrow.

We thought, as we hollow'd his narrow bed
    And smoothed down his lonely pillow,
That the foe and the stranger would tread o'er his head,
    And we far away on the billow!

Lightly they'll talk of the spirit that's gone
    And o'er his cold ashes upbraid him, –
But little he'll reck, if they let him sleep on
    In the grave where a Briton has laid him.

But half of our heavy task was done
    When the clock struck the hour for retiring
And we heard the distant and random gun
    That the foe was sullenly firing.

Slowly and sadly we laid him down,
    From the field of his fame fresh and gory;
We carved not a line and we raised not a stone,
    But we left him alone with his glory.

CHARLES WOLFE (1817)

Casabianca

The boy stood on the burning deck
    Whence all but he had fled.
The flame that lit the battle's wreck
    Shone round him o'er the dead.

Yet beautiful and bright he stood,
    As born to rule the storm;
A creature of heroic blood,
    A proud, though childlike form

The flames rolled on – he would not go
    Without his father's word;
That father, faint in death below,
    His voice no longer heard.

He called aloud: – 'Say, father, say
   If yet my task is done?'
He knew not that the chieftain lay
   Unconscious of his son.

'Speak, Father!' once again he cried,
   'If I may yet be gone!'
And yet the booming shots replied,
   And fast the flames roll'd on.

Upon his brow he felt their breath,
   And in his waving hair,
And look'd from that lone post of death
   In still, yet brave, despair.

And shouted but once more aloud,
   'My Father, must I stay?'
While o'er him fast, through sail and shroud,
   The wreathing fires made way.

They wrapped the ship in splendour wild,
   They caught the flag on high,
And stream'd above the gallant child,
   Like banners in the sky.

There came a burst of thunder sound –
   The boy, oh! where was he?
Ask of the winds that far around
   With fragments strew the sea! –

With mast, and helm, and pennon fair,
   That well had borne their part,
But the noblest thing that perished there
   Was that young faithful heart!

FELICIA HEMANS (1829)

A Waterloo Ballad

To Waterloo, with sad ado,
    And many a sigh and groan,
Amongst the dead came Patty Head
    To look for Peter Stone.

'O prithee tell, good sentinel,
    If I shall find him here?
I've come to weep upon his corse,
    My Ninety-Second dear!

'Into our town a serjeant came,
    With ribands all so fine
A flaunting in his cap – alas!
    His bow enlisted mine!

'They taught him how to turn his toes,
    And stand as stiff as starch;
I thought that it was love in May,
    But it was love in March!

'A sorry March indeed to leave
    The friends he might have kep', –
No March of intellect it was,
    But quite a foolish step.

'O prithee tell, good sentinel,
    If hereabouts he lies?
I want a corpse with reddish hair,
    And very sweet blue eyes.'

Her sorrow on the sentinel
    Appear'd to deeply strike:
'Walk in,' he said, 'among the dead,
    And pick out which you like.'

And soon she picked out Peter Stone,
    Half turned into a corse;
A cannon was his bolster, and
    His mattress was a horse.

'O Peter Stone, O Peter Stone,
   Lord, here has been a skrimmage!
What have they done to your poor breast,
   That used to hold my image?'

'O Patty Head, O Patty Head,
   Your come to my last kissing;
Before I'm set in the Gazette
   As wounded, dead, and missing.

'Alas, a splinter of a shell
   Right in my stomach sticks;
French mortars don't agree so well
   With stomachs as French bricks.

'This very night a merry dance
   At Brussels was to be; –
Instead of opening a ball,
   A ball has opened me.

'Its billet every bullet has,
   And well does it fulfil it; –
I wish mine hadn't come so straight,
   But been a "crooked billet".

'And then there came a cuirassier
   And cut me on the chest; –
He had no pity in his heart,
   For he had *steel'd his breast*.

'Next thing a lancer, with his lance
   Began to thrust away;
I called for quarter, but, alas!
   It was not Quarter day.

'He ran his spear right through my arm,
   Just here above the joint: –
O Patty dear, it was no joke,
   Although it had a point.

'With loss of blood I fainted off
   As dead as women do –
But soon, by charging over me,
   The Coldstreams brought me to.

'With kicks and cuts, and balls and blows,
    I throb and ache all over;
I'm quite convinced the field of Mars
    Is not a field of clover!

'O why did I a soldier turn,
    For any royal Guelph?
I might have been a butcher and
    In business for myself!

'O why did I the bounty take?
    (And here he gasped for breath)
My shillingworth of 'list is nail'd
    Upon the door of death.

'Without a coffin I shall lie,
    And sleep my sleep eternal:
Not even a *shell* – my only chance
    Ofbeing made a *Kernel*.

'O Patty dear, our wedding bells
    Will never ring at Chester!
Here I must lie in Honour's bed,
    That isn't worth a *tester!*

'Farewell my regimental mates,
    With whom I used to dress!
My corps is changed, so I am now,
    In quite another mess .

'Farewell, my Patty dear, I have
    No dying consolations,
Except, when I am dead, you'll go
    And see th'illuminations.'

THOMAS HOOD (1839)

from Amours de Voyage

V – CLAUDE TO EUSTACE

Yes, we are fighting at last, it appears. This morning, as
    usual.
Murray, as usual in hand, I enter the Caffè Nuovo;
Seating myself with a sense as it were of a change in the
    weather,
Not understanding, however, but thinking mostly of Murray,
And, for today is their day, of the Campidoglio Marbles;
Caffè-latte! – I call to the waiter, – and *Non c'e latte,*
This is the answer he makes me, and this is the sign of a
    battle.
So I sit; and truly they seem to think anyone else more
Worthy than me of attention. I wait for my milkless *nero*,
Free to observe undistracted all sorts and sizes of persons,
Blending civilian and soldier on strangest costume, coming
    in and
Gulping in hottest haste, still standing, their coffee, –
    withdrawing
Eagerly, jangling a sword on the steps, or jogging a musket
Slung to the shoulder behind. They are fewer, moreover, than
    usual,
Much, and silenter far; and so I begin to imagine
Something is really afloat. Ere I leave, the Caffè is empty,
Empty, too, the streets, in all its length the Corso
Empty, and empty I see to my right and left the Condotti.

Twelve o'clock, on the Pincian Hill, with lots of English,
Germans, Americans, French, – the Frenchmen, too, are
    protected, –
So we stand in the sun, but afraid of a probable shower;
So we stand and stare, and see, to the left of St Peter's,
Smoke, from the cannon, white, – but that is at intervals
    only, –
Black, from a burning house, we suppose by the
    Cavelleggieri;
And we believe we discern some lines of men descending

Down through the vineyard slopes, and catch a bayonet
    gleaming.
Every ten minutes, however, – in this there is no
    misconception, –
Comes a great white puff of smoke from behind Michael
    Angelo's dome, and
After a space the report of a real big gun, – not the
    Frenchman's! –
That must be doing some work. And so we watch and
    conjecture.
Shortly an Englishman comes, who says he's been to St
    Peter's,
Seen the Piazza and troops, but that is all he can tell us;
So we watch and sit, and, indeed, it begins to be tiresome. –
All this smoke is outside; when it has come to the inside,
It will be time, perhaps, to descend and retreat to our houses.

    Half past one, or two. The report of small arms frequent,
Sharp and savage indeed; that cannot all be for nothing:
So we watch and wonder; but guessing is tiresome, very.
Weary of wondering, watching and guessing, and gossiping
    idly,
Down I go, and pass through the quiet streets with the
    knots of
National Guards patrolling, and flags hanging out at the
    windows,
English, American, Danish, – and after offering to help an
Irish family moving *en masse* to the Maison Serny,
After endeavouring idly to minister balm to the trembling
Quinquagenarian fears of two lone British spinsters,
Go to make sure of my dinner before the enemy enter.
But by this there were signs of stragglers returning; and voices
Talk, though you don't believe it, of guns and prisoners taken;
And on the walls you read the first bulletin of the morning. –
This is all that I saw and all I know of the battle.

ARTHUR HUGH CLOUGH (1849)

(CANTO II, Lines 97–146)

The Roman Republic was only briefly victorious, and was later
overwhelmed by the French troops.

The Charge of the Light Brigade

Half a league, half a league
  Half a league onward,
All in the valley of Death
  Rode the six hundred.
'Charge,' was the captain's cry;
Theirs not to reason why,
Theirs not to make reply,
Theirs but to do and die,
Into the valley of Death
  Rode the six hundred.

Cannon to right of them
Cannon to left of them,
Cannon in front of them,
  Volley'd and thunder'd;
Stormed at with shot and shell,
Boldly they rode and well;
Into the jaws of Death,
Into the mouth of Hell,
  Rode the six hundred.

Flash'd all their sabres bare,
Flash'd all at once in air,
Sabring the gunners there,
Charging an army, while
  All the world wonder'd;
Plung'd in the battery-smoke
Fiercely the line they broke;
Strong was the sabre-stroke;
Making an army reel
  Shaken and sunder'd.
Then they rode back, but not,
  Not the six hundred.

Cannon to right of them,
Cannon to left of them,
Cannon behind them

Volley'd and thunder'd;
Stormed at with shot and shell,
They that had struck so well
Rode through the jaws of Death,
Half a league back again,
Up from the mouth of Hell,
All that was left of them,
    Left of six hundred.
Honour the brave and bold!
Long shall the tale be told,
Yea, when the babes are old –
    How they rode onward.

ALFRED, LORD TENNYSON (1855)

Couplet

'Come, cheer up my lads, 'tis to glory we steer' –
As the soldier remarked whose post lay in the rear.

CHRISTINA ROSSETTI

Battle Hymn of the Republic

Mine eyes have seen the glory of the coming of the Lord:
He is trampling out the vineyard where the grapes of wrath are
    stored
He hath loosed the fateful lightning of his terrible swift sword:
           His truth is marching on.

I have seen Him in the watchfires of a hundred circling camps;
They have builded Him an altar in the evening dews and damps;
I can read his righteous sentence by the dim and flaring lamps.
           His day is marching on.

I have read a fiery gospel built in burnished rows of steel:
'As ye deal with my contemners, so with you my grace shall deal;
Let the Hero, born of woman, crush the serpent with his heel,
           Since God is marching on.'

He has sounded forth the trumpet that shall never call retreat;
He is sifting out the hearts of men before his judgement seat:
'Oh! be swift, my soul, to answer Him! be jubilant, my feet!
           Our God is marching on.

In the beauty of the lilies Christ was born across the sea,
With a glory in his bosom that transfigures you and me:
As he died to make men holy, let us die to make men free,
           While God is marching on.

JULIA WARD HOWE (1861)

The marching song of Union troops in the American Civil War,
which is the subject of the next two poems. It was written to be
sung to the tune of 'John Brown's Body'.

When I was Small a Woman Died

When I was small a woman died
Today her only boy
Went up from the Potomac
His face all victory

To look at her. How slowly
The seasons must have turned
Till bullets clipt an angle
And he passed quickly round!

If pride shall be in Paradise,
Ourself cannot decide;
Of their imperial conduct
No person testified,

But, proud in apparition,
That woman and her boy
Pass back and forth, before my brain
As even in the sky.

I'm confident that bravoes
Perpetual break abroad
For braveries, remote as this
In scarlet Maryland.

EMILY DICKINSON (*c.* 1862)

The Wound Dresser

1

An old man bending I come among new faces,
Years looking backward resuming in answer to children,
Come tell us old man, as from young men and maidens that
    love me,
(Arous'd and angry, I'd thought to beat the alarum, and urge
    relentless war,
But soon my fingers fail'd me, my face droop'd and I
    resign'd myself

To sit by the wounded and soothe them, or silently watch
    the dead;)
Years hence of these scenes, of these furious passions, these
    chances,
Of unsurpass'd heroes, (was one side brave? the other was
    equally brave;)
Now be witness again, paint the mightiest armies of earth,
Of those armies so rapid so wondrous what saw you to tell
    us?
What stays with you latest and deepest? of curious panics
Of hard-fought engagements or sieges tremendous what
    deepest remains?

2

O maidens and young men I love and that love me,
What you ask of my days those the strangest and sudden
    your talking recalls,
Soldier alert I arrive after a long march cover'd with sweat
    and dust,
In the nick of time I come, plunge in the fight, loudly shout
    in the rush of successful charge
Enter the captur'd works — yet lo, like a swif running river
    they fade,
Pass and are gone, they fade — I dwell not on soldiers' perils
    or soldiers' joys,
(Both I remember well — many the hardships, few the joys,
    yet I was content.)

But in silence in dreams' projections,
While the world of gain and appearance and mirth goes on,
So soon what is over forgotten, and waves wash the imprints
    off the sand,
With hinged knees returning I enter the doors (while for
    you up there,
Whoever you are, follow without noise and be of strong
    heart.)

Bearing the bandages, water and sponge,
Straight and swift to my wounded I go,
Where they lie on the ground after the battle brought in,
Where their priceless blood reddens the grass the ground,

Or to the rows of the hospital tent, or under the roof'd
  hospital,
To the long rows of cots up and down each side I return,
To each and all one after another I draw near, not one do
  I miss.

An attendant follows holding a tray, he carries a refuse pail,
Soon to be filled with clotted rags and blood, emptied and
  filled again.

I onward go, I stop
With hinged knees and steady hands to dress wounds,
I am firm with each, the pangs are sharp yet unavoidable;
One turns to me his appealing eyes – poor boy! I never
  knew you,
Yet I think I could not refuse this moment to die for you,
  if that would save you.

3

On, on I go (open doors of time! open hospital doors!)
The crush'd head I dress, (poor crazed hand tear not the
  bandage away,)
The neck of the cavalryman with the bullet through and
  through I examine,
Hard the breathing rattles, quite glazed already the eye, yet
  life struggles hard,
(Come sweet death! be persuaded O beautiful death!
In mercy come quickly.)

From the stump of the arm, the amputated hand,
I undo the clotted lint, remove the slough, wash off the
  matter and blood,
Back on his pillow the soldier bends with curv'd neck and
  side-falling head,
His eyes are clos'd, his face is pale, he dares not look on the
  bloody stump,
And has not yet looked on it.

I dress a wound in the side, deep, deep,
But a day or two more, for see the frame all wasted and
  sinking,
And the yellow blue countenance see.

I dress the perforated shoulder, the foot with the bullet
    wound,
Cleanse the one with a gnawing and putrid gangrene, so
    sickening, so offensive,
While the attendant stands behind aside me holding the
    tray and pail.

I am faithful, I do not give out,
The fractur'd thigh, the knee, the wound in the abdomen,
These and more I dress with impassive hand, (yet deep in
    my breast a fire, a burning flame.)

4

Thus in silence, in dream's projections,
Returning, returning, I thread my way through the hospitals,
The hurt and the wounded I pacify with soothing hand,
I sit by the restless all the dark night, some are so young,
Some suffer so much, I recall the experience sweet and sad,
(Many a soldier's loving arms about this neck have crossed
    and rested.
Many a soldier's kiss dwells on these bearded lips.)

WALT WHITMAN (1865)

The Revenge

A Ballad of the Fleet

1

At Flores in the Azores Sir Richard Grenville lay
And a pinnace, like a fluttered bird, came flying from far
    away:
'Spanish ships of war at sea! we have sighted fifty-three!'
Then sware Lord Thomas Howard: 'Fore God I am no
    coward;
But I cannot meet them here, for my ships are out of gear,
And the half my men are sick. I must fly, but follow quick.
We are six ships of the line; can we fight with fifty-three?'

2

Then spake Sir Richard Grenville: 'I know you are no
  coward;
You fly them for a moment to fight with them again.
But I've ninety men and more that are lying sick ashore.
I should count myself the coward, if I left them, my Lord
  Howard,
To these Inquisition dogs and the devildoms of Spain.'

3

So Lord Howard past away with five ships of war that day,
Till he melted like a cloud in the silent summer heaven;
But Sir Richard bore in hand all his sick men from the land
Very carefully and slow,
Men of Bideford in Devon,
And we laid them on the ballast down below;
For we brought them all aboard,
And they blest him in their pain that they were not left to
  Spain,
To the thumbscrew and the stake, for the glory of the Lord.

4

He had only a hundred seamen to work the ship and fight,
And he sailed away from Flores till the Spaniard came in
  sight,
With his huge sea-castles heaving upon the weather bow.
'Shall we fight or shall we fly?
Good Sir Richard, tell us now,
For to fight is but to die!
There'll be little of us left by the time this sun has set.'
And Sir Richard said again: 'We be all good Christian men.
Let us bang these dogs of Seville, the children of the devil,
For I never turned my back upon Don or devil yet.'

5

Sir Richard spoke and he laugh'd, and we roared a hurrah,
  and so
The little *Revenge* ran on sheer into the heart of the foe,
With her hundred fighters on deck and her ninety sick
  below;

For half of their fleet to the right, and half to the left were
    seen,
And the little *Revenge* ran on thro' the long sea-lane
    between.

6

Thousands of their soldiers look'd down from their decks
    and laugh'd
Thousands of their seamen made mock at the mad little craft
Running on and on, till delay'd
By the mountain-like *San Philip* that, of fifteen hundred
    tons,
And up-shadowing high above us, with her yawning tiers of
    guns,
Took the breath from our sails, and we stay'd.

7

And while now the great *San Philip* hung above us like a
    cloud
Whence the thunderbolt will fall
Long and loud,
Four galleons drew away
From the Spanish fleet that day,
And two upon the larboard and two upon the starboard lay,
And the battle thunder broke from them all.

8

But anon the great *San Philip*, she bethought herself and
    went
Having that within her womb that had left her ill content;
And the rest they came aboard us, and fought us hand to
    hand,
For a dozen times they came, with their pikes and
    musqueteers,
And a dozen times we shook 'em off, as a dog that shakes
    his ears
When he leaps from the water to the land.

9

And the sun went down, and the stars came out, far over the
    summer sea,
But never a moment ceased the fight on the one and the
    fifty-three.
Ship after ship, the whole night long, their high-built
    galleons came,
Ship after ship, the whole night long, drew back with her
    dead and her shame.
For some were sunk and many were shatter'd, and so could
    fight no more –
God of battles, was ever a battle like this in the world
    before?

10

For he said 'Fight on! fight on!
Though his vessel was all but a wreck;
And it chanced that, when half of the short summer night
    was gone,
With a grisly wound to be drest he had left the deck,
But a bullet struck him that was dressing it suddenly dead,
And himself he was wounded again in the side and the
    head,
And he said 'Fight on! fight on!'

11

And the night went down, and the sun smiled out, far over
    the summer sea,
And the Spanish fleet with broken sides lay round us all in a
    ring;
But they dared not touch us again, for they feared that we
    still could sting,
So they watch'd what the end would be.
And we had not fought them in vain,
But in perilous plight were we,
Seeing forty of our poor hundred were slain,
And half of the rest of us maimed for life
In the crash of the cannonades and the desperate strife;
And the sick men in the hold were most of them stark and
    cold,

And the pikes were all broken or bent, and the powder was
    all of it spent;
And the masts and the rigging were lying over the side;
But Sir Richard cried in his English pride,
'We have fought such a fight for a day and a night
As may never be fought again!
We have won great glory, my men!
And a day or more
At sea or ashore,
We die – does it matter when?
Sink me the ship, Master Gunner – sink her, split her in
    twain!
Fall into the hands of God, not into the hands of Spain!

12

And the gunner said 'Ay, ay,' but the seamen made reply:
'We have children, we have wives,
And the Lord has spared our lives.
We will make the Spaniard promise, if we yield, to let us go;
We shall live to fight again and to strike another blow.'
And the lion lay there dying, and they yielded to the foe.

13

And the stately Spanish men to their flagship bore him then,
Where they laid him by the mast, old Sir Richard caught at
    last,
And they praised him to his face, with their courtly foreign
    grace;
But he rose upon their decks, and he cried:
'I have fought for Queen and Faith like a valiant man and
    true;
I have only done my duty as a man is bound to do:
With a joyful spirit I Sir Richard Grenville die!'
And he fell upon their decks and he died.

14

And they stared at the dead that had been so valiant and
    true,
And had holden the power and glory of Spain so cheap
That he dared her with one little ship and his English few;

Was he devil or man? He was devil for aught they knew,
But they sank his body with honour down into the deep,
And they manned the *Revenge* with a swarthier alien crew,

And away she sail'd with her loss, and long'd for her own;
When a wind from the lands they had ruin'd awoke from
    sleep,
And the water began to heave and the weather to moan,
And or ever that evening had ended a great gale blew,
And a wave like the wave that is raised by an earthquake
    grew,
Till it smote on their hulls and their sails and their masts and
    their flags,
And the whole sea plung'd and fell on the shot-shatter'd navy
    of Spain,
And the little *Revenge* herself went down by the island crags
To be lost evermore in the main.

ALFRED, LORD TENNYSON (Published 1888)

The lone battle of Sir Richard Grenville's ship against the Spanish
fleet in 1591 was one of the incidents in British naval history used to
inspire schoolboys to equivalent acts of heroism.

Gunga Din

You may talk o' gin and beer
When you're quartered safe out 'ere,
And you're sent to penny fights and aldershot it;
But when it comes to slaughter
You will do your work on water
And you'll lick the bloomin' boots of 'im that's got it.
Now in Injia's sunny clime,
Where I used to spend my time
A-serving of 'er Majesty the Queen,
Of all them black-faced crew
The finest man I knew
Was our regimental *bhisti*, Gunga Din;   [water-carrier]
    He was 'Din! Din! Din!

You limpin' lump o' brick dust, Gunga Din!
  Hi! Slippy *hitherao*!
Water, get it! *Panee lao*,   [fetch water]
You squidgy nosed old idol, Gunga Din.'

The uniform 'e wore
Was nothing much before,
And rather less than 'alf o' that be'ind,
For a piece o' twisty rag
And a goatskin water-bag
Was all the field equipment 'e could find.
When the sweating troop-train lay
In a sidin' through the day,
Where the 'eat would make your bloomin'
  eyebrows crawl,
   We shouted 'Harry By!'   [O brother]
Till our throats were bricky-dry,
Then we wopped 'im 'cause 'e couldn't serve us all.
   It was 'Din! Din! Din!
You 'eathen, where the mischief 'ave you been?
   You put some *juldee* in it   [haste]
   Or I'll *marrow* you this minute [beat]
If you don't fill up my helmet, Gunga Din!'

'E would dot an' carry one
Till the longest day was done;
And 'e didn't seem to know the use o' fear.
If we charged or broke or cut,
You could bet your bloomin' nut
'Ed be waiting fifty paces right flank rear.
   Wi' 'is *mussick* on 'is back, [water-skin]
'E would skip with our attack,
And watch us till the bugles made 'Retire,'
And for all 'is dirty 'ide
'E was white, clear white, inside
When 'e went to tend the wounded under fire!
   It was 'Din! Din! Din!'
With the bullets kicking dust spots on the green,
   When the cartridges ran out,
   You could hear the front-ranks shout,
'Hi, ammunition mules an' Gunga Din!'

I shan't forgit the night
When I dropped be'ind the fight
With a bullet where my belt-plate should 'a been.
I was chokin' mad with thirst,
An' the man that spied me first
Was our good old grinning grunting Gunga Din.
'E lifted up my 'ead,
An' 'e plugged me where I bled,
An' 'e guv me 'arf-a-pint o' water green.
It was crawlin' and it stunk,
But of all the drinks I've drunk,
I'm gratefullest to one from Gunga Din.
            It was 'Din! Din! Din!
Ere's a beggar with a bullet through 'is spleen;
            'E's chawin' up the ground,
            An' 'es kickin' all around:
'For Gawd's sake git the water Gunga Din!'

'E carried me away
To where a *dooli* lay,   [litter]
An' a bullet came and drilled the beggar clean.
'E put me safe inside,
'An just before 'e died,
'I 'ope you like your drink,' sez Gunga Din.
So I'll meet 'im later on
At the place where 'e is gone –
Where there's always double drill an' no canteen.
'E'll be squatting on the coals
Givin' drink to poor damned souls,
An, I'll get a swig in Hell from Gunga Din!
            Yes, Din! Din! Din!
You Lazarushian leather Gunga Din!
            Though I've belted you and flayed you,
            By the livin' Gawd that made you,
You're a better man than I am, Gunga Din!

RUDYARD KIPLING (Published 1892)

Vitaï Lampada

There's a breathless hush in the Close tonight –
    Ten to make and the match to win –
A bumping pitch and a blinding light,
    An hour to play and the last man in.
And it's not for the sake of a ribboned coat,
    Or the selfish hope of a season's fame,
But his Captain's hand on his shoulder smote –
    'Play up! play up! and play the game!'

The sand of the desert is sodden red, –
    Red with the wreck of a square that broke; –
And the Gatling's jammed and the Colonel dead,
    And the regiment blind with dust and smoke.
The river of death has brimmed his banks,
    And England's far, and Honour a name,
But the voice of a schoolboy rallies the ranks:
    'Play up! play up! and play the game!'

This is the word that year by year,
    While in her place the School is set,
Every one of her sons must hear,
    And none that hears it dare forget.
This they all with a joyful mind
    Bear through life like a torch in flame,
And falling fling to the host behind –
    'Play up! play up! and play the game!'

                              SIR HENRY NEWBOLT (1897)

11
THE WORLD OF
NONSENSE AND
PARODY

Jabberwocky

'Twas brillig and the slithy toves
    Did gyre and gimbol in the wabe;
All mimsy were the borogroves,
    And the mome raths outgrabe.

'Beware the Jabberwock, my son!
    The jaws that bite, the claws that catch!
Beware the Jubjub bird and shun
    The frumious Bandersnatch!'

He took his vorpal sword in hand,
    Long time the manxome foe he sought –
So rested he by the Tumtum tree,
    And stood awhile in thought.

And as in uffish thought he stood,
    The Jabberwock, with eyes of flame,
Came whiffling through the tulgey wood,
    And burbled as it came!

One, two! One! two! And through and through
    The vorpal blade went snicker-snack!
He left it dead, and with its head
    He went galumphing back.

'And hast thou slain the Jabberwock?
    Come to my arms, my beamish boy!
O frabjous day, Callo! Callay!'
    He chortled in his joy.

'Twas brillig and the slithy toves
    Did gyre and gimbol in the wabe;
All mimsy were the borogroves,
    And the mome raths outgrabe.

LEWIS CARROLL (Written 1855)

The Aged Aged Man

I'll tell thee everything I can:
    There's little to relate.
I saw an aged, aged man,
    A-sitting on a gate.
'Who are you, aged man?' I said,
    'And how is it you live?'
And his answer trickled through my head,
    Like water through a sieve.

He said 'I look for butterflies
    That sleep among the wheat:
I make them into mutton-pies
    And sell them in the street.
I sell them unto men,' he said
    'Who sail on stormy seas;
And that's the way I get my bread –
    A trifle, if you please.'

But I was thinking of a plan
    To dye one's whiskers green,
And always use so large a fan
    That they could not be seen.
So having no reply to give
    To what the old man said,
I cried 'Come, tell me how you live!'
    And thumped him on the head.

His accents mild took up the tale:
    He said 'I go my ways
And, when I find a mountain-rill,
    I set it in a blaze;
And thence they make a stuff they call
    Rowland's Macassar Oil –
Yet twopence-halfpenny is all
    They give me for my toil.'

But I was thinking of a way
    To feed oneself on batter,
And so go on from day to day

Getting a little fatter.
I shook him well from side to side,
    Until his face was blue:
'Come tell me how you live,' I cried
    'And what it is you do!'

He said 'I hunt for haddocks' eyes
    Among the heather bright,
And work them into waistcoat buttons
    In the silent night.
And these I do not sell for gold
    Or coin of silvery shine,
But for a copper halfpenny,
    And that will purchase nine.

'I sometimes dig for buttered rolls,
    Or set limed twigs for crabs;
I sometimes search the grassy knolls
    For wheels of Hansom-cabs.
And that's the way' (he gave a wink)
    'By which I get my wealth –
And very gladly will I drink
    Your Honour's noble health.'

I heard him then, for I had just
    Completed my design
To keep the Menai Bridge from rust
    By boiling it in wine.
I thanked him much for telling me
    The way he got his wealth,
But chiefly for his wish that he
    Might drink my noble health.

And now, if e'er by chance I put
    My fingers into glue,
Or madly squeeze a right hand foot
    Into a left hand shoe,
Or if I drop upon my toe
    A very heavy weight,
I weep, for it reminds me so
Of that old man I used to know –
Whose look was mild, whose speech was slow,

Whose hair was whiter than the snow,
Whose face was very like a crow,
With eyes like cinders, all aglow,
Who seemed distracted with his woe,
Who rocked his body to and fro,
And muttered mumblingly and low,
As if his mouth were full of dough,
Who snorted like a buffalo –
That summer evening long ago,
   A-sitting on a gate.

LEWIS CARROLL (Published 1871)

'The Aged Aged Man' is a parody of Wordsworth's *Resolution and Independence*, see Section 14.

The Dong with a Luminous Nose

When awful darkness and silence reign
Over the great Gromboolian plain,
Through the long, long wintry nights,
When the angry breakers roar
As they beat on the rocky shore;
   When Storm-clouds brood on the towering heights
Of the hills of the Chankly Bore, –

Then, through the vast and gloomy dark
There moves what seems a fiery spark, –
   A lonely spark with silvery rays
   Piercing the coal-black night, –
A Meteor strange and bright;
Hither and thither the vision strays,
    A single lurid light.

Slowly it wanders, pauses, creeps, –
Anon it sparkles, flashes and leaps;
And ever as onward it gleaming goes
A light on the Bong-tree stems it throws.
And those who watch at that midnight hour
From Hall or Terrace or lofty Tower,

Cry, as the wild light passes along, –
 The Dong! the Dong!
The wandering Dong through the forest goes!
 The Dong! the Dong!
The Dong with a luminous Nose!'

 Long years ago
 The Dong was happy and gay,
Till he fell in love with a Jumbly Girl
 Who came to those shores one day.
For the Jumblies came in a sieve, they did, –
Landing at eve near the Zemmery Fidd
 Where the Oblong Oysters grow.
And the rocks are smooth and gray.
And all the woods and the valleys rang
With the Chorus they daily and nightly sang, –
 '*Far and few, far and few*
 Are the lands where the Jumblies live;
 Their heads are green and their hands are blue,
 And they went to sea in a sieve.'

Happily, happily passed those days!
 While the cheerful Jumblies staid;
 They danced in circlets all night long
 To the plaintive pipe of the lively Dong,
 In moonlight, shine or shade.
For, day and night, he was always there
By the side of the jumbly Girl so fair,
With her sky blue hands and her sea-green hair;
Till the morning came of that hateful day
When the Jumblies sailed in their sieve away,
And the Dong was left on the cruel shore
Gazing, gazing for evermore, –
Ever keeping his weary eyes on
That pea-green sail on the far horizon, –
Singing the Jumbly Chorus still
As he sate all day on the grassy hill, –
 '*Far and few, far and few,*
 Are the lands where the Jumblies live;
 Their heads are green and their hands are blue,
 And they went to sea in a sieve.'

But when the sun was low in the West,
   The Dong arose, and said, –
'What little sense I once possessed
   Has quite gone out of my head!'
And since that day he wanders still
By lake and forest, marsh and hill,
Singing, 'O somewhere, in valley or plain,
Might I find my Jumbly Girl again!
For ever I'll seek, by lake and shore
Till I find my Jumbly Girl once more!'

   Playing a pipe with silvery squeaks,
   Since then his jumbly Girl he seeks;
   And because by night he could not see,
   He gathered the bark of the Twangum Tree
     On the flowery plain that grows,
     And he wove him a wondrous Nose, –
   A Nose as strange as a Nose could be!
Of vast proportions and painted red,
And tied with cords to the back of his head,
     In a hollow rounded space it ended
     With a luminous Lamp within suspended,
       All fenced about
       With a bandage stout
       To prevent the wind from blowing it out;
     And with holes all round to send the light
     In gleaming rays on the dismal light.

And now each night, and all night long,
Over those plains still roams the Dong;
And above the wail of the Chimp and Snipe
You may hear the squeak of his plaintive pipe,
While ever he seeks, but seeks in vain,
To meet with his Jumbly Girl again,
Lonely and wild, all night he goes, –
The Dong with a luminous Nose!
And all who watch at that midnight hour,
From Hall or Terrace or lofty Tower,
Cry as they trace the Meteor bright,
Moving along through the dreary night, –
     'This is the hour when forth he goes,

The Dong with a luminous Nose!
Yonder, over the plain he goes, –
   He goes!
   He goes, –
The Dong with a luminous Nose!'

EDWARD LEAR (Published 1877)

The Two Old Bachelors

Two old Bachelors were living in one house;
One caught a Muffin, the other caught a Mouse.
Said he who caught the Muffin to him who caught the
   Mouse, –
This happens just in time, for we've nothing in the house,
Save a tiny slice of lemon and a teaspoonful of honey,
And what to do for dinner, – since we haven't any money?
And what can we expect if we haven't any dinner,
But to lose our teeth and eyelashes and keep on growing
   thinner?
Said he who caught the Mouse to him who caught the
   Muffin, –
'We might cook this little Mouse if we only had some
   stuffin'!
If we had but Sage and Onions we could do extremely well,
But how to get that Stuffin' it is difficult to tell!'

Those two old Bachelors ran quickly to the Town
And asked for Sage and Onions as they wandered up and
   down;
They borrowed two large Onions, but no Sage was to be
   found
In the Shops or in the Market or in all the Gardens round.

But someone said, 'A hill there is, a little to the north,
And to its purpledicular top a narrow way leads forth; –
And there among the rugged rocks abides an ancient Sage, –
An earnest man who reads all day a most perplexing page.
Climb up and seize him by the toes, all studious as he sits, –

And pull him down, and chop him into endless little bits!
Then mix him with your Onion (cut up likewise into
    scraps),
And your Stuffin' will be ready, and very good – perhaps.'

Those two old Bachelors, without loss of time,
The nearly purpledicular crags at once began to climb;
And at the top among the rocks, all seated in a nook,
They saw that Sage a-wrestling with a most enormous book.
'You earnest Sage!' aloud they cried, 'your book you've read
    enough in!
We wish to chop you into bits and mix you into Stuffin'!'
But that old Sage looked calmly up, and with his awful book
At those two Bachelors' bald heads a certain aim he took; –
All over crag and precipice they rolled promiscuous down, –
At once they rolled and never stopped in lane or field or
    town;
And when they reached their house they found (besides
    their want of Stuffin')
The Mouse had fled; – and previously had eaten up the
    Muffin.

They left their home in silence by the once convivial door;
And from that hour those Bachelors were never heard of
    more.

EDWARD LEAR (1877)

The Mad Gardener's Song

He thought he saw an Elephant,
    That practised on a fife;
He looked again and saw it was
    A letter from his wife.
'At length I realise,' he said,
    'The bitterness of Life!'

He thought he saw a Buffalo
    Upon the chimney-piece;
He looked again, and found it was
    His Sister's Husband's Niece,
'Unless you leave this house,' he said,
    'I'll send for the Police!'

He thought he saw a Rattlesnake
    That questioned him in Greek;
He looked again, and found it was
    The Middle of Next Week.
'The one thing I regret,' he said,
    'Is that it cannot speak!'

He though he saw a Banker's clerk
    Descending from the 'bus;
He looked again, and found it was
    A Hippopotamus.
'If this should stay to dine,' he said,
    'There won't be much for us!'

He thought he saw a Kangaroo
    That worked a coffee-mill;
He looked again and found it was
    A Vegetable Pill.
'Were I to swallow this,' he said,
    'I should be very ill!'

He thought he saw a Coach-and-Four
    That stood beside his bed;
He looked again and found it was
    A Bear without a Head.
'Poor thing,' he said, 'Poor silly thing!
    'It's waiting to be fed!'

He thought he saw an Albatross
    That fluttered round the lamp;
He looked again, and found it was
    A Penny Postage Stamp.
'You'd best be getting home,' he said,
    'The nights are very damp!'

He thought he saw a Garden-Door
   That opened with a key;
He looked again and found it was
   A Double Rule of Three;
'And all its mystery,' he said,
   'Is clear as day to me!'

He thought he saw an Argument
   That proved he was the Pope;
He looked again, and found it was
   A Bar of Mottled Soap.
'A fact so dread,' he faintly said,
   'Extinguishes all hope!'

LEWIS CARROLL (Published 1889)

Fragment of a Greek Tragedy

Chorus: O suitably attired in leather boots
       Head of a traveller, wherefore seeking whom
       Whence by what way how purposed art thou come
       To this well-nightingaled vicinity?
       My object in inquiring is to know.
       But if you happen to be deaf and dumb
       And do not understand a word I say,
       Then wave your hand to signify as much.
   Alc: I journeyed hither a Boeotian road.
Chorus: Sailing on horseback, or with feet for oars?
   Alc: Plying with speed my partnership of legs.
Chorus: Beneath a shining or a rainy Zeus?
   Alc: Mud's sister, not himself adorns my shoes.
Chorus: To learn your name would not displease me much.
   Alc: Not all that men desire do they obtain.
Chorus: Might I then hear at what thy presence shoots?
   Alc: A shepherd's questioned mouth informed me that –
Chorus: What? for I know not yet what you will say.
   Alc: Nor will you ever if you interrupt.
Chorus: Proceed, and I will hold my speechless tongue.
   Alc: This house was Eriphyla's, no one's else.

Chorus: Nor did he shame his throat with shameful lies.
    Alc: May I then enter, passing through the door?
Chorus: Go chase into the house a lucky foot.
        And, O my son, be, on the one hand, good,
        And do not, on the other hand, be bad;
        For that is very much the safest plan.
    Alc: I go into the house with heels and speed.

Chorus:

STROPHE

In speculation
I would not willingly acquire a name
  For ill digested thought
  But after pondering much
To this conclusion I at last have come:
  Life is uncertain.
This truth I have written deep
  In my reflective midriff
  In tablets not of wax,
Nor with a pen did I inscribe it there,
For many reasons: *Life*, I say, *is not*
  A stranger to uncertainty
Not from the flight of omen-yelling fowls
  This fact did I discover,
Nor did the Delphine tripod bark it out,
  Nor yet Dodona.
Its native ingenuity sufficed
  My self-taught diaphragm.

ANTISTROPHE

Why should I mention
The Inachean daughter, loved of Zeus?
  Her whom of old the gods,
  More provident than kind,
Provided with four hoofs, two horns, one tail,
  A gift not asked for,
  And sent her forth to learn
  The unfamiliar science
  Of how to chew the cud.
She therefore, all about the Argive fields,
Went cropping pale green grass and nettle-tops,
  Nor did they disagree with her.

But yet, howe'er nutritious, such repasts
  I do not hanker after:
Never may Cypris for her seat select
  My dappled liver!
Why should I mention Io? Why indeed?
  I have no notion why.

EPODE

But now does my boding heart,
Unhired, unaccompanied, sing
A strain not meet for the dance.
Yea even the palace appears
To my yoke of circular eyes
(The right, nor omit I the left)
Like a slaughterhouse, so to speak,
Garnished with woolly deaths
And many shipwrecks of cows.
I therefore in a Cissian strain lament;
    And to the rapid
Loud, linen-tattering thumps upon my chest
  Resounds in concert
The battering of my unhappy head.

Eri: *(within)* O I am smitten with a hatchet's jaw;
    And that in deed, and not in word alone.
Chorus: I thought I heard a sound within the house
    Unlike the voice of one that jumps for joy.
Eri: He splits my skull, not in a friendly way,
    Once more; he purposes to kill me dead.
Chorus: I would not be reputed rash, but yet
    I doubt if all be gay within the house.
Eri: O! O! another stroke! that makes the third.
    He stabs me to the heart against my wish.
Chorus: If that be so, thy state of health is poor;
    But thine arithmetic is quite correct.

A. E. HOUSMAN (1893)

This parody of a Greek tragedy in a bad translation reflects very well the comical strangeness of Ancient Greek idioms to modern English readers coming upon them for the first time. It can serve here as a suitable bridge to the next section which reflects in verse the hold that Classical culture still had on the nineteenth-century imagination

12
ECHOES OF GREECE
& ROME

The World is Too Much with Us

The world is too much with us; late and soon
Getting and spending we lay waste our powers;
Little we see in Nature that is ours;
We have given our hearts away, a sordid boon!
This Sea that bares her bosom to the moon;
The winds that will be howling at all hours,
And are upgathered now, like sleeping flowers;
For this, for everything, we are out of tune;
It moves us not. – Great God! I'd rather be
A Pagan, suckled in a creed outworn;
So might I, standing on this pleasant lea,
Have glimpses that would make me less forlorn;
Have sight of Proteus, rising from the sea;
Or hear old Triton blow his wreathed horn.

WILLIAM WORDSWORTH (*c.* 1804)

Written after Swimming
from Sestos to Abydos

If in the month of dark December,
   Leander, who was nightly wont
(What maid will not the tale remember?)
   To cross thy stream, broad Hellespont!

If when the wintry tempest roared
   He sped to Hero, nothing loth,
And thus of old thy current poured,
   Fair Venus, how I pity both!

For me, degenerate modern wretch,
   Though in the genial month of May,
My dripping limbs I faintly stretch,
   And think I've done a feat today.

But since he cross'd the rapid tide,
   According to the doubtful story,
To woo – and – Lord knows what beside,
   And swam for Love, as I for Glory;

'Twere hard to say who fared the best:
   Sad mortals, thus the gods still plague you!
He lost his labour, I my jest:
   For he was drown'd, and I've the ague.

GEORGE GORDON, LORD BYRON (1810)

On first looking into Chapman's Homer

Much have I travelled in the realms of gold,
   And many goodly states and kingdoms seen;
   Round many western islands have I been
Which bards in fealty to Apollo hold.
Oft of one wide expanse had I been told,
   Which deep-browed Homer ruled as his demesne;
   Yet did I never breathe its pure serene
Till I heard Chapman speak out loud and bold:
Then felt I like some watcher of the skies
   When a new planet swims into his ken;
Or like stout Cortez, when with eagle eyes
   He stared at the Pacific, – and all his men
Looked at each other with a wild surmise –
   Silent, upon a peak in Darien.

JOHN KEATS (1816)

George Chapman's Elizabethan translation suited Romantic tastes better than Pope's characteristically polished eighteenth-century translation in heroic couplets.

Ode to Psyche

O Goddess! hear these tuneful numbers wrung
  By sweet enforcement and remembrance dear,
And pardon that thy secrets should be sung
  Even into thine own soft conched ear;
Surely I dreamt today, or did I see
  The winged Psyche with awakened eyes?
I wandered in a forest thoughtlessly,
  And, on the sudden, fainting with surprise,
Saw two fair creatures, couched side by side
  In deepest grass, beneath the whisp'ring roof
  Of leaves and trembled blossoms, where there ran
    A brooklet, scarce espied:

Mid hushed, cool-rooted flowers, fragrant-eyed,
  Blue, silver-white and budded Tyrian,
They lay, calm-breathing on the bedded grass;
  Their arms embraced, and their pinions too;
  Their lips touched not, but had not bade adieu,
As if disjoined by soft-handed slumber,
And ready still past kisses to outnumber:
  At tender eye-dawn of aurorean love
    The winged boy I knew;
But who wast thou, O happy, happy dove?
      His Psyche true!

O latest both and loveliest vision far
  Of all Olympus faded hierarchy!
Fairer than Phoebe's sapphire-region'd star   [the moon]
  Or Vesper, amorous glow-worm of the sky;
Fairer than these, though temple thou hast none,
  Nor altar heap'd with flowers;
No virgin choir to make delicious moan
  Upon the midnight hours;
No voice, no lute, no pipe, no incense sweet
  From chain-swung censer teeming;
No shrine, no grove, no oracle, no heat
  Of pale mouth'd prophet dreaming.

O brightest, though too late for antique vows,
    Too late, too late for the fond believing lyre
When holy were the haunted forest boughs,
    Holy the air, water, and the fire;
Yet even in these days so far retir'd
    From happy pieties, thy lucent fans,
Fluttering among the faint Olympians,
    I see, and sing, by my own eyes inspired.
So let me be thy choir, and make a moan
        Upon the midnight hours;
Thy voice, thy lute, thy pipe, thy incense sweet
    From swinged censer teeming;
Thy shrine, thy grove, thy oracle, thy heat
    Of pale-mouth'd prophet dreaming.

Yes, I will be thy priest and build a fane
    In some untrodden region of my mind,
Where branched thoughts new-grown with pleasant pain,
    Instead of thoughts shall murmur in the wind;
Far, far around shall those dark-cluster'd trees
    Fledge the wild-ridged mountains steep by steep;
And there by zephyrs, streams and birds and bees,
    The moss-lain Dryads shall be lull'd to sleep;
And, in the midst of this wide quietness
        A rosy sanctuary will I dress
With the wreathed trellis of a working brain,
    With buds and bells, and stars without a name,
With all the gardener Fancy e'er could feign,
    Who, breeding flowers, will never breed the same:
And there shall be for thee all soft delight
        That shadowy thought can win,
A bright torch, and a casement ope at night
        To let the warm Love in.

                                        JOHN KEATS (1819)

The preceding poem was inspired by the very late Classical story of the love of Cupid (the God of Love) and the mortal Psyche (which means 'soul'). In the story Cupid visits Psyche only in the dark, and she is not aware of his identity until she is induced to look at him by lamplight and wakes him. He disappears, but later they are reunited and she becomes an immortal.

Ode on a Grecian Urn

Thou still unravished bride of quietness,
   Thou foster child of silence and slow time,
Sylvan historian, who canst thus express
   A flowery tale more sweetly than our rhyme:
What leaf-fringed legend haunts about thy shape
   Of deities or mortals, or of both,
     In Tempe or the vales of Arcady?
   What men or gods are these? What maidens loth?
What mad pursuit? What struggle to escape?
   What pipes and timbrels? What wild ecstasy?

Heard melodies are sweet, but those unheard
   Are sweeter; therefore, ye soft pipes, play on;
Not to the sensual ear, but, more endeared,
   Pipe to the spirit ditties of no tone:
Fair youth, beneath the trees, thou canst not leave
   Thy song, nor ever can those trees be bare;
     Bold Lover, never, never canst thou kiss,
Though winning near the goal – yet do not grieve;
   She cannot fade, though thou hast not thy bliss,
     For ever wilt thou love and she be fair!

Ah, happy, happy boughs! that cannot shed
   Your leaves, nor ever bid the Spring adieu;
And, happy melodist, unwearied,
   For ever piping songs for ever new;
More happy love! more, happy, happy love!
   For ever warm and still to be enjoy'd,
     For ever panting, and for ever young;
All breathing human passion far above,
   That leaves a heart high-sorrowful and cloy'd,
     A burning forehead, and a parching tongue.

Who are these coming to the sacrifice?
   To what green altar, O mysterious priest,
Lead'st thou that heifer lowing at the skies,
   And all her silken flanks with garlands drest?

What little town by river or sea shore,
   Or mountain-built, with peaceful citadel
     Is emptied of its folk this pious morn?
And, little town, thy streets for evermore
   Will silent be; and not a soul to tell
     Why thou art desolate, can e'er return.

O Attic shape! Fair attitude! with brede
   Of marble men and maidens overwrought,
With forest branches and the trodden weed;
   Thou, silent form, dost tease us out of thought
As doth eternity: Cold Pastoral!
   When old age shall this generation waste,
     Thou shalt remain, in midst of other woe
    Than ours, a friend to man, to whom thou say'st,
'Beauty is truth, truth beauty,' – that is all
     Ye know on earth, and all ye need to know.

JOHN KEATS (1819)

Hymn of Pan

From the forests and highlands
   We come, we come;
From the river-girt islands,
   Where loud waves are dumb
     Listening to my sweet pipings.
The wind in the leaves and the rushes,
   The bees on the bells of thyme,
The birds on the myrtle bushes,
   The cicale above the lime,
And the lizard below in the grass,
Were as silent as ever old Tmolus was,
   Listening to my sweet pipings.

Liquid Peneus was flowing,
   And all dark Tempe lay
In Pelion's shadow, outgrowing
   The light of the dying day,

Speeded by my sweet pipings.
The Sileni, and Sylvans and Fauns,
 And the Nymphs of the woods and the waves,
To the edge of the moist river-lawns
 And the brink of the dewy caves,
And all that did then attend and follow,
Were silent with love, as you now Apollo,
 With envy of my sweet pipings.

I sang of the dancing stars,
 I sang of the daedal Earth,
And of Heaven – and the giant wars,
 And Love, and Death, and Birth, –
  And then I changed my pipings, –
Singing how, down the vale of Maenalus
 I pursued a maiden and clasped a reed.
Gods and men, we are all deluded thus!
 It breaks in our bosom and then we bleed;
All wept, as I think both ye now would,
If age or envy had not frozen your blood,
 At the sorrow of my sweet pipings.

PERCY BYSSHE SHELLEY (1820)

The Isles of Greece

1

The isles of Greece, the isles of Greece,
 Where burning Sappho loved and sung,
Where grew the arts of war and peace,
 Where Delos rose, and Phoebus sprung!
Eternal summer gilds them yet,
But all except their sun, is set.

2

The Scian and the Teian muse,
 The hero's harp, the lover's lute,
Have found the fame your shores refuse:
 Their place of birth alone is mute
To sounds which echo further west
Than your sires' 'Islands of the Blest.'

3

The mountains look on Marathon –
    And Marathon looks on the sea;
And musing there an hour alone,
    I dreamt that Greece might still be free;
For standing on the Persians' grave
I could not deem myself a slave.

4

A king sate on a rocky brow
    Which looks on seaborne Salamis;
And ships by thousands lay below,
    And men in nations; – all were his!
He counted them at break of day –
And when the sun set, where were they?

5

And where are they? and where art thou,
    My country? On thy voiceless shore
The heroic lay is tuneless now –
    The heroic bosom beats no more!
And must thy lyre, so long divine,
Degenerate into hands like mine?

6

'Tis something, in the dearth of fame,
    Though link'd among a fetter'd race,
To feel at least a patriot's shame,
    Even as I sing, suffuse my face;
For what is left the poet here?
For Greeks a blush, for Greeks a tear.

7

Must we but weep o'er days more blest?
    Must we but blush? – Our fathers bled.
Earth! render back from out thy breast
    A remnant of thy Spartan dead!
Of the three hundred grant but three
To make a new Thermopylae!

8

What, silent still? and silent all?
    Ah no! the voices of the dead
Sound like a distant torrent's fall,
    And answer, Let one living head,
But one arise, – we come, we come!
'Tis but the living who are dumb.

9

In vain – in vain: strike other chords;
    Fill high the cup of Samian wine!
Leave battles to the Turkish hordes,
    And shed the blood of Scio's vine!
Hark! rising to the ignoble call –
How answers each bold Bacchanal!

10

You have the Pyrrhic dance as yet;
    Where is the Pyrrhic phalanx gone?
Of two such lessons, why forget
    The nobler and the manlier one?
You have the letters Cadmus gave –
Think ye he meant them for a slave?

11

Fill high the bowl with Samian wine!
    We will not think of themes like these!
It made Anacreon's song divine;
    He served – but served Polycrates –
A tyrant; but our masters then
Were still, at least, our countrymen.

12

The tyrant of the Chersonese
    Was freedom's best and bravest friend;
That tyrant was Miltiades!'
    O that the present hour would lend
Another despot of the kind!
Such chains as his were sure to bind.

13

Fill high the bowl with Samian wine;
   On Suli's rock and Parga's shore,
Exists the remnant of a line
   Such as the Doric mothers bore;
And there, perhaps, some seed is sown,
That Heracleidan blood might own.

14

Trust not for freedom to the Franks –
   They have a king who buys and sells;
In native swords, and native ranks,
   The only hope of courage dwells;
But Turkish force and Latin fraud,
Would break your shield, however broad.

15

Fill high the cup with Samian wine!
   Our virgins dance beneath the shade –
I see their glorious black eyes shine;
   But, gazing on each glowing maid,
My own the burning tear-drop laves,
To think such breast must suckle slaves.

16

Place me on Sunium's marbled steep,
   Where nothing, save the waves and I,
May hear our mutual murmurs sweep;
   There, swan-like, let me sing and die:
A land of slaves shall ne'er be mine –
Dash down yon cup of Samian wine!

*   *   *   *   *

Thus sung, or would, or could, or should have sung
   The modern Greek, in tolerable verse;
If not like Orpheus quite, when Greece was young,
   Yet in these times he might have done much worse . . .

GEORGE GORDON, LORD BYRON (By 1823)

(from *Don Juan*, Canto III)

Marathon, Salamis and Thermopylae were all sites of heroic battles between the ancient Greeks and the Persians. Byron is lamenting the reluctance of nineteenth-century Greeks to free themselves from Turkish rule, a cause for which he was to meet his death at Missolonghi.

Dirce

Stand close around, ye Stygian set,
    With Dirce in one boat conveyed!
Or Charon seeing might forget
    That he is old, and she a shade.

WALTER SAVAGE LANDOR (1831)

Ianthe

Past ruin'd Ilion Helen lives,
    Alcestis rises from the shades;
Verse calls them forth; 'tis verse that gives
    Immortal youth to mortal maids.

Soon shall Oblivion's deepening veil
    Hide all the peopled hills you see,
The gay, the proud, while lovers hail
    In distant ages you and me.

The tear for fading beauty check,
    For passing glory cease to sigh;
One form shall rise above the wreck,
    One name, Ianthe, shall not die.

WALTER SAVAGE LANDOR (1831)

The next two contrasting poems, by Tennyson, are both connected with Homer's *Odyssey*. The first imagines the thoughts of Ulysses' crew as they ate the fruit of the legendary lotus, which made them, like a modern mind-altering drug, forget their troubles and responsibilities. The second shows us the aged hero Ulysses, long after the events covered by the *Odyssey*, deciding to set out on a final mission from which he may not return.

Choric Song from the Lotos-Eaters

1

There is sweet music here that softer falls
Than petals from blown roses on the grass,
Or night-dews on still waters between walls
Of shadowy granite, in a gleaming pass;
Music that gentlier on the spirit lies,
Than tired eyelids upon tired eyes;
Music that brings sweet sleep down from the blissful skies.
Here are cool mosses deep,
And through the moss the ivies creep,
And in the stream the long-leaved flowers weep,
And from the craggy ledge the poppy hangs in sleep.

2

Why are we weighed upon with heaviness,
And utterly consumed with sharp distress,
While all things else have rest from weariness?
We only toil, who are the first of things,
And make perpetual moan,
Still from one sorrow to another thrown;
Nor ever fold our wings,
And cease from wanderings,
Nor steep our brows in slumber's holy balm;
Nor hearken what the inner spirit sings,
'There is no joy but calm!'
Why should we only toil, the roof and crown of things?

3

Lo! in the middle of the wood
The folded leaf is wooed from out the bud
With winds upon the branch, and there
Grows green and broad, and takes no care,
Sun-steeped at noon, and in the moon
Nightly dew-fed; and turning yellow
Falls, and floats adown the air.
Lo! sweetened with summer light,
The full-juiced apple, waxing over-mellow,

Drops in a silent autumn night.
All its allotted length of days
The flower ripens in its place,
Ripens and fades, and falls, and hath no toil,
Fast-rooted in the fruitful soil.

4

Hateful is the dark blue sky,
Vaulted o'er the dark blue sea.
Death is the end of life; ah why
Should life all labour be?
Let us alone. Time driveth onward fast,
And in a little while our lips are dumb.
Let us alone. What is it that will last?
All things are taken from us, and become
Portions and parcels of the dreadful past.
Let us alone. What pleasure can we have
To war with evil? Is there any peace
In ever climbing up the climbing wave?
All things have rest, and ripen toward the grave
In silence – ripen, fall and cease;
Give us long rest or death, dark death or dreamful ease.

5

How sweet it were, hearing the downward stream,
With half-shut eyes ever to seem
Falling asleep in a half dream!
To dream and dream like yonder amber light
Which will not leave the myrrh-bush on the height;
To hear each other's whispered speech;
Eating the Lotos day by day,
To watch the crisping ripples on the beach,
And tender curving lines of creamy spray;
To lend our hearts and spirits wholly
To the influence of mild-minded melancholy;
To muse and live again in memory,
With those old faces of our infancy
Heaped over with a mound of grass,
Two handfuls of white dust, shut in an urn of brass!

6

Dear is the memory of our wedded lives,
And dear the last embraces of our wives
And their warm tears, but all hath suffered change;
For surely now our household hearths are cold,
Our sons inherit us, our looks are strange,
And we should come like ghosts to trouble joy.
Or else the island princes, overbold
Have eat our substance, and the minstrel sings
Before them of the ten years' war in Troy,
And our great deeds as half forgotten things.
Is there confusion in our little isle?
Let what is broken so remain.
The Gods are hard to reconcile;
Tis hard to settle order once again.
There is confusion, worse than death,
Trouble on trouble, pain on pain,
Long labour unto aged breath,
Sore task to hearts worn out by many wars
And eyes grown dim with gazing on the pilot stars.

7

But, propped on beds of amaranth and moly,
How sweet – while warm airs lull us, blowing lowly –
With half-dropped eyelid still,
Beneath a heaven dark and holy,
To watch the long, bright river drawing slowly
His waters from the purple hill –
To hear the dewy echoes calling
From cave to cave through the thick-twined vine –
To watch the emerald-coloured water falling
Through many a woven acanthus leaf divine!
Only to hear and see the far-off sparkling brine,
Only to hear were sweet, stretched out beneath the pine.

8

The Lotos blooms below the barren peak;
The Lotos blows by every winding creek;
All day the wind breathes low with mellower tone;
Through every hollow cave and valley lone

Round and round the spicy downs the yellow Lotos dust
   is blown.
We have had enough of action, and of motion we,
Rolled to starboard, rolled to larboard, when the surge
   was seething free,
Where the wallowing monster spouted his foam-fountains
   in the sea.
Let us swear an oath, and keep it with an equal mind,
In the hollow Lotos land to live and lie reclined
On the hills like Gods together, careless of mankind.
For they lie beside their nectar, and the bolts are hurled
Far below them in the valleys, and the clouds are lightly
   curled
Round their golden houses, girdled with the gleaming
   world;
While they smile in secret, looking over wasted lands,
Blight and famine, plague and earthquake, roaring deeps,
   and fiery sands,
Clanging fights, and flaming towns, and sinking ships,
   and praying hands.
But they smile, they find a music centred in a doleful
   song,
Steaming up, a lamentation and an ancient tale of wrong,
Like a tale of little meaning, though the words are strong;
Chanted from an ill-used race of men that cleave the soil,
Sow the seed and reap the harvest with enduring toil,
Storing yearly little dues of wheat, and wine and oil;
Till they perish and they suffer – some, 'tis whispered –
   down in hell
Suffer endless anguish, others in Elysian valleys dwell,
Resting weary limbs at last on beds of asphodel.
Surely, surely, slumber is more sweet than toil, the shore
Than labour in the deep mid-ocean, wind and wave
   and oar;
O rest ye, brother mariners, we will not wander more.

ALFRED, LORD TENNYSON (1832)

Ulysses

It little profits that an idle king,
By this still hearth, among these barren crags,
Match'd with an aged wife, I mete and dole
Unequal laws unto a savage race,
That hoard and sleep and feed, and know not me.
I cannot rest from travel; I will drink
Life to the lees: all times I have enjoy'd
Greatly, have suffer'd greatly, both with those
That loved me, and alone; on shore and when
Thro' scudding drifts the rainy Hyades
Vext the dim sea; I am become a name;
For always roaming with a hungry heart.
Much have I seen and known: cities of men
And manners, climates, councils, governments,
Myself not least, but honoured of them all;
And drunk delight of battle with my peers,
Far on the ringing plains of windy Troy.
I am a part of all that I have met;
Yet all experience is an arch wherethro'
Gleams that untravell'd world, whose margin fades
Forever and forever when I move.
How dull it is to pause, to make an end,
To rust unburnish'd, not to shine in use!
As tho' to breathe were life. Life piled on life
Were all too little, and of one to me
Little remains; but every hour is saved
From that eternal silence, something more,
A bringer of new things; and vile it were
For some three suns to hoard and store myself
And this gray spirit yearning in desire
To follow knowledge like a sinking star,
Beyond the utmost bound of human thought.
This is my son, mine own Telemachus,
To whom I leave the sceptre and the isle –
Well loved of me, discerning to fulfil
This labour, by slow prudence to make mild
A rugged people, and thro' soft degrees

Subdue them to the useful and the good.
Most blameless is he, centred in the sphere
Of common duties, decent not to fall
In offices of tenderness, and pay
Meet adoration to my household gods,
When I am gone. He works his work, I mine.
There lies the port, the vessel puffs her sail:
There gloom the dark broad seas. My mariners,
Souls that have toil'd and wrought and thought
    with me –
That ever with a frolic welcome took
The thunder and the sunshine, and opposed
Free hearts, free foreheads – you and I are old;
Old age hath yet his honour and his toil;
Death closes all: but something ere the end,
Some work of noble note may yet be done,
Not unbecoming men that strove with Gods.
The lights begin to twinkle from the rocks:
The long day wanes: the slow moon climbs: the deep
Moans round with many voices. Come, my friends,
'Tis not too late to seek a newer world.
Push off, and sitting well in order smite
The sounding furrows; for my purpose holds
To sail beyond the sunset, and the battle
Of all the western stars, until I die.
It may be that the gulfs will wash us down;
It may be we shall touch the Happy Isles
And see the great Achilles, whom we knew.
Tho' much is taken, much abides; and tho'
We are not now that strength which in old days
Mov'd earth and heaven; that which we are we are:
One equal temper of heroic hearts,
Made weak by time and fate, but strong in will
To strive, to seek to find and not to yield.

                   ALFRED, LORD TENNYSON (1832)

To Helen

Helen, thy beauty is to me
   Like those Nicaean barks of yore,
That gently o'er a perfumed sea,
   The weary, way-worn wanderer bore
   To his own native shore.

On desperate seas long wont to roam,
   Thy hyacinth hair, thy classic face,
Thy Naiad airs have bought me home
   To the glory that was Greece
And the grandeur that was Rome.

Lo! in yon brilliant window-niche
   How statue-like I see thee stand,
   The agate lamp within thy hand!
Ah, Psyche, from the regions which
    Are Holy Land!

EDGAR ALLAN POE (1845 REVISION)

A Musical Instrument

1

What was he doing, the great god Pan,
   Down in the reeds by the river?
Spreading ruin and scattering ban,
Splashing and paddling with hoofs of a goat,
And breaking the golden lilies afloat
   With the dragon-fly on the river.

2

He tore out a reed, the great god Pan,
   From the deep cool bed of the river.
The limpid water turbidly ran,
And the broken lilies a-dying lay,
And the dragon-fly had fled away,
   Ere he brought it out of the river.

3

High on the shore sat the great god Pan
   While turbidly flowed the river;
And hacked and hewed as a great god can,
With his hard bleak steel at the patient reed,
Till there was not a sign of the leaf indeed
   To prove it fresh from the river.

4

He cut it short, did the great god Pan,
   (How tall it grew in the river!)
Then drew the pith, like the heart of a man,
Steadily from the outside ring,
And notched the poor dry empty thing
   In holes, as he sat by the river.

5

'This is the way,' laughed the great god Pan
   (Laughed while he sat by the river),
The only way, since gods began,
To make sweet music, they could succeed.'
Then, dropping his mouth to a hole in the reed,
   He blew in power by the river.

6

Sweet, sweet, sweet, O Pan!
   Piercing sweet by the river!
Blinding sweet, O great god Pan!
The sun on the hill forgot to die,
And the lilies revived, and the dragon-fly
   Came back to dream on the river.

7

Yet half a beast is the great god Pan,
   To laugh as he sits by the river,
Making a poet out of a man:
The true gods sigh for the cost and pain, –
For the reed which grows nevermore again
   As a reed with the reeds in the river.

ELIZABETH BARRETT BROWNING (1860)

The nature god Pan was supposed to have invented the pan-pipes
in memory of the nymph Syrinx, who had been turned into a reed

Hymn to Proserpine

After the Proclamation in Rome of the Christian Faith

VICISTI GALILEÆ

I have lived long enough, having seen one thing, that love hath
    an end,
Goddess and maiden and queen, be near me now and befriend.
Thou art more than the day or the morrow, the seasons that
    laugh or that weep;
For these give joy and sorrow; but thou, Proserpina, sleep.
Sweet is the treading of wine, and sweet the feet of the dove;
But a goodlier gift is thine than foam of the grapes or love.
Yea, is not even Apollo, with hair and harpstring of gold,
A bitter god to follow, a beautiful god to behold?
I am sick of singing; the bays burn deep and chafe. I am fain
To rest a little from praise and grievous pleasure and pain.
For the gods we know of, who give us our daily breath,
We know they are cruel as love or life, and lovely as death.

O gods dethroned and deceased, cast forth, wiped out in a day
From your wrath is the world released, redeemed from your
    chains, men say.
New gods are crowned in the city; their flowers have broken
    your rods;
They are merciful, clothed with pity, the young compassionate
    gods.
But for me their new device is barren, the days are bare;
Things long past over suffice, and men forgotten that were.
Time and the gods are at strife; ye dwell in the midst thereof,
Draining a little life from the barren breasts of love.
I say to you, cease, take rest, yea I say to you all, be at peace,
Till the bitter milk of her breast and the barren bosom shall
    cease.
Wilt thou yet take all, Galilean? But these thou shalt not take –
The laurel, the palms and the paean, the breasts of the nymphs
    in the brake,

Breasts more soft than a dove's, that tremble with tenderer
    breath,
And all the wings of the Loves, and all the joy before death;
And the feet of the hours that sound as a single lyre,
Dropped and deep in the flowers, with strings that flicker like
    fire.
More than these wilt thou give, things fairer than all these
    things?
Nay, for a little we live, and life hath mutable wings.
A little while and we die; shall life not thrive as it may?
For no man under the sky lives twice, outliving his day.
And grief is a grievous thing, and a man hath enough of his
    tears;
Why should he labour, and bring fresh grief to blacken his
    years?

Thou hast conquered, O pale Galilean, the world has grown
    gray from thy breath,
We have drunken of things Lethean, and fed on the stillness of
    death.
Laurel is green for a season, and love is sweet for a day;
But love grows bitter with treason, and laurel outlives not May.
Sleep, shall we sleep after all? for the world is not sweet in the
    end;
For the old faiths loosen and fall, the new years ruin and rend.
Fate is a sea without shore, and the soul is a rock that abides;
But her ears are vexed with the roar and her face with the foam
    of the tides,
O lips that the live blood faints in, the leavings of racks and of
    rods!
O ghastly glories of saints, dead limbs of gibbeted gods!
Though all men abase you before them in spirit, and all knees
    bend,
I kneel not, neither adore you, but standing look to the end.

All delicate days and pleasant, all spirits and sorrows are cast
Far out with the foam of the present that sweeps to the surf of
    the past;
Where beyond the extreme sea wall, and between the remote
    sea gates,

Waste water washes, and tall ships founder, and deep death
  waits;
Where, mighty with deepening sides, clad about with the seas
  as wings
And impelled of invisible tides, and fulfilled of unspeakable
  things,
White-eyed and poisonous-finned, shark-toothed and
  serpentine-curled,
Rolls under the whitening wind of the future, the wave of the
  world.
The depths stand naked in sunder behind it, the storms flee
  away;
In the hollow before it the thunder is taken and snared as a
  prey;
In its sides is the north wind bound; and its salt is of all men's
  tears,
With light of ruin, and sound of changes and pulse of years;
With travail of day after day, and with trouble of hour upon
  hour.
And bitter as blood is the spray; and the crests are as fangs that
  devour;
And its vapor and storm of its steam as the sighing of spirits to
  be;
And its noise as the noise in a dream; and its depths as the
  roots of the sea;
And the height of its heads as the height of the utmost stars of
  the air;
And the ends of the earth at the might thereof tremble, and
  time is made bare.
Will ye bridle the deep sea with reins, will ye chasten the high
  sea with rods?
Will ye take her to chain her with chains, who is older than all
  ye gods?
All ye as a wind shall go by, as a fire shall ye pass and be past;
Ye are gods, and behold, ye shall die, and the waves be upon
  you at last.
In the darkness of time, in the deeps of the years, in the
  changes of things,
Ye shall sleep as a slain man sleeps, and the world shall forget
  you or kings.

Though the feet of thine high priests tread where thy lords and
    our forefathers trod
Though these that were gods are dead, and thou being dead art
    a god,
Though before thee the throned Cytherean be fallen, and
    hidden her head,
Yet thy kingdom shall pass, Galilean, thy dead shall go down to
    thee dead.

Of the maiden thy mother men sing as a goddess with grace
    clad around,
Thou art crowned where another was king, where another was
    queen she is crowned.
Yea, once we had sight of another; but now she is queen, say
    these.
Not as thine, not as thine was my mother, a blossom of
    flowering seas,
Clothed round with the world's desire as with raiment, and fair
    as the foam.
And fleeter than kindled fire, and a goddess, and mother of
    Rome.
For thine came pale and a maiden, and sister to sorrow, but
    ours,
Her deep hair heavily laden with odour and colour of flowers,
White rose of the rose-white water, a silver splendour, a flame,
Bent down unto us that besought her, and earth grew sweet
    with her name.
For thine came weeping, a slave among slaves, and rejected,
    but she
Came flushed from the full-flushed wave, and imperial, her foot
    on the sea.
And the wonderful waters knew her, the winds and the
    viewless ways,
And the rosier, and bluer the sea-blue stream of the days.

Ye are fallen, our lords, by what token? we wist that ye should
    not fall.
Ye were all so fair that are broken; and one more fair than ye all.
But I turn to her still, having seen she shall surely abide in the
    end;

Goddess and maiden and queen, be near me now and befriend.
O daughter of earth, of my mother, her crown and blossom of
    birth,
I am also, I also, thy brother; I go as I came unto earth.
In the night where thine eyes are as moons are in heaven, the
    night where thou art,
Where the silence is more than all tunes, where sleep overflows
    from the heart,
Where the poppies are sweet as the rose in our world, and the
    red rose is white,
And the wind falls faint as it blows with the fume of the flowers
    of the night,
And the murmur of spirits that sleep in the shadow of gods
    from afar
Grows dim in thine ears and deep as the deep dim soul of a
    star,
In the sweet low light of thy face, under heavens untrod by the
    sun,
Let my soul with their souls find place, and forget what is done
    and undone.
Thou art more than the gods who number the days of our
    temporal breath,
For these give labor and slumber; but thou, Proserpina, death.
Therefore now at thy feet I abide for a season in silence. I know
I shall die as my fathers died, and sleep as they sleep,
        even so.
For the glass of the years is brittle, wherein we gaze for a span.
A little soul for a litttle bears up this corpse, which is man.
So long I endure, no longer; and laugh not again, neither weep.
For there is no god found stronger than death, and death is a
    sleep.

ALGERNON CHARLES SWINBURNE (1866)

Proserpina, the consort of Pluto, God of the Underworld, was
therefore queen of the Classical kingdom of the dead. The 'throned
Cytherean' is Venus, Goddess of Love, who arose from the foam of
the sea, and is the subject of the next poem.

Song from the Hill of Venus

Before our lady came on earth,
Little there was of joy or mirth;
About the borders of the sea
The sea-folk wandered heavily;
About the wintry river side,
The weary fishers would abide.

Alone, within the weaving room
The girls would sit before the loom,
And sing no song and play no play
Alone from dawn to hot mid-day.

From mid-day unto evening,
The men afield would work, nor sing,
'Mid weary thoughts of man and God,
Before thy feet the wet ways trod.

Unkissed the merchant bore his care,
Unkissed the knights went out to war
Unkissed the mariner came home,
Unkissed the minstrelmen did roam,

Or in the stream the maids would stare,
Nor know why they were made so fair;
Their yellow locks, their bosoms white,
Their limbs well wrought for all delight,
Seemed foolish things that waited death,
As hopeless as the flowers beneath
The weariness of unkissed feet:
No life was bitter then, or sweet.

Therefore, O Venus, well may we
Praise the green ridges of the sea
O'er which, upon a happy day,
Thou cam'st to take our shame away.
Well may we praise the curdling foam
Amidst the which thy feet did bloom,
Flowers of the gods; the yellow sand
They kissed atwixt the sea and land;

The bee-beset ripe seeded grass,
Through which thy fine limbs first did pass;
The purple-dusted butterfly,
First blown against thy quivering thigh;
The first red rose that touched thy side,
And over-blown and fainting died;
The flickering of thy orange shade,
Where first in sleep thy limbs were laid;
The happy day's sweet life and death,
Whose air caught first thy balmy breath –
Yea, all these things well praised may be,
But with what words shall we praise thee –
O Venus, O thou love alive,
Born to give peace to souls that strive?

WILLIAM MORRIS (c. 1869)

Failure

We are much bound to them that do succeed;
    But, in a more pathetic sense are bound
    To such as fail. They all our loss expound;
They comfort us for work that will not speed,
And life – itself a failure. Ay, his deed,
    Sweetest in story, who the dusk profound
    Of Hades flooded with entrancing sound,
Music's own tears, was failure. Doth it read
Therefore the worse? Ah no! So much to dare,
    He fronts the regnant Darkness on its throne, –
So much to do; impetuous even there,
    He pours out love's disconsolate sweet moan –
He wins; but few for that his deed recall;
Its power is in the look which costs him all.

JEAN INGELOW (By 1886)

The allusion is, of course, to the legend of Orpheus and Euridice, and Orpheus's success in freeing his wife Euridice from the Underworld only to lose her on the way out because he could not resist looking back at her before they reached the surface.

Heraclitus

They told me, Heraclitus, they told me you were dead;
They brought me bitter news to hear and bitter tears to shed.
I wept as I remembered how often you and I
Had tired the sun with talking, and sent him down the sky.

And now that you are lying, my dear old Carian guest,
A handful of grey ashes, long long ago at rest.
Still are thy pleasant voices, thy nightingales awake,
For Death he taketh all away, but them he cannot take.

WILLIAM CORY (Published 1858)

This is a translation from the Greek poet Callimachus.

To Virgil

Roman Virgil, thou that singest
    Ilion's lofty temples robed in fire
Ilion falling, Rome arising,
    wars, and filial faith, and Dido's pyre;

Landscape-lover, lord of language
    more than he who sang the 'Works and Days',
All the chosen coins of fancy
    flashing out from many a golden phrase;

Thou that singest wheat and woodland
    tilth and vineyard, hive and horse and herd;
All the charm of all the Muses
    often flowering in a lonely word;

Poet of the happy Tityrus
    piping underneath his beechen bowers;
Poet of the poet-satyr
    whom the laughing shepherd bound with flowers;

Chanter of the Pollio, glorying
     in the blissful years again to be,
Summers of the snakeless meadow,
     unlaborious earth and oarless sea;

Thou that seest Universal
     Nature moved by Universal Mind;
Thou majestic in thy sadness
     at the doubtful doom of human kind;

Light amongst the vanish'd ages;
     star that gildest yet this phantom shore;
Golden branch amongst the shadows,
     kings and realms that pass to rise no more;

Now thy Forum roars no longer,
     fallen every purple Caesar's dome –
Tho' thine ocean-roll of rhythm
     sound forever of Imperial Rome –

Now the Rome of slaves hath perish'd
     and the Rome of freemen holds her place,
I, from out the Northern Island,
     sunder'd once from all the human race,

I salute thee, Mantovano,
     I that loved thee since my day began
Wielder of the stateliest measure
     ever moulded by the lips of man.

ALFRED, LORD TENNYSON (1882)

The first stanza refers to Virgil's epic masterpiece the *Aeneid*. The *Works and Days* was the title of a poem by the Greek poet Hesiod who preceded Virgil in writing about rural life. Tityrus was a shepherd in Virgil's early pastoral work the *Eclogues*. This included the famous Fourth (Pollio) Eclogue often taken to prophesy the coming of Christ.

Parnassus

Exegi monumentum . . .
Quod non . . .
Possit diruere . . . innumerabilis
Annorum series et fuga temporum – Horace

1

What be those crowned forms high over the sacred
    fountain?
Bards, that the mighty Muses have raised to the heights of
    the mountain,
And over the flight of the ages! O Goddesses, help me up
    thither!
Lightning may shrivel the laurel of Caesar, but mine would
    not wither.
Steep is the mountain, but you, you will help me to
    overcome it,
And stand with my head in the zenith, and roll my voice
    from the summit,
Sounding for ever and ever thro' Earth and her listening
    nations,
And mixed with the great Sphere music of stars and of
    constellations.

2

What be those two shapes high over the sacred mountain,
Taller than all the Muses, and huger than all the mountain?
On those two known peaks they stand, ever spreading and
    heightening;
Poets, that evergreen laurel is blasted by more than
    lightning!
Look, in their deep double shadows the crowned ones all
    disappearing!
Sing like a bird and be happy, nor hope for a deathless
    hearing!
'Sounding for ever and ever?' pass on! the sight confuses –
These are Astronomy and Geology, terrible Muses!

3

If the lips were touch'd with the fire from off a pure Pierian
    altar,
Though their music here be mortal, need the singer greatly
    care?
Other songs for other worlds! the fire within him would
    not falter;
Let the golden Iliad vanish, Homer here is Homer there.

ALFRED, LORD TENNYSON (Published 1889)

The superscription comes from the end of Book III of Horace's
Odes, where he claims to have founded, in his poetry, a monument
that time will not destroy.

Cynara

Non sum qualis eram bonae sub regno Cynarae

Last night, ah, yesternight, betwixt her lips and mine
There fell thy shadow, Cynara! thy breath was shed
Upon my soul between the kisses and the wine;
And I was desolate, and sick of an old passion,
    Yea, I was desolate, and bowed my head:
I have been faithful to thee, Cynara, in my fashion.

All night upon mine heart I felt her warm heart beat,
Night-long within mine arms in love and sleep she lay;
Surely the kisses of her bought red mouth were sweet;
But I was desolate, and sick of an old passion,
    When I awoke, and found the dawn was gray:
I have been faithful to thee, Cynara, in my fashion.

I have forgot much, Cynara, gone with the wind,
Flung roses, roses riotously with the throng,
Dancing, to put thy pale lost lilies out of mind;
But I was desolate, and sick of an old passion,
   Yea, all the time, because the dance was long:
I have been faithful to thee, Cynara, in my fashion.

I cried for madder music, and stronger wine,
But when the feast is finished and the lamps expire,
Then falls thy shadow, Cynara! the night is thine;
And I am desolate, and sick of an old passion,
   Yea, hungry for the lips of my desire:
I have been faithful to thee, Cynara, in my fashion.

ERNEST DOWSON (1891)

They are Not Long

Vitae summa brevis spem nos vetat incohare longam

They are not long, the weeping and the laughter,
    Love and desire and hate;
I think they have no portion in us after
    We pass the gate.

They are not long, the days of wine and roses:
    Out of a misty dream
Our path emerges for a while, then closes
    Within a dream.

ERNEST DOWSON (1896)

These two poems have been included here, (although the first could well have come under 'Varieties of Love') because of their essentially pagan quality, emphasised by the quotations from Horace's *Odes* which preface them. The first is from *Odes* IV, i: 'I am not the same as I was under the rule of Cynara the good'; the second from *Odes* I, iv: 'The shortness of life forbids us to begin to have long-term hopes.'

On Wenlock Edge

On Wenlock Edge the wood's in trouble;
  His forest fleece the Wrekin heaves;
The gale it plies the saplings double,
  And thick on Severn snow the leaves.

'Twould blow like this through holt and hanger
  When Uricon the city stood:
'Tis the old wind in the old anger,
  But then it threshed another wood.

Then, 'twas before my time, the Roman
  At yonder heaving hill would stare:
The blood that warms an English yeoman,
  The thoughts that hurt him, they were there.

Then, like the wind through woods in riot,
  Through him the gale of life blew high;
The tree of man was never quiet:
  Then 'twas the Roman, now 'tis I.

The gale, it plies the saplings double,
  It blows so hard, 'twill soon be gone:
Today the Roman and his trouble
  Are ashes under Uricon.

A. E. HOUSMAN (1896)

Uricon was a Roman city near Shrewsbury and the two Shropshire hills, Wenlock Edge and the Wrekin, referred to in the poem.

13
MEDIEVALISM, LEGEND, DREAM, NIGHTMARE & THE SUPERNATURAL

Darkness

I had a dream which was not all a dream.
The bright sun was extinguish'd and the stars
Did wander darkling in the eternal space,
Rayless and pathless, and the icy earth
Swung blind and blackening in the moonless air;
Morn came and went and came and brought no day,
And men forgot their passions in the dread
Of this their desolation; and all hearts
Were chill'd into a selfish prayer for light:
And they did live by watchfires – and the thrones,
The palaces of crowned kings – the huts,
The habitations of all things which dwell,
Were burnt for beacons; cities were consumed,
And men were gather'd round their blazing homes
To look once more into each other's face;
Happy were those which dwelt within the eye
Of the volcanoes, and their mountain torch:
A fearful hope was all the world contain'd;
Forests were set on fire – but hour by hour
They fell and faded – and the crackling trunks
Extinguish'd with a crash, and all was black.
The brows of men by the despairing light
Wore an unearthly aspect, as by fits
The flashes fell upon them; some lay down
And hid their eyes and wept; and some did rest
Their chins upon their clenched hands and smiled;
And others hurried to and fro, and fed
Their funeral pyres with fuel, and looked up
With mad disquietude on the dull sky,
The pall of a past world; and then again
With curses cast them down upon the dust,
And gnashed their teeth and howl'd; the wild birds shriek'd
And terrified did flutter on the ground,
And flap their useless wings; the wildest brutes
Came tame and tremulous; and vipers crawl'd
And twin'd themselves among the multitude,

Hissing, but stingless – they were slain for food.
And War, which for a moment was no more,
Did glut himself again: – a meal
Was bought with blood, and each sate sullenly apart
Gorging himself in gloom: no love was left;
All earth was but one thought, and that was death
Immediate and inglorious; and the pang
Of famine fed upon all entrails – men
Died, and their bones were tombless as their flesh;
The meagre by the meagre were devour'd,
Even dogs assailed their masters, all save one,
And he was faithful to a corse, and kept
The birds and beasts and savage men at bay,
Till hunger clung them, or the dropping dead
Lured their lank jaws; himself sought out no food,
But, with a piteous and perpetual moan,
And a quick desolate cry, licking the hand
Which answered not with a caress – he died.
The crowd was famish'd by degrees; but two
Of an enormous city did survive,
And they were enemies: they met beside
The dying embers of an altar-place
Where had been heap'd a mass of holy things
For an unholy usage; they raked up,
And shivering scrap'd with their cold skeleton hands
The feeble ashes, and their feeble breath
Blew for a little life, and made a flame
Which was a mockery; then they lifted up
Their eyes as it grew lighter and beheld
Each other's aspects – saw, and shriek'd, and died –
Even of their mutual hideousness they died,
Unknowing who he was upon whose brow
Famine had written Fiend. The world was void,
The populous and powerful was a lump,
Seasonless, herbless, treeless, manless, lifeless,
A lump of death – a chaos of hard clay.
The rivers, lakes and oceans all stood still,
And nothing stirred within their silent depths;
Ships sailorless lay rotting on the sea,
And their masts fell down piecemeal: as they dropp'd,

They slept on the abyss without a surge –
The waves were dead; the tides were in their grave,
The moon, their mistress had expired before;
The winds were wither'd in the stagnant air,
And the clouds perish'd; Darkness had no need
Of aid from them – She was the Universe.

GEORGE GORDON, LORD BYRON (1816)

La Belle Dame sans Merci

O what can ail thee, knight at arms,
    Alone and palely loitering?
The sedge is withered from the lake
        And no birds sing.

O what can ail, thee, knight at arms,
    So haggard and so woe begone?
The squirrel's granary is full,
        And the harvest's done.

I see a lilly on thy brow
    With anguish moist and fever dew
And on thy cheeks a fading rose
        Fast withereth too.

'I met a lady in the meads,
    Full beautiful, a faery's child,
Her hair was long, her foot was light,
        And her eyes were wild.

I made a garland for her head,
    And bracelets too, and fragrant zone;
She looked at me as she did love,
        And made sweet moan.

I set her on my pacing steed,
    And nothing else saw all day long,
For sideways would she bend and sing
        A Faery's song.

She found me roots of relish sweet,
    And honey wild, and manna dew,
And sure in language strange she said,
       'I love thee true'.

She took me to her elfin grot,
    And there she wept, and sigh'd full sore,
And there I shut her wild wild eyes,
       With kisses four.

And there she lulled me asleep,
    And there I dreamed – Ah woe betide!
The latest dream that e'er I dreamed
       On the cold hill side.

I saw paie kings and warriors pale
    Pale warriors, death pale were they all,
They cried – '*La Belle Dame sans Merci*
       Hath thee in thrall!'

I saw their starved lips in the gloam,
    With horrid warning gaped wide,
And I awoke and found me here
       On the cold hill's side.

And this is why I sojourn here,
    Alone and palely loitering,
Though the sedge is wither'd from the lake,
       And no birds sing.

JOHN KEATS (1819)

La Belle Dame can be seen as a personification of death, in the form of the consumption from which Keats died.

The Kraken

Below the thunders of the upper deep,
Far, far beneath in the abysmal sea,
His ancient, dreamless, uninvaded sleep
The Kraken sleepeth: faintest sunlights flee
About his shadowy sides; above him swell
Huge sponges of millennial growth and height,
And far away into the sicky light
From many a wondrous grot and secret cell
Unnumbered and enormous polypi
Winnow with giant arms the slumbering green.
There hath he lain for ages, and will lie
Battening upon huge sea worms in his sleep,
Until the latter fire shall heat the deep;
Then once by man and angels to be seen,
In roaring he shall rise and on the surface die.

ALFRED LORD, TENNYSON (1830)

Childe Roland to the Dark Tower Came

(See Edgar's song in Lear*)*

1

My first thought was, he lied in every word.
    That hoary cripple, with malicious eye
    Askance to watch the working of his lie
On mine, and mouth scarce able to afford
Suppression of his glee, that pursed and scored
    Its edge, at one more victim gained thereby.

2

What else should he be set for, with his staff?
   What, save to waylay with his lies, ensnare
    All travellers who might find him posted there
And ask the road? I guessed what skull-like laugh
Would break, what crutch 'gin write my epitaph
   or pastime in the dusty thoroughfare,

3

If at his counsel I should turn aside
   Into that ominous tract which, all agree,
    Hides the Dark Tower. Yet acquiescingly
I did turn as he pointed; neither pride
Nor hope rekindling at the end descried,
   So much as gladness that some end might be.

4

For, what with my whole world-wide wandering,
   What, with my search drawn out thro' years, my hope
    Dwindled into a ghost not fit to cope
With that obstreperous joy success would bring,
I hardly tried now to rebuke the spring
   My heart made, finding failure in its scope.

5

As when a sick man, very near to death
   Seems dead indeed, and feels begin and end
    The tears and takes the farewell of each friend,
And hears one bid the other go, draw breath
Freelier outside, ('since all is o'er,' he saith,
   And the blow fall'n no grieving can amend;')

6

While some discuss if near the other graves
   Be room enough for this, and when a day
    Suits best for carrying the corpse away,
With care about the banners, scarves and staves;
And still the man hears all, and only craves
   He may not shame such tender love and stay.

7

Thus, I had so long suffered in this quest,
  Heard failure prophesied so oft, been writ
  So many times amongst 'The Band' – to wit,
The knights who to the Dark Tower's search addressed
Their steps – that just to fail as they, seemed best,
  And all the doubt was now – should I be fit?

8

So, quiet as despair, I turned from him,
  That hateful cripple, out of his highway
  Into the path he pointed. All the day
Had been a dreary one at best, and dim
Was settling to its close, yet shot one grim
  Red leer to see the plain catch its estray.

9

For mark! no sooner was I fairly found
  Pledged to the plain, after a pace or two,
  Than, pausing to throw backward a last view
O'er the safe road, 'twas gone; grey plain all round:
Nothing but plain to the horizon's view.
  I might go on; nought else remained to do.

10

So, on I went. I think I never saw
  Such starved, ignoble nature; nothing throve:
  For flowers – as well expect a cedar grove!
But cockle, spurge, according to their law
Might propagate their kind, with none to awe,
  You'd think; a burr had been a treasure trove.

11

No, penury, inertness and grimace,
  In some strange sort were the land's portion. 'See
  'Or shut your eyes,' said Nature peevishly,
'It nothing skills: I cannot help my case:
' 'Tis the Last Judgement's fire must cure this place.
  'Calcine its clods and set my prisoners free.'

12

If there pushed any ragged thistle-stalk
   Above its mates, the head was chopped; the bents
   Were jealous else. What made those hole and rents
In the dock's harsh swarth leaves, bruised as to baulk
All hope of greenness? 'Tis a brute must walk
   Pashing their life out, with a brute's intents.

13

As for the grass, it grew as scant as hair
   In leprosy; thin dry blades pricked the mud
   Which underneath looked kneaded up with blood.
One stiff blind horse, his every bone a-stare,
Stood stupefied, however he came there:
   Thrust out past service from the devil's stud!

14

Alive? He might be dead for aught I know,
   With that red gaunt and colloped neck a-strain
   And shut eyes underneath the rusty mane;
Seldom went such grotesqueness with such woe;
I never saw a beast I hated so;
   He must be wicked to deserve such pain.

15

I shut my eyes and turned them on my heart,
   As a man calls for wine before he fights,
   I asked one draught of earlier, happier sights,
Ere fitly I could hope to play my part.
Think first, fight afterwards – the soldiers art:
   One taste of the old time sets all to rights.

16

Not it! I fancied Cuthbert's reddening face
   Beneath its garniture of curly gold,
   Dear fellow, till I almost felt him fold
An arm in mine to fix me to the place
That way he used. Alas, one night's disgrace!
   Out went my heart's new fire, and left it cold.

17

Giles, then, the soul of honour – there he stands
  Frank as ten years ago, when knighted first.
  What honest man should dare (he said) he durst.
Good – but the scene shifts – faugh! what hangman's hands
Pin to his breast a parchment? His own bands
    Read it. Poor traitor, spit upon and curst.

18

Better this present than a past like that;
  Back, therefore, to my darkening path again!
  No sound, no sight, as far as eye could strain.
Will the night send a howlet or a bat?
I asked; when something on the dismal flat
    Came to arrest my thoughts and change their train.

19

A sudden little river crossed my path,
  As unexpected as a serpent comes,
  No sluggish tide congenial to the glooms;
This, as it frothed by, might have been a bath
For the fiend's glowing hoof – to see the wrath
    Of its black eddy bespate with flukes and spumes.

20

So petty, yet so spiteful! All along,
  Low scrubby alders kneeled down over it;
  Drenched willows flung them headlong in a fit
Of mute despair, a suicidal throng:
The river, which had done them all the wrong,
    Whate'er that was, rolled by, deterred no whit.

21

Which, while I forded, – good saints, how I feared
  To set my foot upon a dead man's cheek,
  Each step, or feel the spear I thrust to seek
For hollows, tangled in his hair or beard!
It may have been a water-rat I speared,
    But, ugh!, it sounded like a baby's shriek.

22

Glad was I when I reached the other bank.
　　Now for a better country. Vain presage!
　　Who were the strugglers, what war did they wage,
Whose savage trample thus could pad the dank
Soil to a plash? Toads in a poisoned tank,
　　Or wildcats in a red-hot iron cage –

23

The fight must so have seemed in that fell cirque.
　　What penned them there, with all the plain to choose?
　　No footprint leading to that horrid mews,
None out of it. Mad brewage set to work
Their brains, no doubt, like galley slaves the Turk
　　Pits for his pastime, Christians against Jews.

24

And more than that – a furlong on – why, there!
　　What use was that bad engine for, that wheel,
　　Or brake, not wheel – that harrow fit to reel
Men's bodies out like silk? with all the air
Of Tophet's tool, on earth left unaware,
　　Or brought to sharpen its rusty teeth of steel.

25

Then came a bit of stubbed ground, once a wood,
　　Next a marsh, it would seem, and now mere earth
　　Desperate and done with; (so, a fool finds mirth,
Makes a thing and then mars it, till his mood
Changes and off he goes!) within a rood –
　　Bog, clay and rubble, sand and stark black dearth.

26

Now blotches rankling, coloured gay and grim,
　　Now patches where some leanness of the soil's
　　Broke into moss or substances like boils;
Then came some palsied oak, a cleft in him
Like a distorted mouth that splits its rim
　　Gaping at death, and dies while it recoils.

27

And just as far as ever from the end!
   Nought in the distance but the evening, nought
   To point my footstep further! At the thought,
A great black bird, Apollyon's bosom-friend
Sailed past, nor beat his wide wing dragon-penned
   That brushed my cap – perchance the guide I sought.

28

  For, looking up, aware I somehow grew,
    'Spite of the dusk, the plain had given place
    All round to mountains – with such name to grace
Mere ugly heaps and heights now stolen in view.
How thus they had surprised me, solve it, you!
    How to get from them was no clearer case.

29

Yet half I seemed to recognize some trick
    Of mischief happened to me, God knows when –
    In a bad dream perhaps. Here ended, then
Progress this way. When in the very nick
Of giving up, one time more, came a click
    As when a trap shuts – you're inside the den!

30

Burningly it came on me all at once,
    This was the place! those two hills on the right,
    Crouched like two bulls locked horn in horn in fight;
While, to the left, a tall scalped mountain . . . Dunce,
Dotard, a-dozing at the very nonce,
    After a life spent training for the sight!

31

What in the midst lay, but the Tower itself?
    That round, squat turret, blind as the fool's heart,
    Built of brown stone, without a counterpart
In the whole world. The tempest's mocking elf
Points to the shipman thus the unseen shelf
    He strikes on, only when the timbers start.

32

Not see? because of night, perhaps – why, day
  Came back again for that! before it left,
  The dying sunset kindled through a cleft:
The hills like giants at a hunting lay
Chin upon chin to see the game at bay, –
  'Now stab and end the creature – to the heft!'

33

Not hear? when noise was everywhere! it rolled
  Increasing like a bell. Names in my ears
  Of all the lost adventurers, my peers, –
How such a one was strong, and such was bold,
And such was fortunate, yet each of old
   Lost, lost! One moment knelled the woe of years.

34

Thus they stood, ranged along the hillsides, met
  To view the last of me, a living frame
  For one more picture! In a sheet of flame
I saw them, and I knew them all. And yet
Dauntless, the slughorn to my lips I set,
   And blew. *'Childe Roland to the Dark Tower came.'*

ROBERT BROWNING (Published 1855)

This haunting and highly atmospheric poem about a heroic
encounter with unknown and sinister forces provided the inspiration
for Louis MacNeice's much praised radio drama *The Dark Tower*.
Many might find the original poem far superior.

The Vampire

1

I found a corpse, with glittering hair,
Of a woman whose face, tho' dead,
The white death in it had left still fair,
  Too fair for an earthly bed!
So I loosened each fold of her bright curls roll'd
From forehead to foot in a rush of red gold,
And kissed her lips till her lips were red,
And warm and light on her eyelids white
I breath'd, and pressed unto mine her breast,
  Till the blue eyes oped and the breast grew warm,
  And this woman, behold! arose up bold,
    And lifelike lifting a wilful arm,
With steady feet from the winding sheet
  Stepp'd forth to a mutter'd charm.

2

And now beside me, whatever betide me,
  This woman is, night and day.
For she cleaves to me so, that, wherever I go
  She is with me the whole of the way.
And her eyes are so bright in the dead of the night,
  That they keep me awake with dread;
While my life blood pales in my veins and fails,
  Because her red lips are so red
That I fear 'tis my heart she must eat for her food;
  And it makes my whole flesh creep
To think she is drinking and draining my blood,
  Unawares, if I chance to sleep.

3

It were better for me, ere I came nigh her, –
  This corpse, – ere I looked upon her, –
Had they burn'd my body with penal fire
  With a sorcerer's dishonour.
For when the devil has made his lair

In the living eyes of a dear dead woman,
(To bind a man's strength by her golden hair,
   And break his heart, if his heart be human),
Is there any penance, or any prayer,
   That may save the sinner whose soul he tries
To catch in the curse of the constant stare
   Of those heartbreaking bewildering eyes, –
Comfortless, cavernous glowworms that glare
   From the gaping grave where a dead hope lies?
It is more than the soul of a man may bear.
   For the misery worst of all miseries
Is Desire eternally feeding Despair
   On the flesh, or the blood, that forever supplies
Life more than enough to keep fresh in repair
   The death ever dying, which yet never dies.

'OWEN MEREDITH', LORD LYTTON (Published 1858)

The only ghost I ever saw

The only ghost I ever saw
Was dressed in mechlin, – so;
He wore no sandal on his foot,
And stepped like flakes of snow .

His gait was soundless, like the bird,
But rapid, like the roe,
His fashions, quaint mosaic,-
Or haply, mistletoe.

His conversation seldom,
His laughter like the breeze
That dies away in dimples
Among the pensive trees.

Our interview was transient, –
Of me, himself was shy;
And God forbid I look behind
Since that appalling Day!

EMILY DICKINSON (c. 1861)

from *Goblin Market*

Laura has been tempted by the goblins to buy some of their enchanted fruit with a lock of her golden hair. Returning to her sister Lizzie, who, remembering how another girl, Jeanie, had died from the effects of the fruit, has resisted the goblins' call, she begins to pine away. The poem, with its forbidden fruit, has been related to Christina's own agony over her temptation to elope with her former fiancé, James Collinson, which her sister helped her to overcome.

> Tender Lizzie could not bear
> To watch her sister's cankerous care,
> Yet not to share.
> She night and morning
> Caught the goblins' cry:
> 'Come buy our orchard fruits,
> Come buy, come buy:' –
> Beside the brook, along the glen,
> She heard the tramp of goblin men,
> The voice and stir
> Poor Laura could not hear;
> Longed to buy fruit to comfort her,
> But feared to pay too dear.
> She thought of Jeanie in her grave,
> Who should have been a bride;
> But who for joys brides hope to have
> Fell sick and died
> In her gay prime,
> In earliest winter time,
> With the first glazing rime,
> With the first snow-fall of crisp winter time.
>
> Till Laura dwindling
> Seemed knocking at Death's door.
> Then Lizzie weighed no more
> Better and worse;
> But put a silver penny in her purse,
> Kissed Laura, crossed the heath with clumps of furze
> At twilight, halted by the brook:

And, for the first time in her life
Began to listen and look.

Laughed every goblin
When they spied her peeping:
Came towards her hobbling,
Flying, running, leaping,
Puffing and blowing,
Chuckling, clapping, crowing,

Clucking and gobbling,
Mopping and mowing,
Full of airs and graces,
Pulling wry faces,
Demure grimaces,
Cat-like and rat-like,
Ratel-like and wombat-like,
Snail-paced in a hurry,
Parrot-voiced and whistler,
Helter-skelter, hurry skurry,
Chattering like magpies,
Fluttering like pigeons,
Gliding like fishes, –
Hugged her and kissed her:
Squeezed and caressed her:
Stretched up their dishes,
Panniers and plates:
'Look at our apples,
Russet and dun,
Bob at our cherries,
Bite at our peaches,
Citrons and dates,
Grapes for the asking,
Pears red with basking
Out in the sun,
Plums on their twigs;
Pluck them and suck them, –
Pomegranates, figs.'

'Good folk,' said Lizzie,
Mindful of Jeanie:
'Give me much and many:' –
Held out her apron,
Tossed them her penny.
'Nay, take a seat with us,
Honour and eat with us,'
The answered, grinning:
'Our feast is but beginning.
Night yet is early,
Warm and dew-pearly,
Wakeful and starry:
Such fruits as these
No man can carry;
Half their bloom would fly,
Half their dew would dry,
Half their flavour would pass by.
Sit down and feast with us,
Be welcome guest with us,
Cheer you and rest with us.' –
'Thank you,' said Lizzie: 'But one waits
At home alone for me:
So without further parleying,
If you will not sell me any
Of your fruits though much and many,
Give me back my silver penny
I tossed you for a fee.' –
They began to scratch their pates,
No longer wagging, purring,
But visibly demurring,
Grunting and snarling.
One called her proud,
Cross-grained, uncivil;
Their tones waxed loud,
Their looks were evil.
Lashing their tails
They trod and hustled her,
Elbowed and jostled her,
Clawed with their nails,
Barking, mewing, hissing, mocking,

Tore her gown and soiled her stocking,
Twitched her hair out by the roots,
Stamped upon her tender feet,
Held her hands and squeezed their fruits
Against her mouth to make her eat.
White and golden Lizzie stood,
Like a lily in a flood, –
Like a rock of blue-veined stone
Lashed by tides obstreperously, –
Like a beacon left alone
In a hoary roaring sea,
Sending up a golden fire, –
Like a fruit-crowned orange tree
White with blossoms honey sweet,
Sore beset by wasp and bee, –
Like a royal virgin town
Topped with gilded dome and spire
Close beleaguered by a fleet
Mad to tug her standard down.

One may lead a horse to water,
Twenty cannot make him drink.
Tho' the goblins cuffed and caught her,
Coaxed and fought her,
Bullied and besought her,
Scratched her, pinched her black as ink,
Kicked and knocked her,
Mauled and mocked her,
Lizzie uttered not a word;
Would not open lip from lip
Lest they should cram a mouthful in:
But laughed in heart to feel the drip
Of juice that syruped all her face,
And lodged in dimples of her chin,
And streaked her neck which quaked like curd.
At last the evil people,
Worn out by her resistance,
Flung back her penny, kicked their fruit
Along whichever road they took,
Not leaving root or stone or shoot;

Some writhed into the ground,
Some dived into the brook
With ring and ripple,
Some scudded on the gale without a sound,
Some vanished in the distance.
In a smart, ache, tingle,
Lizzie went her way;
Knew not was it night or day;
Sprang up the bank, tore through the furze,
Threaded copse and dingle,
And heard her penny jingle
Bouncing in her purse, —
Its bounce was music to her ear.
She ran and ran
As if she felt some goblin man
Dogged her with gibe and curse
Or something worse:
But not one goblin skurried after,
Nor was she pricked by fear;
The kind heart made her windy-paced
That urged her home quite out of breath with haste
And inward laughter.

She cried, 'Laura,' up the garden,
'Did you miss me?
Come and kiss me.
Never mind my bruises,
Hug me, suck my juices
Squeezed from goblin fruits for you,
Goblin pulp and goblin dew.
Eat me, drink me, love me;
Laura, make much of me;
For your sake I have braved the glen,
And had to do with goblin merchant men.'

Laura started from her chair,
Flung her arms up in the air,
Clutched her hair:
'Lizzie, Lizzie, have you tasted,
For my sake the fruit forbidden?

Must your light like mine be hidden,
Your young life like mine be wasted,
Undone in my undoing,
And ruined in my ruin,
Thirsty, cankered, goblin-ridden?' –
She clung about her sister,
Kissed and kissed and kissed her:
Tears once again
Refreshed her sunken eyes,
Dropping like rain
After long sultry drouth;
Shaking with aguish fear and pain,
She kissed and kissed her with a hungry mouth.

Her lips began to scorch,
That juice was wormwood to her tongue,
She loathed the feast:
Writhing as one possessed she leapt and sung,
Rent all her robe, and wrung
Her hands in lamentable haste,
And beat her breast.
Her locks streamed like the torch
Borne by a racer at full speed,
Or like the mane of horses in their flight,
Or like an eagle when she stems the light
Straight toward the sun,
Or like a caged thing freed,
Or like a flying flag when armies run.

Swift fire spread through her veins, knocked
        at her heart,
Met the fire smouldering there
And overbore its lesser flame;
She gorged on bitterness without a name:
Ah fool, to choose such part
Of soul-consuming care!
Sense failed in the mortal strife:
Like the watch-tower of a town
Which an earthquake shatters down,
Like lightning stricken mast,

Like a wind-uprooted tree
Spun about,
Like a foam-topped waterspout
Cast down headlong in the sea,
She fell at last;
Pleasure past and anguish past,
Is it death or is it life?

Life out of death.
That night long Lizzie watched by her,
Counted her pulse's flagging stir,
Felt for her breath
Held water to her lips and cooled her face
With tears and fanning leaves.
But when the first birds chirped about their eaves,
And early reapers plodded to the place
Of golden sheaves,
And dew wet grass
Bowed in the morning winds so brisk to pass,
And new buds with new day
Opened of cup-like lilies on the stream,
Laura awoke as from a dream,
Laughed in the innocent old way,
Hugged Lizzie but not twice or thrice;
Her gleaming locks showed not one trace of grey,
Her breath was sweet as May,
And light danced in her eyes.

Days, weeks months years
Afterwards, when both were wives
With children of their own;
Their mother hearts beset with fears,
Their lives bound up in tender lives;
Laura would call the little ones
And tell them of her early prime,
Those pleasant days long gone
Of not-returning time:
Would talk about the haunted glen,
The wicked quaint fruit-merchant men,
Their fruits like honey to the throat

But poison to the blood
(Men sell not such in any town)
Would tell them how her sister stood
In deadly peril to do her good,
And win the fiery antidote;
Then joining hands top little hands
Would bid them cling together, –
'For there is no friend like a sister
In calm or stormy weather;
To cheer one on the tedious way,
To fetch one if one goes astray,
To lift one if one totters down,
To strengthen while one stands.'

                    CHRISTINA ROSSETTI (Published 1862)

The Berg

A Dream

I saw a ship of martial build
(Her standards and her brave apparel on)
Directed as by madness mere
Against a solid iceberg steer,
Nor budge it, though the infatuate ship went down.
The impact made huge ice-cubes fall
Sullen, in tons that crashed the deck;
But that one avalanche was all –
No other movement save the floundering wreck.

Along the spurs of ridges pale,
Not any slenderest shaft and frail,
A prism over glass-green gorges lone,
Toppled; nor lace of traceries fine,
Nor pendant drops in grot or mine
Were jarred when the stunned ship went down.
Nor sole the gulls in cloud that wheeled
Circling one snow-flanked field afar,

But nearer fowl the floes that skimmed
And crystal beaches felt no jar.
No thrill transmitted stirred the lock
Of jack-straw needle-ice at base;
Towers undermined by waves – the block
Atilt impending – kept their place.
Seals, dozing sleek on sliddery ledges
Slipt never, when by loftier edges
Through very inertia overthrown,
The impetuous ship in bafflement went down.

Hard Berg (methought), so cold, so vast,
With mortal damps self-overcast;
Exhaling still thy dankish breath –
Adrift dissolving, bound for death;
Though lumpish thou, a lumbering one –
A lumbering lubbard, loitering slow,
Impingers rue thee and go down,
Sounding thy precipice below,
Nor stir the slimy slug that sprawls
Along thy dead indifference of walls.

HERMAN MELVILLE

Although Melville's dream vessel appears to be a warship, this is an uncanny anticipation of what happened to the *Titanic*, many years later. In fact Hardy's poem on the loss of the liner, 'The Convergence of the Twain', seems to recall Melville's sea-slug.

from *The Passing of Arthur*

So all day long the noise of battle rolled
Among the mountains by the winter sea;
Until King Arthur's table, man by man,
Had fallen in Lyonesse about their lord,
King Arthur. Then, because his wound was deep,
The old Sir Bedivere uplifted him

And bore him to a chapel nigh the field,
A broken chapel with a broken cross,
That stood in a dark strait of barren land:
On one side lay the Ocean, and on one
Lay a great water, and the moon was full.

Then spake King Arthur to Sir Bedivere:
'The sequel of today unsolders all
The goodliest fellowship of famous knights
Whereof this world holds record. Such a sleep
They sleep – the men I loved. I think that we
Shall nevermore, at any future time,
Delight our souls with talk of knightly deeds,
Walking about the gardens and the halls
Of Camelot, as in the days that were.
I perish by this people that I made, –
Though Merlin sware that I should come again
To rule once more; but let what will be, be,
I am so deeply smitten through the helm
That without help I cannot last till morn.
Thou therefore take my sword Excalibur,
Which was my pride, for thou rememberest how
In those old days, one summer noon, an arm
Rose up from out the bosom of the lake,
Clothed in white samite, mystic, wonderful,
Holding the sword – and how I row'd across
And took it and have worn it like a king;
And wheresoever I am sung or told
In aftertime, this also shall be known:
But now delay not: take Excalibur,
And fling him far into the middle mere:
Watch what thou seest, and lightly bring me word.'

To him replied the bold Sir Bedivere:
'It is not meet, Sir King, to leave thee thus,
Aidless, alone, and smitten thro' the helm –
A little thing may harm a wounded man;
Yet I thy hest will all perform at full,
Watch what I see, and lightly bring thee word.'

So saying, from the ruin'd shrine he stept,
And, in the moon, athwart the place of tombs,
Where lay the mighty bones of ancient men,
Old knights, and over them the sea-wind sang,
Shrill, chill, with flakes of foam. He, stepping down
By ziz-zag paths and juts of pointed rock,
Came on the shining levels of the lake.

There drew he forth the brand Excalibur,
And o'er him drawing it, the silver moon,
Brightening the skirts of a long cloud, ran forth
And sparkled keen with frost against the hilt:
For all the haft twinkled with diamond sparks,
Myriads of topaz-lights, and jacinth-work
Of subtlest jewellery. He gazed so long
That both his eyes were dazzled as he stood,
This way and that dividing the swift mind,
In act to throw: but at the last it seemed
Better to leave Excalibur conceal'd
There in the many-knotted water-flags
That whistled stiff and dry about the marge.
So strode he back slow to the wounded King.

Then spake King Arthur to Sir Bedivere:
'Hast thou performed my mission which I gave?
What is it thou hast seen? or what hast heard?'

And answer made the bold Sir Bedivere:
'I heard the ripple washing in the reeds,
And the wild water lapping on the crag.'

To whom replied King Arthur, faint and pale:
Thou hast betrayed thy nature and thy name,
Not rendering true answer, as beseem'd
Thy fealty, nor like a noble knight:
For surer sign had follow'd, either hand
Or voice, or else a motion of the mere.
This is a shameful thing for men to lie.
Yet now I charge thee, quickly go again,
As thou art lief and dear, and do the thing
I bade thee, watch and lightly bring me word.'

Then went Sir Bedivere the second time
Across the ridge, and paced beside the mere,
Counting the dewy pebbles, fix'd in thought;
But when he saw the wonder of the hilt,
How curiously and strangely chased, he smote
His palms together, and he cried aloud:

'And if indeed I cast the brand away,
Surely a precious thing, one worthy note,
Should thus be lost for ever from the earth
Which might have pleased the eyes of many men.
What good should follow this if this were done?
What harm, undone? Deep harm to disobey,
Seeing obedience is the bond of rule.
Were it well to obey then, if a king demand
An act unprofitable, against himself?
The King is sick, and knows not what he does.
What record or what relic of my lord
Should be to aftertime, but empty breath
And rumours of a doubt? But were this kept,
Stored in some treasure-house of mighty kings,
Someone might show it at a joust of arms,
Saying, 'King Arthur's sword, Excalibur,
Wrought by the lonely maiden of the Lake.
Nine years she wrought it, sitting in the deeps,
Under the hidden bases of the hills.'
So might some old man speak in the aftertime
To all the people, winning reverence.
But now much honour and much fame were lost.'

So spake he, clouded with his own conceit,
And hid Excalibur the second time,
And so strode back slow to the wounded King.

Then spake King Arthur, breathing heavily:
'What is it thou hast seen and what hast heard?'

And answer made the bold Sir Bedivere:
'I heard the water lapping on the crag.
And the long ripple washing in the reeds.'

To whom replied King Arthur, much in wrath:
'Ah miserable and unkind, untrue,
Unknightly, traitor-hearted! Woe is me!
Authority forgets a dying king,
Laid widow'd of the power in his eye
That bow'd the will. I see thee what thou art,
For thou, the latest-left of all my knights,
In whom should meet the offices of all,
Thou wouldst betray me for the precious hilt;
Either from lust of gold, or like a girl
Valuing the giddy pleasure of the eyes.
Yet, for a man may fail in duty twice
And the third time may prosper, get thee hence:
But, if thou spare to fling Excalibur,
I will arise and slay thee with my hands.'

Then quickly rose Sir Bedivere and ran,
And, leaping down the ridges lightly, plung'd
Among the bulrush beds, and clutch'd the sword,
And strongly wheel'd and threw it. The great brand
Made lightnings in the splendour of the moon,
And flashing round and round, and whirl'd in an arch,
Shot like a streamer of the northern morn,
Seen where the moving tides of winter shock
By night with noises of the Northern Sea.
So flash'd and fell the brand Excalibur:
But ere he dipt the surface, rose an arm,
Clothed in white samite, mystic, wonderful,
And caught him by the hilt, and brandish'd him
Three times, and drew him under in the mere.
Then lightly went the other to the King.

Then spoke King Arthur, drawing thicker breath:
'Now see I by thine eyes that this is done.
Speak out: what is it thou hast heard, or seen?'

And answer made the bold Sir Bedivere:
'Sir King, I closed mine eyelids, lest the gems
Should blind my purpose, for I never saw,
Nor shall see here or elsewhere till I die

So great a miracle as yonder hilt.
Then with both hands I flung him, wheeling him;
But when I look'd again, behold an arm
Cloth'd in white samite, mystic, wonderful
That caught him by the hilt and brandish'd him
Three times, and drew him in under the mere.'

And answer made King Arthur, breathing hard:
'My end draws nigh; 'tis time that I were gone.
Make broad thy shoulders to receive my weight,
And bear me to the margin; yet I fear
My wound hath taken cold, and I shall die.'

So saying, from the pavement he half rose,
Slowly, with pain, reclining on his arm,
And, looking wistfully with wide blue eyes
As in a picture. Him Sir Bedivere
Remorsefully regarded thro' his tears,
And would have spoken, but he found not words;
Then took with care, and kneeling on one knee,
O'er both his shoulders drew the languid hands,
And rising, bore him thro' the place of tombs.

But, as he walked, King Arthur panted hard,
Like one that feels a nightmare on his bed
When all the house is mute. So sighed the King
'Muttering and murmuring at his ear, 'Quick, quick,
I fear it is too late and I shall die.'
But the other swiftly strode from ridge to ridge
Cloth'd with his breath, and looking as he walk'd,
Larger than human on the frozen hills.
He heard the deep behind him, and a cry
Before. His own thought drove him like a goad.
Dry clash'd his harness in the icy caves
And barren chasms, and all to left and right
The bare black cliff clang'd round him as he bas'd
His feet on juts of slippery rock that rang
Sharp smitten with the dint of armed heels. –
And, on a sudden, lo! the level lake,
And the long glories of the winter moon.

Then saw they how there hove a dusky barge,
Dark as a funeral scarf from stem to stern,
Beneath them; and descending they were ware
That all the decks were dense with stately forms,
Black-stoled, black hooded, like a dream – by these
Three Queens with crowns of gold: and from them rose
A cry that shiver'd to the tingling stars,
And, as it were one voice, an agony
Of lamentation, like a wind that shrills
All night in a waste land where no one comes,
Or hath come since the making of the world.

Then murmur'd Arthur, 'Place me in the barge.'
So to the barge they came. There those three Queens
Put forth their hands, and took the King, and wept.
But she that rose the tallest of them all
And fairest, laid his head upon her lap,
And loos'd the shatter'd casque, and chafed his hands,
And call'd him by his name, complaining loud,
And dropping bitter tears against a brow
Strip'd with dark blood: for all his face was white
And colourless, and like the wither'd moon
Smote by the fresh beam of the springing east;
And all his greaves and cuisses dash'd with drops
Of onset; and the light and lustrous curls –
That made his forehead like a rising sun
High from the dais-throne – were parch'd with dust;
Or clotted into points and hanging loose,
Mix'd with the knightly growth that fring'd his lips.
So like a shatter'd column lay the King;
Not like that Arthur who, with lance in rest,
From spur to plume a star of tournament,
Shot through the lists at Camelot, and charged
Before the eyes of ladies and of knights.

Then loudly cried the bold Sir Bedivere:
'Ah! my Lord Arthur, whither shall I go?
Where shall I hide my forehead and my eyes?
For now I see the true old times are dead,
When every morning brought a noble chance,

And every chance brought out a noble knight.
Such times have been not since the light that led
The holy Elders with the gift of myrrh.
But now the whole Round Table is dissolved
Which was an image of the mighty world,
And I, the last, go forth companionless,
And the days darken round me, and the years,
Among new men, strange faces, other minds.'

And slowly answer'd Arthur from the barge:
'The old order changeth, giving place to new,
And God fulfils himself in many ways,
Lest one good custom should corrupt the world.
Comfort thyself: what comfort is in me?
I have lived my life, and that which I have done
May he within himself make pure! but thou,
If thou shouldst never see my face again
Pray for my soul. More things are wrought by prayer
Than this world dreams of. Wherefore, let thy voice
Rise like a fountain for me night and day.
For what are men better than sheep or goats
That nourish a blind life within the brain,
If, knowing God, they lift not hands of prayer
Both for themselves and those who call them friend?
For so the whole round earth is every way
Bound by gold chains about the feet of God.
But now, farewell. I am going a long way
With these thou seest – if indeed I go
(For all my mind is clouded with a doubt) –
To the island-valley of Avilion;
Where falls not hail, or rain, or any snow,
Nor ever wind blows loudly; but it lies
Deep-meadow'd, happy, fair, with orchard lawns,
And bowery hollows crown'd with summer sea,
Where I will heal me of my grievous wound.'

So said he, and the barge with oar and sail
Mov'd from the brink, like some full-breasted swan
That, fluting a wild carol ere her death,
Ruffles her pure white plume, and takes the flood
With swarthy webs. Long stood Sir Bedivere

Revolving many memories, till the hull
Look'd one black dot against the verge of dawn,
And on the mere the wailing died away.

But when that moan had past for evermore
The stillness of the dead world's winter dawn
Amaz'd him, and he groan'd, 'The King is gone.'
And therewithal came on him the weird rhyme,
'From the great deep to the great deep he goes'

Whereat he slowly turn'd and slowly clomb
The last hard footstep of that iron crag;
Thence mark'd the black hull moving yet and cried,
'He passes to be King among the dead,
And after healing of his grievous wound
He comes again; but – if he come no more –
O me, be yon dark Queens in yon black boat,
Who shriek'd and wail'd, the three whereat we gaz'd
On that high day, when, cloth'd with living light,
They stood before his throne in silence, friends Of
    Arthur, who should help him at his need?'

Then from the dawn it seem'd there came, but faint
As from beyond the limits of the world,
Like the last echo born of a great cry,
Sounds, as if some fair city were one voice
Around a king, returning from his wars.

Thereat once more he moved about and clomb
Ev'n to the highest he could climb, and saw,
Straining his eyes beneath an arch of hand,
Or thought he saw, the speck that bare the King,
Down that long water opening on the deep
Somewhere far off, pass on and on and go
From less to less and vanish into light,
And the new sun rose bringing the new year.

ALFRED, LORD TENNYSON (1833–69)

The Card-dealer

Could you not drink her gaze like wine?
    Yet, though its splendour swoon
Into the silence languidly
    As a tune into a tune,
Those eyes unravel the coiled night
    And know the stars at noon.

The gold that's heaped beside her hand,
    In truth rich prize it were;
And rich the dreams that wreathe her brows
    With magic stillness there;
And he were rich who should unwind
    That woven golden hair.

Around her, where she sits, the dance
    Now breathes its eager heat;
And not more lightly or more true
    Fall there the dancers' feet
Than fall her cards on the bright board
    As 'twere an heart that beat.

Her fingers let them softly through,
    Smooth-polished silent things;
And each one as it falls reflects
    In swift light-shadowings,
Blood-red and purple, green and blue,
    The great eyes of her rings.

Whom plays she with? With thee who lov'st
    Those gems upon her hand;
With me, who search her secret brows;
    With all men, bless'd or bann'd.
We play together, she and we,
    Within a vain strange land:

A land without any order, –
    Day even as night, (one saith,) –
Where who lieth down ariseth not
    Nor the sleeper awakeneth;

A land of darkness as darkness itself
   And of the shadow of death.

What be her cards, you ask? Even these: –
   The heart, that doth but crave
More, having fed; the diamond,
   Skilled to make base seem brave;
The club, for smiting in the dark;
   The spade, to dig a grave.

And do you ask what grave she plays?
   With me 'tis lost or won;
With thee it is playing still; with him
   It is not well begun;
But 'tis a game she plays with all
   Beneath the sway o' the sun.

Thou seest the card that falls, – she knows
   The card that followeth:
Her game in thy tongue is called Life,
   As ebbs thy daily breath:
When she shall speak, thou'lt learn her tongue
   And know she calls it Death.

DANTE GABRIEL ROSSETTI (Published 1870)

Shameful Death

There were four of us about that bed;
 The mass-priest knelt at the side,
I and his mother stood at the head,
 Over his feet lay the bride;
We were quite sure that he was dead,
 Though his eyes were open wide.

He did not die in the night,
 He did not die in the day,
But in the morning twilight
 His spirit passed away,
When neither sun or moon was bright,
 And the trees were merely grey.

He was not slain with the sword,
 Knight's axe or knightly spear,
Yet spoke he never a word
 After he came in here;
I cut away the cord
 From the neck of my brother dear.

He did not strike one blow,
 For the recreants came behind,
In a place where rthe hornbeams grow,
 A path right hard to find,
For the hornbeam boughs swing so
 That the twilight makes it blind.

They lighted a great torch then,
 When his arms were pinion'd fast,
Sir John the knight of the Fen,
 Sir Guy of the Dolorous Blast,
With knights threescore and ten,
 Hung brave Sir Hugh at last,

I am threescore and ten,
 And my hair is all turn'd grey,

But I met Sir John of the Fen
    Long ago on a summer day,
And am glad to think of the moment when
    I took his life away.

I am threescore and ten,
    And my strength is mostly pass'd,
But long ago I and my men
    When the sky was overcast,
And the smoke rose over the reeds of the fen
    Slew Guy of the Dolorous Blast,

And now, knights all of you,
    I pray you pray for Sir Hugh,
A good knight and a true,
    And for Alice his wife pray too.

WILLIAM MORRIS

Lucifer in Starlight

On a starred night Prince Lucifer uprose,
Tired of his dark dominion, swung the fiend
Above the rolling ball, in cloud part screened,
Where sinners hugged their spectre of repose.
Poor prey to his hot fit of pride were those.
And now upon his weatern wing he leaned,
Now his huge bulk o'er Afric's sands careened,
Now the black planet shadowed Arctic snows.
Soaring through wider zones that pricked his scars
With memory of the old revolt from Awe,
He reached a middle height, and at the stars,
Which are the brain of heaven, he looked, and sank.
Around the ancient track marched, rank on rank,
The army of unalterable law.

GEORGE MEREDITH (Published 1883)

The Song of Wandering Aengus

I went out to the hazel wood
Because a fire was in my head,
And curt and peeled a hazel wand,
And hooked a berry to a thread;
And when white moths were on the wing,
And moth-like stars were flickering out,
I dropped the berry in a stream
And caught a little silver trout.

When I had laid it on the floor
I went to blow the fire aflame,
But something rustled on the floor,
And someone called me by my name:
It had become a glimmering girl
With apple blossom in her hair
Who called me by my name and ran
And faded through the brightening air.

Though I am old with wandering
Through hollow lands and hilly lands,
I will find out where she has gone,
And kiss her lips and take her hands;
And walk among long dappled grass,
And pluck till times and time are done
The silver apples of the moon,
The golden apples of the sun

WILLIAM BUTLER YEATS (1899)

14
PORTRAITS
& ENCOUNTERS

Resolution and Independence

1

There was a roaring in the wind all night
The rain came heavily and fell in floods;
But now the sun is rising, calm and bright,
the birds are singing in the distant woods,
Over his own sweet voice the Stock-dove broods,
The jay makes answer as the Magpie chatters,
And all the air is filled with pleasant noise of waters.

2

All things that love the sun are out of doors,
The sky rejoices in the morning's birth;
The grass is bright with rain-drops, – on the moors
The hare is running races in her mirth;
And with her feet she from the plashy earth
Raises a mist; that, glittering in the sun,
Runs with her all the way, wherever she doth run.

3

I was a Traveller then, upon the moor;
I saw the hare that raced about with joy;
I heard the woods and distant waters roar;
Or heard them not, as happy as a boy:
The pleasant season did my heart employ:
My old remembrances went from me wholly;
And all the ways of men, so vain and melancholy.

4

But, as it sometimes chanceth, from the might
Of joy in minds that can no further go,
As high as we have mounted in delight
In our dejection do we sink as low;
To me that morning did it happen so;
And fears and fancies thick upon me came;
Dim sadness – and blind thoughts
I knew not, nor could name.

5

I heard the sky-lark warbling in the sky,
And I bethought me of the playful hare:
Even such a happy Child of earth am I,
Even as these blissful creatures do I fare;
Far from the world I walk, and from all care;
But there may come another day to me –
Solitude, pain of heart, distress and poverty.

6

My whole life I have lived in pleasant thought,
As if life's business were a summer mood,
As if all needful things would come unsought
To genial faith, still rich in genial good;
But how can he expect that others should
Build for him, sow for him, and at his call
Love him, who for himself will take no heed at all?

7

I thought of Chatterton, the marvellous Boy,
The sleepless Soul that perished in his pride,
Of him who walked in glory and in joy
Following his plough, along the mountain-side.
By our own spirits are we deified:
We Poets in our youth begin in gladness;
But thereof come in the end despondency and madness.

8

Now whether it were by peculiar grace,
A leading from above, a something given,
Yet it befel that in this lonely place,
When I with these untoward thoughts had striven,
Beside a pool bare to the eye of heaven
I saw a Man before me unawares:
The oldest man he seemed that ever wore grey hairs.

9

As a huge stone is sometimes seen to lie,
Couched on the bald top of an eminence;
Wonder to all who do the same espy
By what means it could thither come and whence;
So that it seems a thing endowed with sense:
Like a sea-beast crawled forth, that on a shelf
Of rock or sand reposeth, there to sun itself;

10

Such seemed this Man, not all alive nor dead,
Not all asleep in his extreme old age:
His body was bent double, feet and head
Coming together in life's pilgrimage;
As if some dire constraint of pain, or rage
Of sickness felt by him in times long past,
A more than human weight upon his frame had cast.

11

Himself he propped, limbs, body and pale face,
Upon a long grey staff of shaven wood:
And still as I drew near with gentle pace,
Upon the margin of that moorish flood
Motionless as a cloud the old man stood,
That heareth not the loud winds when they call,
And moveth all together, if it move at all.

12

At length, himself unsettling, he the pond
Stirred with his staff, and fixedly did look
Upon the muddy water, which he conned,
As if he had been reading in a book:
And now a stranger's privilege I took,
And drawing to his side to him did say,
'This morning gives us promise of a glorious day.'

13

A gentle answer did the old Man make,
In courteous speech which forth he slowly drew:
And him with further words I thus bespake,
'What occupation do you there pursue?
This is a lonesome place for one like you.'
Ere he replied, a flash of mild surprise
Broke from the sable orbs of his yet-vivid eyes.

14

His words came feebly, from a feeble chest,
But each in solemn order followed each,
With something of a lofty utterance drest –
Choice word and measured phrase, above the reach
Of ordinary men; a stately speech;
Such as grave Livers do in Scotland use,
Religious men, who give to God and man their dues.

15

He told that to these waters he had come
To gather leeches, being old and poor:
Employment hazardous and wearisome!
And he had many hardships to endure:
From pond to pond he roamed, from moor to moor;
Housing, with God's good help, by choice or chance,
And in this way he gained an honest maintenance.

16

The old Man still stood talking by my side;
But now his voice to me was like a stream
Scarce heard; nor word from word I could divide;
And the whole body of the Man did seem
Like one whom I had met with in a dream,
Or like a man, from some far region sent,
To give me human strength, by apt admonishment.

17

My former thoughts returned, the fear that kills,
And hope that is unwilling to be fed;
Cold, pain and labour, and all earthly ills,
And mighty Poets in their misery dead.
– Perplexed, and longing to be comforted,
My question eagerly did I renew,
'How is it that you live, and what is it you do?'

18

He with a smile did then his words repeat;
And said, that, gathering leeches far and wide
He travelled, stirring thus about his feet
The waters of the pools where they abide.
'Once I could meet with them on every side;
But they have dwindled long, by slow decay,
Yet still I persevere, and find them where I may.'

19

While he was talking thus, the lonely place;
The old Man's shape and speech – all troubled me.
In my mind's eye I seemed to see him pace
About the weary moors continually,
Wandering about alone and silently.
While I these thoughts within myself pursued,
He, having made a pause, the same discourse renewed.

20

And soon with this he other matter blended,
Cheerfully uttered, with demeanour kind,
But stately in the main; and when he ended,
I could have laughed myself to scorn to find,
In that decrepit Man so firm a mind.
'God,' said I, 'Be my help and stay secure;
I'll think of the Leech-Gatherer on the lonely moor!'

WILLIAM WORDSWORTH (1802)

The Solitary Reaper

Behold her, single in the field,
Yon solitary Highland Lass!
Reaping and singing by herself;
Stop here, or gently pass!
Alone she cuts and binds the grain,
And sings a melancholy strain;
O listen! for the Vale profound
Is overflowing with the sound.

No Nightingale did ever chaunt
More welcome notes to weary bands
Of travellers in some shady haunt,
Among Arabian sands;
A voice so thrilling ne'er was heard
In spring-time from the Cuckoo-bird
Breaking the silence of the seas
Among the farthest Hebrides.

Will no one tell me what she sings? –
Perhaps the plaintive numbers flow
From old, unhappy, far-off things,
And battles long ago:
Or is it some more humble lay,
Familiar matter of today?
Some natural sorrow, loss, or pain,
That has been, and may be again?

Whate'er the theme, the Maiden sang
As if her song could have no ending;
I saw her singing at her work,
And o'er the sickle bending; –
I listened, motionless and still;
And, as I mounted up the hill,
The music in my heart I bore,
Long after it was heard no more.

WILLIAM WORDSWORTH (1804)

Gipsies

The snow falls deep; the forest lies alone;
The boy goes hasty for his load of brakes,
Then thinks upon his fire and hurries back;
The gipsy knocks his hands and tucks them up,
And seeks his squalid camp, half hid in snow,
Beneath the oak which breaks away the wind,
And bushes close in snow, like hovel warm;
There tainted mutton wastes upon the coals,
And the half wasted dog squats close and rubs,
Then feels the heat too strong and goes aloof;
He watches well, but none a bit can spare,
And vainly waits the morsel thrown away.
'Tis thus they live – a picture to the place,
A quiet, pilfering, unprotected race.

JOHN CLARE

My Last Duchess

That's my last duchess painted on the wall,
Looking as if she were alive. I call
That piece a wonder now; Fra Pandolf's hands
Worked busily a day, and there she stands.
Wilt please you sit and look at her? I said
'Fra Pandolf' by design, for never read
Strangers like you that pictured countenance,
The depth and passion of that earnest glance,
But to myself they turned (since none puts by
The curtain I have drawn for you but I)
And seemed as they would ask me, if they durst,
How such a glance came there; so not the first
Are you to turn and ask thus. Sir, 'twas not
Her husband's presence only, called that spot
Of joy into the Duchess' cheek: perhaps
Fra Pandolf chanced to say 'Her mantle laps
Over my lady's wrist too much,' or 'Paint
Must never hope to reproduce the faint

Half flush that dies along her throat:' such stuff
Was courtesy, she thought, and cause enough
For calling up that spot of joy. She had
A heart – how shall I say? – too easily made glad,
Too easily impressed; she liked whate'er
She looked on, and her looks went everywhere.
Sir, 'twas all one! My favour at her breast,
The dropping of the daylight in the West,
The bough of cherries some officious fool
Broke in the orchard for her, the white mule
She rode with round the terrace – all and each
Would draw from her alike the approving speech,
Or blush, at least. She thanked, men, – good! but thanked
Somehow – I know not how – as if she ranked
My gift of a nine hundred years-old name
With anybody's gift. Who'd stoop to blame
This sort of trifling? Even had you skill
In speech – (which I have not) – to make your will
Quite clear to such an one, and say, 'Just this
Or that in you disgusts me; here you miss,
Or here exceed the mark' – and if she let
Herself be lessoned so, nor plainly set
Her wits to yours, forsooth, and made excuse,
– E'en then would be some trifling; and I choose
Never to stoop. Oh, Sir, she smiled, no doubt,
Whene'er I passed her; but who passed without
Much the same smile? This grew; I gave commands;
Then all smiles stopped together. There she stands
As if alive. Wilt please you rise? We'll meet
The company below, then. I repeat,
The Count your master's known munificence
Is ample warrant that no just pretence
Of mine for dowry will be disallowed;
Though his fair daughter's self, as I avowed
At starting, is my object. Nay, we'll go
Together down, sir. Notice Neptune, though,
Taming a seahorse, thought a rarity,
Which Claus of Innsbruck cast in bronze for me!

                              ROBERT BROWNING (1842)

How it Strikes a Contemporary

I only knew one poet in my life:
And this, or something like it, was his way.

You saw go up and down Valladolid,
A man of mark, to know next time you saw.
His very serviceable suit of black
Was courtly once and conscientious still,
And many might have worn it, though none did;
The cloak, that somewhat shone and showed the
    threads,
Had purpose, and the ruff significance.
He walked and tapped the pavement with his cane,
Scenting the world, looking it full in face,
An old dog, pale and blindish at his heels.
They turned up, now, the alley by the church,
That leads nowhither; now they breathed themselves
On the main promenade just at the wrong time:
You'd come upon his scrutinizing hat,
Making a peaked shade blacker than itself
Against the single window spared some house
Intact yet with its mouldered Moorish work, –
Or else surprise the ferrule of his stick
Trying the mortar's temper 'tween the chinks
Of some new shop a-building, French and fine.
He stood and watched the cobbler at his trade,
The man who slices lemons into drink,
The coffee-roaster's brazier, and the boys
That volunteer to help him turn its winch.
He glanced o'er books on stalls with half an eye,
And fly-leaf ballads on the vendor's string,
And broad-edge bold-print posters by the wall.
He took such cognizance of men and things,
If any beat a horse, you felt he saw;
If any cursed a woman, he took note;
Yet stared at nobody, – you stared at him,
And found, less to your pleasure than surprise,
He seemed to know you and expect as much.

So, next time that a neighbour's tongue was loosed,
It marked the shameful and notorious fact,
We had amongst us, not so much a spy,
As a recording chief inquisitor,
The town's true master, if the town but knew!
We merely kept a governor for form,
While this man walked about and took account
Of all thought, said and acted, then went home,
And wrote it fully to our Lord the King,
Who has an itch to know things, he knows why,
And reads them in his bedroom of a night.
Oh, you might smile! there wanted not a touch,
A tang of . . . well, it was not wholly ease
As back into your mind the man's look came,
Stricken in years a little, – such a brow
His eyes had to live under! clear as flint
On either side the formidable nose
Curved, cut and coloured like an eagle's claw.
Had he to do with A's surprising fate?
When altogether old C. disappeared
And young C. got his mistress, – was't our friend,
His letter to the King, that did it all?
What paid the bloodless man for so much pains?
Our Lord the King has favourites manifold,
And shifts his ministry some once a month;
Our city gets new governors at whiles, –
But never word or sign that I could hear,
Notified to this man about the streets
The King's approval of those letters conned
The last thing duly at the dead of night.
Did the man love his office? Frowned our Lord,
Exhorting when none heard – 'Beseech me not!
'Too far above my people – beneath me!
'I set the watch, – how should the people know?
'Forget them, keep me all the more in mind!'
Was some such understanding 'twixt the two?

I found no truth in one report at least –
That, if you tracked him to his home down lanes
Beyond the Jewry, and as clean to pace,

You found he ate his supper in a room
Blazing with lights, four Titians on the wall,
And twenty naked girls to change his plate!
Poor man, he lived another kind of life
In that new stuccoed third house by the bridge,
Fresh painted, rather smart than otherwise!
The whole street might o'erlook him as he sat,
Leg crossing leg, one foot on the dog's back,
Playing a decent cribbage with his maid
(Jacynth you're sure his name was) o'er the cheese
And fruit, three red halves of starved winter-pears,
Or treat of radishes in April. Nine,
Ten, struck the church clock, straight to bed went he.

My father, like the man of sense he was,
Would point him out to me a dozen times;
' 'St – 'St,' he'd whisper, 'the Corregidor!'
I had been used to think that personage
Was one with lacquered breeches, lustrous belt
And feathers like a forest in his hat,
Who blew a trumpet and proclaimed the news,
Announced the bull fights, gave each church
    its turn,
And memorized the miracle in vogue!
He had a great observance from the boys;
We were in error; that was not the man.

I'd like now, yet have haply been afraid,
To have just looked when this man came to die,
And seen who lined the clean gay garret sides
And stood about the neat low truckle bed,
With the heavenly manner of relieving guard.
Here had been, mark, the general in chief,
Thro' a whole campaign of the world's life and
    death,
Done the King's work all the dim day long,
In his old coat, and up to knees in mud,
Smoked like a herring, dining on a crust, –
And now the day was won, relieved at once!
No further show or need for that old coat,

You are sure, for one thing! Bless us, all the while,
How sprucely we are dressed out, you and I!
A second, and the angels alter that.
Well, I could never write a verse, – could you?
Let's to the Prado and make the most of time.

ROBERT BROWNING (Published 1855)

Browning's picture here of the poet as a man who blends into the
social background and observes his fellow men is a corrective to the
popular view of the poet as an impressive, romantically cloaked
figure in the manner of Yeats or Tennyson.

In an Artist's Studio

One face looks out from all his canvases,
    One selfsame figure stands or walks or leans,
    We found her hidden just behind those screens,
That mirror gave back all her loveliness.
A queen in opal or in ruby dress,
    A nameless girl in freshest summer greens,
    A saint, an angel, – every canvas means
The same one meaning, neither more nor less.
He feeds upon her face by day and night,
    And she with true kind face looks back on him
Fair as the moon, and joyful as the light:
    Not wan with waiting, not with sorrow dim;
Not as she is, but was when hope shone bright,
    Not as she is, but as she fills his dream.

CHRISTINA ROSSETTI (1856)

Almost certainly referring to her brother's model and future wife,
Elizabeth Siddal, writer of the poem 'Worn Out' in Section 9.

A Face devoid of Love or Grace

A face devoid of love or grace
A hateful, hard, successful face,
A face with which a stone
Would feel as thoroughly at ease
As were they old acquaintances –
First time together thrown.

EMILY DICKINSON

from *Jenny*

Lazy, languid, laughing Jenny
Fond of a kiss and fond of a guinea,
Whose head upon my knee tonight
Rests for a while, as if grown light
With all our dances and the sound
To which the wild tunes spun you round:
Fair Jenny mine, the thoughtless queen
Of kisses, which the blush between
Could hardly make much daintier;
Whose eyes are as blue skies, whose hair
Is countless gold incomparable:
Fresh flower, scarce touched with signs
        that tell
Of Love's exuberant hotbed: – Nay,
Poor flower left torn since yesterday
Until tomorrow leave you bare;
Poor handful of bright spring-water
Flung in the whirlpool's shrieking face;
Poor shameful Jenny, full of grace
Thus with your head upon my knee; –
Whose person or whose purse may be
The lodestar of your reverie?

This room of yours, my Jenny, looks
A change from mine, so full of books,
Whose serried ranks hold fast, forsooth,
So many captive hours of youth, –
The hours they thieve from day and night
To make one's cherished work come right,
And leave it wrong for all one's theft,
Even as tonight my work was left:
Until I vowed that since my brain
And eyes of dancing seemed so fain,
My feet should have some dancing too: –
And thus it was I met with you.
Well, I suppose 'twas hard to part,
For here I am. And now, sweetheart,
You seem too tired to get to bed.

   It was a careless life I led
When rooms like this were scarce so strange
Not long ago. What breeds the change, –
The many aims, or the few years?
Because tonight it all appears
Something I do not know again.

   The cloud's not danced out of my brain, –
The cloud that made it turn and swim
While hour by hour the books grew dim.
Why, Jenny, as I watch you there, –
For all your wealth of loosened hair,
Your silk ungirdled and unlac'd
And warm sweets open to the waist,
All golden in the lamplight's gleam,
You know not what a book you seem,
Half read by lamplight in a dream!
How should you know, my Jenny? Nay,
And I should be ashamed to say: –
Poor beauty, so well worth a kiss!
But while my thought runs on like this
With wasteful whims more than enough,
I wonder what you're thinking of.

If of myself you think at all,
What is the thought? – conjectural
On sorry matters best unsolved? –
Or inly is each grace revolved
To fit me with a lure? – or (sad
To think!) perhaps you're merely glad
That I'm not drunk or ruffianly
And let you rest upon my knee.

For sometimes, were the truth confess'd,
You're thankful for a little rest, –
Glad from the crush to rest within,
From the heart-sickness and the din
Where envy's voice at virtue's pitch
Mocks you because your gown is rich;
And from the pale girl's dumb rebuke,
Whose ill-clad grace and toil-worn look
Proclaim the strength that keeps her weak,
And other nights than yours bespeak;
And from the wise, unchildish elf,
To schoolmate lesser than himself
Pointing you out, what thing you are: –
Yes, from the daily jeer and jar,
From shame, and shame's outbraving, too,
Is rest sometimes not sweet to you? –
But most from the hatefulness of man
Who spares not to end what he began,
Whose acts are ill and his speech ill,
Who, having used you at his will,
Thrusts you aside, as when I dine,
I serve the dishes and the wine.

Well, handsome Jenny mine, sit up;
I've filled our glasses, let us sup,
And do not let me think of you,
Lest shame of yours suffice for two.
What, still so tired? Well, well then, keep
Your head there, so you do not sleep;
But that the weariness may pass
And leave you merry, take this glass.
Ah, lazy lily hand, more bless'd

If ne'er in rings it had been dress'd
Nor ever by a glove conceal'd!

Behold the lilies of the field,
They toil not, neither do they spin;
(So doth the ancient text begin, –
Not of such rest as one of these
Can share.) Another rest and ease,
Along each summer sated path
From its new lord the summer hath,
Than that whose spring in blessings ran
Which praised the bounteous husbandman,
Ere yet in days of hankering breath,
The lilies sickened unto death.

What, Jenny, are your lilies dead?
Aye, and the snow-white leaves are spread
Like winter on the garden bed.
But you had roses left in May, –
They were not gone too, Jenny, nay,
But must your roses die, and those
Their purfled buds that should unclose?
Even so; the leaves are curled apart,
Still read, as from the broken heart,
And here's the naked stem of thorns.

Nay, nay, mere words. Here nothing warns,
As yet of winter. Sickness here
Or want alone could waken fear, –
Nothing but passion wrings a tear,
Except when there may rise unsought
Haply at times a passing thought
Of the old days which seem to be
Much older than any history
That is written in any book;
When she would lie in fields and look
Along the ground through the blown grass,
And wonder where the city was,
Far out of sight, whose broil and bale
They told her then for a child's tale.

Jenny, you know the city now,
A child can tell the tale there, how
Some things which are not yet enroll'd
In market lists are bought and sold
Even till the early Sunday light,
When Saturday is market-night
Everywhere, be it dry or wet,
And market night in the Haymarket,
Our learned London children know,
Poor Jenny, all your pride and woe;
Have seen your lifted silken skirt
Advertise dainties through the dirt;
Have seen your coach-wheels splash rebuke
On virtue, and have known your look
When, wealth and health slipped past, you stare
Along the streets alone, and there,
Round the long park, across the bridge,
The cold lamps at the pavement's edge
Wind on together and apart,
A fiery serpent for your heart.

Let the thoughts pass, an empty cloud!
Suppose I were to think aloud, –
What if to her all this were said?
Why, as a volume seldom read
Being opened halfway shuts again,
So might the pages of her brain
Be parted at such words, and thence
Close back upon the dusty sense.
For is there hue or shape defin'd
In Jenny's desecrated mind,
Where all contagious currents meet,
A Lethe of the middle street?
Nay, it reflects not any face,
Nor sound is in its sluggish pace,
But as they coil, those eddies clot,
And night and day remembers not.

Why Jenny, you're asleep at last! –
Asleep, poor Jenny, hard and fast, –

So young and soft and tired; so fair
With chin thus nestled in your hair,
Mouth quiet, eyelids almost blue
As if some sky of dreams shone through!

* * * * *

So on the wings of day decamps
My last night's frolic. Glooms begin
To shiver off as lights creep in
Past the gauze curtains half drawn-to,
And the lamp's doubled shade grows blue, –
Your lamp, my Jenny, kept alight
Like a wise virgin's, all one night!
And in the alcove coolly spread
Glimmers with dawn your empty bed;
And yonder your fair face I see
Reflected, lying on my knee,
Where teems with first foreshadowings
Your pier-glass scrawled with diamond rings;
And on your bosom all night worn
Yesterday's rose now droops forlorn,
But dies not yet this summer morn.

And now, without, as if some word
Had called upon them that they heard,
The London sparrows far and nigh
Clamour together suddenly;
And Jenny's cage-bird grown awake
Here in their song his part must take,
Because here too the day doth break.

And somehow in myself the dawn
Among stirred clouds and veils withdrawn
Strikes greyly on her. Let her sleep.
But will it wake her if I heap
These cushions thus beneath her head
Where my knee was? No, – there's your bed,
My Jenny, while you dream. And there
I lay among your golden hair
Perhaps the subject of your dreams,

These golden coins.
              For still one deems
That Jenny's flattering sleep confers
New magic on the magic purse, –
Grim web, how clogged with shrivelled flies!
Between the threads fine fumes arise
And shape their pictures in the brain.
There roll no streets in glare and rain,
Nor flagrant man-swine whets his tusk;
But delicately sighs in musk
The homage of the dim boudoir;
Or like a palpitating star
Thrilled into song, the opera-night
Breathes faint in the quick pulse of light;
Or at the carriage-window shine
Rich wares for choice; or, free to dine,
Whirls though its hour of health (divine
For her) the concourse of the Park.
And, though in the discounted dark
Her functions there and here are one,
Beneath the lamps and in the sun
There reigns at least the acknowledged belle
Apparelled beyond parallel.
Ah, Jenny, yes, we know your dreams.

For even the Paphian Venus seems
A goddess o'er the realms of love
When silver shrined in shadowy grove;
Aye, or let offerings nicely placed
But hide Priapus to the waist.
And whoso looks on him shall see
An eligible deity.

   Why, Jenny, waking here alone
May help you to remember one,
Though all the memory's long outworn
Of many a double-pillowed morn.
I think I see you when you wake,
And rub your eyes for me, and shake
My gold, in rising, from your hair,
A Danae for a moment there.

Jenny, my love rang true! for still
Love at first sight is vague, until
That tinkling makes him audible.

And must I mock you to the last,
Ashamed of my own shame, – aghast
Because some thoughts not born amiss
Rose at a poor fair face like this?
Well, of such thoughts so much I know;
In my life, as in hers, they show,
By a far gleam which I may near,
A dark path I can strive to clear.

Only one kiss. Good-bye, my dear.

DANTE GABRIEL ROSSETTI (Published 1870)

Mona Lisa

She is older than the rocks on which she sits;
Like the Vampire,
She has been dead many times,
And learned the secrets of the grave;
And has been a diver in deep seas,
And keeps their fallen day about her;
And trafficked for strange webs with Eastern
    merchants;
And as Leda,
Was the mother of Helen of Troy,
And as St Anne,
Was the mother of Mary;

And all this has been to her but as the sound
    of lyres and flutes
And lives
Only in the delicacy
With which it has moulded the changing
    lineaments,
And tinged the eyelids and the hands.

WALTER PATER

Rizpah

1

Wailing, wailing, wailing, the wind over land and sea, –
And Willy's voice in the wind, 'O mother, come out to me.'
Why should he call me tonight, when he knows that I
    cannot go?
For the downs are as bright as day, and the full moon stares
    at the snow.

2

We should be seen, my dear; they would spy us out of the
    town.
The loud black night for us, and the storm rushing over the
    down,
When I cannot see my own hand, but am led by the creak of
    the chain,
And grovel and grope for my son till I find myself drenched
    with the rain.

3

Anything fallen again? Nay – what was there left to fall?
I have taken them home, I have numbered the bones, I have
    hidden them all.
What am I saying? and what are *you*? do you come as a spy?
Falls, what falls? who knows? As the tree falls, so must it lie.

4

Who let her in? How long has she been? you – what have
    you heard?
Why did you sit so quiet? you never have spoken a word.
O – to pray with me – yes – a lady – none of their spies –
But the night has crept into my heart, and begun to darken
    my eyes.

5

Ah – you that have lived so soft, what should you know of
    the night,
The blast and the burning shame and the bitter frost and the
    fright?

I have done it, while you were asleep – you were only made
for the day.
I have gathered my baby together – and now you may go
your way.

6

Nay – for it's kind of you, Madam, to sit by an old dying
wife.
But say nothing of my boy, I have only an hour of life.
I kissed my boy in the prison, before he went out to die.
'They dared me to do it,' he said, and he never has told me a
lie.
I whipt him for robbing an orchard once when he was but a
child –
'The farmer dared me to do it,' he said; he was always so
wild –
And idle – and couldn't be idle – my Willy – he never could
rest.
The King should have made him a soldier; he would have
been one of his best.

7

But he lived with a lot of wild mates, and they never would
let him be good;
They swore that he dare not rob the mail, and he swore that
he would;
And he took no life, but he took one purse, and when all
was done
He flung it among his fellows – I'll none of it, said my son.

8

I came into court to the Judge and the lawyers. I told them
my tale,
God's own truth – but they kill'd him, they kill'd him, for
robbing the mail.
They hang'd him in chains for a show – we had always
borne a good name –
To be hang'd for a thief – and then put away – isn't that
enough shame?

Dust to dust – low down – let us hide! but they set him so
   high
That all the ships of the world could stare at him, passing
   by.
God'll pardon the hell-black raven and horrible fowls of the
   air,
But not the black heart of the lawyer who kill'd him and
   hang'd him there.

9

And the jailer forced me away. I had bid him my last
   goodbye;
They had fastened the door of his cell, 'O, mother!' I heard
   him cry.
I couldn't get back, tho' I tried; he had something further to
   say,
And now I shall never know it. The jailer forced me away.

10

Then since I couldn't but hear that cry of my boy that was
   dead,
They seized me and shut me up; they fastened me down on
   my bed.
'Mother, O mother!' he call'd in the dark to me year after
   year –
They beat me for that, they beat me – you know that I
   couldn't but hear;
And then, at the last, they found I had grown so stupid and
   still,
They let me abroad again, but the creatures had worked
   their will.

11

Flesh of my flesh was gone, but bone of my bone was left –
I stole them all from the lawyers – and you, will you call it a
   theft? –
My baby, the bones that had suck'd me, the bones that had
   laugh'd and cried –
Theirs? O no! they are mine, not theirs – they had moved in
   my side.

12

Do you think I was scared by the bones? I kissed 'em, I
    buried 'em all –
I can't dig deep; I am old – in the night, by the churchyard
    wall.
My Willy 'ill rise up whole when the trumpet of judgement
    'ill sound,
But I charge you never to say that I laid him in holy ground.

13

They would scratch him up – they would hang him again on
    the cursed tree.
Sin? O yes – we are all sinners, I know, let all that be,
And read me a Bible verse of the Lord's good will toward
    men –
'Full of compassion and mercy, the Lord' – let me hear it
    again;
'Full of compassion and mercy – long-suffering.' Yes, O yes!
For the lawyer lives but to murder – the Saviour lives but to
    bless.

He'll never put on the black cap except for the worst of the
    worst,
And the first may be last – I have heard it in church – and
    the last may be first,
Suffering – O long-suffering – yes, as the Lord must know,
Year after year in the mist, and the shower and the snow.

14

Heard, have you? what? they have told you he never
    repented his sin.
How do they know it? are *they* his mother are *you* of his kin?
Heard! have you ever heard, when the storm on the down
    began,
The wind that 'ill wail like a child and the sea that 'ill moan
    like a man?

15

Election, Election and Reprobation – it's all very well.
But I go tonight to my boy, and I shall not find him in Hell.
For I cared so much for my boy that the Lord has look'd
    into my care,
And he means me, I'm sure, to be happy with Willy, I know
    not where.

16

And if he be lost – but to save my soul, that is all your
    desire:
Do you think that I care for my soul if my boy be gone to the
    fire?
I have been with God in the dark – go, go, you may leave me
    alone –
You never have borne a child – you are just as hard as stone.

17

Madam, I beg your pardon! I think that you mean to be kind,
But I cannot hear what you say for my Willy's voice in the
    wind –
The snow and the sky so bright – he used but to call in the
    dark,
And he calls to me now from the church and not from the
    gibbet – for hark!
Nay – you can hear it yourself – it is coming – shaking the
    walls –
Willy – the moon's in a cloud – Goodnight. I am going. He
    calls.

ALFRED, LORD TENNYSON (Published 1880)

Harry Ploughman

Hard as hurdle arms, with a broth of golden flue
Breathed round; the rack of ribs; the scooped flank; lank
Rope-over thigh; knee knave; and barrelled shank –
　　　Head and foot, shoulder and shank –
By a grey eye's heed steered well, one crew, fall to;
Stand at stress. Each limb's barrowy brawn, his thew
That onwhere curded, onwhere soared or sank –
　　　Soared ór sánk – ,

Though as a beechbole firm, find his, as at a roll call,
　　rank
And features, in flesh, what deed he each must do –
　　　His sinew-service, where do.

He leans to it, Harry bends, look. Back, elbow and liquid
　　waist
In him all quail to the wallowing o' the plough. 'S cheek
　　crimsons; curls
Wag or crossbridle, in a wind lifted, windlaced –
　　　See his wind-lilylocks-laced;
Churlsgrace, too, child of Amansstrength, how it hangs
　　or hurls
Them – broad in bluff hide his frowning feet lashed!
　　raced
With, along them, cragiron under and cold furls –
　　　With a fountain's shining-shot furls.

GERARD MANLEY HOPKINS (1887)

A Man

1

In Casterbridge there stood a noble pile,
Wrought with pilaster, bay and balustrade
In tactful times when shrewd Eliza swayed. –
    On burgher, squire and clown
It smiled the long street down for near a mile.

2

But evil days beset that domicile;
The stately beauties of its roof and wall
Fell into sordid hands. Condemned to fall
    Were cornice, quoin and cove,
And all that art had wove in antique style.

3

Among the hired dismantlers entered there
One till the moment of his task untold.
When charged therewith he gazed, and answered bold:
    'Be needy I or no,
I will not help lay low a house so fair!

4

Hunger is hard. But since the terms be such –
No wage, or labour stained with the disgrace
Of wrecking what our age cannot replace
    To save its tasteless soul –
I'll do without your dole. Life is not much!'

5

Dismissed with sneers he backed his tools and went,
And wandered workless; for it seemed unwise
To close with one who dared to criticize
    And carp on points of taste:
Rude men should work where placed, and be content.

6

Years whiled. He aged, sank, sickened; and was not:
And it was said, 'A man intractable
And curst is gone.' None sighed to hear his knell,
        None sought his churchyard-place;
His name, his rugged face, were soon forgot.

7

The stones of that fair hall lie far and wide,
And but a few recall its ancient mould;
Yet when I pass the spot I long to hold
        As truth what fancy saith:
'His protest lives where deathless things abide.'

THOMAS HARDY (By 1900)

An interesting case of an early conservationist at a time when the
Victorian passion for tearing down old buildings was at its height.
Casterbridge, as Hardy-lovers will know, is Dorchester.

XIV
GILBERTIAN
INTERLUDE

Gentle Alice Brown

from The Bab Ballads

It was a robber's daughter and her name was Alice Brown
Her father was the terror of a small Italian town;
Her mother was a gentle, weak, but amiable old thing;
But it isn't of her parents that I'm going for to sing.

As Alice was a sitting at her windowsill one day
A beautiful young gentleman he chanced to pass that way;
She cast her eyes upon him, and he looked so good and true,
That she thought, 'I could be happy with a gentleman like
    you!'

And every morning passed her house that cream of
    gentlemen;
She knew she might expect him at a quarter unto ten;
A sorter in the Custom House, it was his daily road
(The Custom House was fifteen minutes walk from her
    abode).

But Alice was a pious girl, who knew it wasn't wise
To look at strange young sorters with expressive purple eyes;
So she sought the village priest to whom her family confessed –
The priest by whom their little sins were carefully assessed.

'Oh holy father,' Alice said, ' 'twould grieve you would it not
To discover that I was a most disreputable lot!
Of all unhappy sinners I'm the most unhappy one!'
The padre said, 'Whatever have you been and gone and
    done?'

'I have helped mamma to steal a little kiddy from its dad;
I've assisted dear papa in cutting up a little lad;
I've planned a little burglary and forged a little cheque,
And slain a little baby for the coral round its neck!'

The worthy pastor heaved a sigh and dropped a silent tear –
And said, 'You mustn't judge yourself so heavily my dear –
'Tis wrong to murder babies, their corals for to fleece;
But sins like these one expiates at half a crown apiece.

'Girls will be girls; you're very young, and flighty in your
    mind,
Old heads upon young shoulders we must not expect to
    find;
We mustn't be too hard upon these little girlish tricks!
Let's see: five crimes at half a crown: exactly twelve and six!'

'Oh father,' little Alice cried, 'your kindness makes me
    weep!
You do these little things for me so singularly cheap!
Your thoughtful liberality I never can forget,
But oh, there is another crime I haven't mentioned yet!

'A pleasant looking gentleman, with pretty purple eyes
I've noticed at my window as I've sat a-catching flies;
He passes by it every day as certain as can be –
I blush to say I've winked at him and he has winked at me!'

'For shame,' said Father Paul, 'my erring daughter! On my
    word
This is the most distressing news that I have ever heard.
Why, naughty girl, your excellent papa has pledged
    your hand
To a promising young robber, the lieutenant of his band!

'This dreadful piece of news will pain your worthy
    parents so!
They are the most remunerative customers I know;
For many many years they've kept starvation from my doors:
I never knew so criminal a family as yours!

'The common country folk of this insipid neighbourhood
Have nothing to confess; they're so ridiculously good!
And if you marry anyone respectable at all,
Why, you'll reform, and what will then become of Father
    Paul?'

The worthy priest, he upped and drew his cowl upon his
    crown,
And started off in haste to tell the news to Robber Brown:
To tell him how his daughter, who was now for marriage fit
Had winked upon a sorter, who reciprocated it.

Good Robber Brown, he muffled up his anger pretty well.
He said 'I have a notion, and that notion I will tell.
I will nab this gay young sorter, terrify him into fits,
And get my gentle wife to chop him into little bits.

'I've studied human nature, and I knows a thing or two –
Though a girl may fondly love a living gent, as many do,
A feeling of disgust upon her senses there will fall
When she looks upon his body chopped particularly small.'

He traced that gallant sorter to a still suburban square;
He watched his opportunity and seized him unaware;
He took a life-preserver, and he hit him on the head,
And Mrs Brown dissected him before she went to bed.

And pretty little Alice grew more settled in her mind;
She never more was guilty of a weakness of the kind,
Until at length good Robber Brown bestowed her pretty
    hand,
On that promising young robber, the lieutenant of his band.

W. S. GILBERT (1869)

The Judge's Song

from Trial by Jury

When first my friends I came to the Bar,
    With an appetite hale and hearty,
I was, as most young barristers are,
    An impecunious party,
I'd a swallowtail coat of a beautiful blue,
A brief that I'd bought of a booby,
A couple of shirts and a collar or two,
    And a ring that looked like a ruby.

At Westminster Hall I danced the dance
    Of a semi-despondent Fury,
And I thought I never should get a chance
    Of addressing a British jury,

But I soon got tired of third-class journeys,
And dinners of bread and water,
So I fell in love with a rich attorney's
    Elderly ugly daughter.

That rich attorney he jumped with joy
    In response to my fond professions.
'You shall reap the reward of your pluck, my boy,
    At the Bailey and the Middlesex sessions,
You may take my girl your bride to be,
And a very nice bride you'll find her.
She may even pass for forty-three,
    In the dark with the light behind her!'

That rich attorney was as good as his word:
    The briefs came trooping daily.
And every day my voice was heard
    At the sessions and the ancient Bailey.
All thieves who could my fees afford
    Relied on my orations,
And many a burglar I've restored
To his friends and his relations!

At length I became as rich as the Gurneys;
    An incubus then I thought her'
So I threw over that rich attorney's
    Elderly ugly daughter.
That rich attorney my character high
    Tried vainly to disparage . . .
And now, if you please, I'm ready to try
This breach of promise of marriage!

                                        W. S. GILBERT (1875)

The Police Sergeant's Song

from The Pirates of Penzance

When a felon's not engaged in his employment,
Or maturing his felonious little plans
His capacity for innocent enjoyment
Is just as great as any honest man's.
Our feelings we with difficulty smother
When constabulary duty's to be done.
Ah, take one consideration with another
A policeman's lot is not a happy one.

When the enterprising burglar's not a-burgling –
When the cutthroat isn't occupied in crime –
He loves to hear the little brook a gurgling
And listen to the merry village chime
When the coster's finished jumping on his mother,
He loves to lie a-basking in the sun –
Ah take one consideration with another –
A policeman's lot is not a happy one.

W. S. GILBERT (1880)

Bunthorne's Confession and Song

from Patience

Am I alone,
     And unobserved? I am!
Then let me own.
     I'm an aesthetic sham!
This air severe
     Is but a mere
          Veneer!

This cynic smile
Is but a wile
Of guile!

This costume chaste
Is but good taste
Misplaced!

Let me confess!
A languid love for lilies does not blight me!
Lank limbs and haggard cheeks do not delight me!
I do not care for dirty greens
By any means.
I do not long for all one sees
That's Japanese.
I am not fond of uttering platitudes
In stained glass attitudes,
In short, my mediaevalism's affectation,
Born of a morbid love of admiration!

SONG

If you're anxious for to shine in the high aesthetic line, as a man
of culture rare
You must get up all the germs of the transcendental terms, and
plant them everywhere,
You must lie upon the daisies and discourse in novel phrases of
your complicated state of mind,
The meaning doesn't matter, if it's only idle chatter of a
transcendental kind.
And everyone will say
As you walk your mystic way,
'If this young man expresses himself in terms too deep for me,
Why what a very singularly deep young man this deep young
man must be!'

Be eloquent in praise of the very dull old days which have long
since passed away,
And convince them if you can, that the reign of good Queen
Anne was Culture's palmiest day.
Of course you will pooh-pooh whatever's fresh and new, and
declare it's crude and mean,

For Art stopped short at the cultivated court of the Empress
    Josephine.
        And everyone will say,
        As you walk your mystic way,
If that's not good enough for him which is good enough for me,
Why what a very cultivated kind of youth this kind of youth
    must be!

Then a sentimental passion of a vegetable passion must excite
    your languid spleen,
An attachment *a la* Plato for a bashful young potato or a not too
    French French bean!
Though the philistines may jostle, you will rank as an apostle in
    the high Aesthetic band,
If you walk down Piccadilly with a poppy or a lily in your
    medieval hand.
        And everyone will say,
        As you walk your flowery way
'If he's content with a vegetable love which would certainly not
    suit me,
Why what a very singularly pure young man this pure young
    man must be!'

W. S. GILBERT (1881)

Patience is a good-humoured satire on Oscar Wilde and the Aesthetic
School of the 1880s. Lady Jane (below) is an ageing aristocratic admirer.

Lady Jane's Song

from Patience

Silvered is the raven hair,
    Spreading is the parting straight,
Mottled the complexion fair
    Halting is the youthful gait,
Hollow is the laughter free,
    Spectacled the limpid eye –
Little will be left of me
    In the coming by and by!

Fading is the taper waist,
　　Shapeless grows each shapely limb,
And although severely laced,
　　Spreading is the figure trim!
Stouter than I used to be,
　　Still more corpulent grow I –
There will be too much of me
　　In the coming by and by!

W. S. GILBERT (1881)

Lord Mountararat's Song

from Iolanthe

When Britain really ruled the waves –
　　(In good Queen Bess's time)
The House of Peers made no pretence
　　To intellectual eminence,
Or scholarship sublime;
　　Yet Britain won her proudest bays
In good Queen Bess's golden days!

When Wellington thrashed Bonaparte
　　As any child can tell,
The house of Lords, throughout the war
　　Did nothing in particular
And did it very well;
　　Yet Britain set the world ablaze
In good King George's golden days!

And while the House of Peers withholds
　　Its legislative hand,
And noble statesmen do not itch
　　To interfere with matters which
They do not understand,
　　As bright will shine Great Britain's rays
As in King George's golden days.

W. S. GILBERT (1882)

The Lord Chancellor's Nightmare

from Iolanthe

When you're lying awake with a dismal headache and repose
    is taboo'd by anxiety,
I assume you may use what expression you choose to
    indulge in without impropriety;
For your brain is on fire – the bedclothes conspire of usual
    slumber to plunder you:
First your counterpane goes, and uncovers your toes, and
    your sheet slips demurely from under you;
Then the blanketing tickles – you feel like mixed pickles –
    so terribly sharp is the pricking,
And you're hot and you're cross, and you tumble and toss
    till there's nothing twixt you and the ticking,
Then the bedclothes all creep to the ground in a heap, and
    you pick them all up in a tangle;
Next your pillow resigns, and politely declines to remain at
    its usual angle!
Well you get some repose in the form of a doze, with hot
    eye-balls and head ever-aching,
But your slumbering teems with such horrible dreams that
    you'd very much better be waking:
For you dream you are crossing the Channel and tossing
    about in a steamer from Harwich –
Which is something between a large bathing machine and a
    very small second-class carriage –
And you're giving a treat (penny ice and cold meat) to a
    party of friends and relations –
They're a ravenous horde and they all came on board at
    Sloane Square and South Kensington stations,
And bound on that journey you find your attorney (who
    started that morning from Devon)
He's a bit undersized, and you don't feel surprised when he
    tells you he's only eleven.
Well you're driving like mad with this singular lad (by the
    by, the ship's now a four-wheeler),

And you're playing round games, and he calls you bad
    names when you tell him that 'ties pay the dealer';
But this you can't stand, so you throw up your hand, and
    you find you're as cold as an icicle,
In your shirt and your socks (the black silk with gold
    clocks), crossing Salisbury Plain on a bicycle;
And he and the crew are on bicycles too, which they've
    somehow or other invested in –
And he's telling the tars all the particulars of a company he's
    interested in –
It's a scheme of devices to get at low prices all goods from
    cough mixtures to cables
(Which tickled the sailors) by treating retailers as though
    they were all vegetables –
You get a good spadesman to plant a small tradesman (first
    take off his boots with a boot-tree),
And his legs will take root, and his fingers will shoot, and
    they'll blossom and bud like a fruit-tree –
From the green-grocer tree you get grapes and green pea,
    cauliflower, pineapple and cranberries,
While the pastry-cook plant cherry brandy will grant, apple
    puffs and three-corners and Banburys –
The shares are a penny, and ever so many are taken by
    Rothschild and Baring,
And just as a few are allotted to you, you awake with a
    shudder despairing –
You're a regular wreck, with a crick in your neck, and no
    wonder you snore, for your head's on the floor, and
    you've needles and pins from your soles to your shins,
    and your flesh is a-creep, for your left leg's asleep, and
    you've cramp in your toes, and a fly on your nose, and
    some fluff in your lung, and a feverish tongue, and a
    thirst that's intense and a general sense that you haven't
    been sleeping in clover;
But the darkness has passed, and it's daylight at last, and
    the night has been long – ditto ditto my song – and
    thank goodness they're both of them over!

W. S. GILBERT (1882)

16
THE CLOSE OF
THE CENTURY

Two very different poets express their feelings about the situation in the last few years of Victoria's reign, with Kipling anxious, with good reason, about the future of the Empire in whose mission he passionately believed and Hardy commenting on the situation of soldiers sent abroad to fight in its service. His 'Drummer Hodge', about a colonial war which exposed Britain's increasing vulnerability, probably inspired Rupert Brooke's very different, because explicitly patriotic, 'The Soldier'. Hardy's farewell to the century in 'The Darkling Thrush' is full of religious imagery from the rituals of a faith which, in common with many others, he found it impossible to sustain after Darwin's discoveries.

Recessional

God of our fathers, known of old,
 Lord of our far flung battle line
Beneath whose awful hand we hold
 Dominion over palm and pine –
Lord God of Hosts, be with us yet
Lest we forget, lest we forget.

The tumult and the shouting dies
 The Captains and the Kings depart;
Still stands thine ancient sacrifice
 An humble and a contrite heart.
Lord God of Hosts, be with us yet,
Lest we forget, lest we forget.

Far called our navies melt away;
 On dune and headland sinks the fire:
Lo all our pomp of yesterday
 Is one with Nineveh and Tyre!
Judge of the Nations, spare us yet,
Lest we forget, lest we forget.

If drunk with sight of power we loose
   Wild tongues that have not thee in awe.
Such boastings as the Gentiles use,
   Or lesser breeds without the Law –
Lord God of Hosts, be with us yet,
Lest we forget, lest we forget.

For heathen heart, that puts in trust
   In reeking tube and iron shard,
All valiant dust that builds on dust,
   And guarding, calls not thee to guard,
For frantic boast and foolish word,
Thy mercy on thy people, Lord.

                           RUDYARD KIPLING (1897)

Written after Queen Victoria's Diamond Jubilee.

The White Man's Burden

Take up the White Man's burden –
   Send forth the best ye breed –
Go bind your sons to exile
   To serve your captives' need;
To wait in heavy harness
   On fluttered folks and wild –
Your new-caught, sullen peoples,
   Half devil, and half child.

Take up the White man's burden –
   In patience to abide,
To veil the threat of terror
   And check the show of pride;
By open speech and simple,
   An hundred times made plain,
To seek another's profit,
   And work another's gain.

Take up the White Man's burden –
    The savage wars of peace –
Fill full the mouth of famine
    And bid the sickness cease;
And when your goal is nearest
    The end for others sought,
Watch Sloth and heathen Folly
Bring all your hope to nought.

Take up the White Man's burden –
    No tawdry rule of kings,
But toil of serf and sweeper –
    The tale of common things.
The ports ye shall not enter,
    The roads ye shall not tread,
Go make them with your living,
    And mark them with your dead!

Take up the White Man's burden –
    And reap his old reward:
The blame of those ye better,
    The hate of those ye guard –
The cry of hosts ye humour
    (Ah, slowly!) toward the light: –
'Why brought ye us from bondage,
    'Our loved Egyptian night?'

Take up the White Man's burden –
    Ye dare not stoop to less –
Nor call too loud on Freedom
    To cloak your weariness;
By all ye cry or whisper,
    By all ye leave or do,
The silent sullen peoples
    Shall weigh your Gods and you.

Take up the White Man's burden –
    Have done with childish days –
The lightly proffered laurel,
    The easy, ungrudged praise.

Comes now, to search your manhood
    Through all the thankless years,
Cold edged with dear-bought wisdom,
    The judgement of your peers!

RUDYARD KIPLING (1899)

Written to urge his friend, Theodore Roosevelt, to make the USA join Britain as a colonial power by taking control of the Philippines after the defeat of Spain in the Spanish–American War. His view of the purpose of empire here is far from the optimistic expansionist one familiar to us, for example, from 'Land of Hope and Glory'.

Drummer Hodge

They throw in Drummer Hodge to rest
    Uncoffined – just as found –
His landmark is a kopje-crest
    That breaks the veldt around,
And foreign constellations west
    Each night above his mound.

Young Hodge the Drummer never knew –
    Fresh from his Wessex home –
The meaning of the broad Karoo,
    The Bush, the dusty loam,
And why uprose to nightly view
    Strange stars amid the gloam.

Yet portion of that unknown plain
    Will Hodge forever be,
His homely Northern breast and brain
    Grow to some Southern tree,
And strange-eyed constellations reign
    His stars eternally.

THOMAS HARDY (1899)

The Darkling Thrush

I leant upon a coppice gate,
    When frost was spectre gray
And Winter's dregs made desolate
    The weakening eye of day.
The tangled bine stems scored the sky
    Like strings of broken lyres,
And all mankind that haunted nigh
    Had sought their household fires.

The land's sharp features seemed to be
    The Century's corpse outleant,
His crypt the cloudy canopy,
    The wind his death lament,
The ancient pulse of germ and birth,
    Was shrunken hard and dry,
And every spirit upon earth
    Seemed fervourless as I.

At once a voice arose among
    The bleak twigs overhead
In a full-throated evensong
    Of joy illimited;
An aged thrush, frail gaunt and small,
    In blast beruffled plume,
Had chosen thus to fling his soul
    Upon the growing gloom.

So little cause for carolings
    Of such ecstatic sound
Was written on terrestrial things
    Afar or near around,
That I could think there trembled through
    His happy good-night air
Some blessed hope of which he knew
    And I was unaware.

THOMAS HARDY (December 31st 1900)

INDEX OF POEM TITLES

INDEX OF FIRST LINES

No city primness train'd my feet 180
No coward soul is mine 70
No worst, there is none. Pitched past pitch of grief 83
Not a drum was heard, not a funeral note 290
Not a line of writing have I 236
Now, even, I cannot think it true 235

O blackbird! sing me something well 126
O Goddess! hear these tuneful numbers wrung 331
O Lyric Love, half-angel and half-bird 222
'O, Melia, my dear, this does everything crown! 50
O suitably attired in leather boots 324
O take this world away from me 67
O what can ail thee, knight at arms 365
O wild West Wind, thou breath of Autumn's being 119
Oh how one ugly trick has spoiled 91
Oh to be in England 134
On a starred night Prince Lucifer uprose 397
On Linden when the sun was low 286
On Wenlock Edge the wood's in trouble 360
One face looks out from all his canvases 412
One more unfortunate 46
Our Adonais has drunk poison – oh 195
Out of the night that covers me 82

Past ruin'd Ilion Helen lives 339
Push hard across the sand 30

Roll forth, my song, like the rushing river 68
Roman Virgil, thou that singest 355

Saint Peter sat by the celestial gate 9
Say not the struggle naught availeth 71
Season of mists and mellow fruitfulness 115
She is older than the rocks on which she sits 420
She was a Phantom of delight 239
Silvered is the raven hair 437

Since all that I can do for thee 265
Since I noo mwore do zee your feäce 221
Since that I may not have 279
So all day long the noise of battle rolled 385
So we'll go no more a-roving 242
Some men to carriages aspire 161
Stand close around, ye Stygian set 339
Stop, for thy tread is on an Empire's dust! 287
Strong Son of God, Immortal Love 205
Sunset and evening star 86
Surprised by joy, impatient as the Wind 195

Take up the White Man's burden 444
Tears, idle tears, I know not what they mean 72
Tender Lizzie could not bear 377
That's my last duchess painted on the wall 407
The age is dull and mean. Men creep 28
The Assyrian came down like a wolf on the fold 285
The bat is dun, with wrinkled wings 144
The boy stood on the burning deck 291
The brawling of a sparrow in the eaves 281
The Child is Father to the Man 165
The isles of Greece, the isles of Greece 335
The jackdaw sat on the Cardinal's chair! 104
The last night that she lived 233
The moon is distant from the sea 276
The mountain sheep are sweeter 97
The only ghost I ever saw 376
The rain set early in tonight 247
The sea is calm tonight 73
The sky is cloudy, yellowed by the smoke 158
The snow falls deep; the forest lies alone 407
The sun from the west glares back 159
The Thames nocturne of blue and gold 160
The world is too much with us; late and soon 329

The Wordsworth Poetry Library

Works of:

Matthew Arnold

William Blake

The Brontë Sisters

Rupert Brooke

Robert Browning

Elizabeth Barrett Browning

Robert Burns

Lord Byron

Geoffrey Chaucer

G. K. Chesterton

John Clare

Samuel Taylor Coleridge

Emily Dickinson

John Donne

John Dryden

Thomas Hardy

George Herbert

Gerard Manley Hopkins

A. E. Housman

James Joyce

John Keats

Rudyard Kipling

D. H. Lawrence

Henry Wadsworth Longfellow

Macaulay

Andrew Marvell

John Milton

Wilfred Owen

'Banjo' Paterson

Edgar Allen Poe

Alexander Pope

John Wilmot, Earl of Rochester

Christina Rossetti

Sir Walter Scott

William Shakespeare

P. B. Shelley

Edmund Spenser

Algernon Swinburne

Alfred Lord Tennyson

Edward Thomas

Walt Whitman

Oscar Wilde

William Wordsworth

W. B. Yeats

Anthologies & Collections

Restoration and
Eighteenth-Century Verse

Nineteenth-Century Verse

Poetry of the First World War

Love Poems

The Metaphysical Poets

The Wordsworth Book of Sonnets